INTEGRATIVE FEMINISMS

D0145049

PERSPECTIVES ON GENDER

Series Editor:
Myra Marx Feree, University of Connecticut

Pleasure, Power, and Technology:
Some Tales of Gender, Engineering, and the Cooperative Workplace
Sally Hacker

Black Feminist Thought:
Knowledge, Consciousness, and the Politics of Empowerment
Patricia Hill Collins

Understanding Sexual Violence:
A Study of Convicted Rapists
Diana Scully

Maid in the U.S.A.
Mary Romero

Feminisms and the Women's Movement:
Dynamics of Change in Social Movement Ideology and Activism
Barbara Ryan

Black Women and White Women in the Professions:
Analysis of Job Segregation by Race and Gender, 1960–1980
Natalie J. Sokoloff

Gender Consciousness and Politics
Sue Tolleson Rinehart

Mothering:
Ideology, Experience, and Agency
Evelyn Nakano Glenn, Grace Change, and Linda Rennie Forcey (editors)

For Richer, For Poorer:
Mothers Confront Divorce
Demie Kurz

Integrative Feminisms
Building Global Visions, 1960s–1990s

Angela Miles

ROUTLEDGE • NEW YORK and LONDON

Published in 1996 by
Routledge
29 West 35th Street
New York, NY 10001

Published in Great Britain by
Routledge
11 New Fetter Lane
London EC4P 4EE

Library of Congress Cataloging-in-Publication Data

Miles, Angela R. (Angela Rose)
    Integrative feminisms : building global visions, 1960s–1990s / Angela   Miles.
        p. cm. — (Perspectives on gender)
    Includes bibliographical references.
    ISBN 0-415-90756-X. — ISBN 0-415-907577-8
    1. Feminist theory.   2. Feminisms—North America.   3. Radicalism—North
America.   I. Title.   II. Series : Perspectives on gender (New York, NY)
HQ1190.M54   1993
305.42'01—dc20   92-33164
                                                         CIP

CONTENTS

ACKNOWLEDGMENTS

In my years of making, studying, and writing about feminist politics I have learned from and been supported by many, many people; most of all by my parents Chickie and Hans Breitenbach, They provided me with a writer's retreat and supplied all my earthly needs for long periods on numerous occasions when I needed to escape daily demands to make progress with my writing.

Brian Milani, partner in politics and life, and Margaret Benston, Somer Brodribb, Linda Christiansen-Ruffman, Frieda Foreman, Pam Harris, Lucille Harper, Carolyn Lehman, Cath McNaughton, Mary O'Brien, and Carole Yawney, long time sister-activists whom I love dearly, have sustained and inspired me over decades of shared, sometimes joyful and always challenging struggles.

I have benefitted beyond measure from my friendships in Toronto Women for a Just and Healthy Planet, the Antigonish Women's Association, the Feminist Party of Canada, and Women Against Violence Against Women; and from my association with colleagues and students at St. Francis Xavier University and The Ontario Institute for Studies in Education.

For this book, feminists from all parts of the world have given time in interviews and discussions, read and commented on the manuscript, shared pre-publication papers, helped me with contacts, and contributed logistical and other aid on research trips. These feminists have provided inspiration and example for my analysis as well as concrete support for my project, but in expressing my gratitude here for kindnesses over decades, I am not claiming their endorsement for the book's main argument: Bisi Adeleya-Fayemi, Haleh Afshar, Ama Ata Aidoo, Paula Gunn Allen, Peggy Antrobus, Berit Ås, Jasodhara Bagchi, Kathy Barry, Pauline Bart, Mary Becker, Sarah Begus, Elise Boulding, Charlotte Bunch, Linda Cardinal, Roxanna Carillo, Deborah Chansonneuve, Emily Culpepper, Mariarosa Dalla Costa, Chhaya Datar, Neera Desai, Suzanne Doerge, Carol Anne Douglas, Andrea Dworkin, Cynthia Enloe, Ramabai Espinet, Honor Ford-Smith, Ulrike Främbs, Ursula Franklin, Gaye Geltner, Anne Gillies, Barbara Godard, Ann Gordon, Pat Gowens, Collette Guillaumin, Jalna Hanmer, Mechthild Hart, Nancy Hartsock, Pat Hughes, Ayesha Imam, Moon Joyce, Danielle Juteau, Kalpana Kannabiran, Ynestra King, Renate Klein, Cheris Kramarae, Lou Lavender, Lisa Leghorn, Molara Ogundipe Leslie, Karen Lindsey, Rozena Maart, Patricia McFadden, Mary Mellor, Maria Mies, Obioma Nnaemeka, Rosiska Darcy d'Oliviera, Kathy Parker, Sheela Patel, Nan Peacock, Ellen Pence, Beth Percival, Sister Sol Perpiñan, Ann Phillips, Hilkka Pietilä, Rhoda Reddock, Diana Russell, Khadiga Safwat, Chela Sandoval, Erella Shadmi, Barbara Smith, Ailbhe Smyth, Liz Stanley, Deborah Stienstra, Peggy Strobel, Kazuko Tanaka, Fiona Thomas, Pura Velasco, Moema Viezzer, Shirley Walters, Betsy Warrior, Brooke Williams, Wu Tsui-Yee, Eve Zaremba.

I would also like to thank the Social Sciences and Humanities Research Council for funding parts of the research for this book and Frances Baker, Joan May, Jeanie Stewart, Lisa Caton, Marie Doyle, Sue Geddis, and Beth Pettigrew for their fine support (in every sense of the word) with manuscript preparation.

INTRODUCTION

We are living in a period of enormous social change and contestation. The world dominance of Western patriarchal nations and capitalist transnational corporations, the accompanying imposition of punitive international and national economic and social arrangements, and the rise of right-wing, militarist, racist, and fundamentalist forces are met by increasing feminist resistance as well as resistance on the part of indigenous and colonized peoples. In individualist, apolitical, and parochial North America[1] it is often hard for feminists to keep a strong political and global sense of their/our[2] movement. The difficulty is exacerbated when feminist theory is divorced from questions of practice and debate within the women's liberation movement[3] is couched in individual and reactive rather than collective and strategic terms. In these times it is easy to lose sight of the essential "politicalness" of feminism, the scope of its vision, and the depth of its challenge to existing patriarchal arrangements. This book presents a theoretical analysis of the politics of feminist radicalism in a global context. It recognizes both the enormity of feminism's project and its triumph in sustaining a growing worldwide movement against great opposition.

In the sixties I was involved in the student, New Left, and antiwar movements in England and Canada. Since the early seventies I have been an active feminist—a founding member of WAVAW (Women against Violence against Women) in Toronto, the Antigonish Women's Association in Nova Scotia, and the Feminist Party of Canada, and a participant in many other groups and activities, including currently, Toronto Women for a Just and Healthy Planet. Since 1976 I have also interviewed many feminist activists, from Canada, the United States, and around the world; I use these interviews as well as my own experience in this engaged study. My intentions are both analytical and exhortatory.

The analysis presented here identifies what I call "integrative feminist politics" and documents the existence of such politics in North America and the "Two-Thirds World"[4] from the 1960s to the 1990s. In making the argument that integrative feminisms offer our best hope for progressive change, I focus on the values and visions they share rather than their differences, which are easier to see. The integrative feminisms of Quebec, English-speaking Canada, and the United States are treated together, as are integrative feminisms from all the varied regions of the "Two-Thirds World." Nevertheless, my analysis is grounded in actual feminist politics as they are lived all over the world by variously self-defined feminists.

The variety of the feminisms discussed here, their resilience, and the extent of their geographical dispersal are inspiring. Although I cannot do justice to particular integrative feminisms or particular countries or ethnicities, I have tried to draw examples from their whole range. In this way I hope that feminists around the world will see themselves in this book and that less informed readers will get a strong (if not systematic) sense of integrative feminisms' differences as well as their commonalities. I am writing as a North American and primarily addressing North American readers, but I hope this information will also be useful to others.

Integrative feminisms in North America (like those elsewhere) have a long and creditable history of struggle. Much current academic and political debate, unfortunately, colludes in the denial of this history and its potential. General dismissals of ill-defined and politically undifferentiated "white Western feminism" or "essentialism" often fail to recognize the progressive potential and radical history of important and much-beleaguered feminisms. They cannot address their real weaknesses in ways that foster this potential. They may even leave women with the immobilizing impression that there is no progressive potential in North American feminism.

Guilt-ridden, angry, self-doubting, or judgmental rejections of North American feminism are politically irresponsible when global solidarity is both an urgent necessity and an increasing possibility. Local struggle is the only and the necessary basis for global solidarity. We diverse women in North America must build the kinds of feminisms that enable us to both benefit from and contribute to global dialogue and networking. Accordingly, we need to recognize the weaknesses in our practice, but we also have to recognize and nurture its radical strengths.

I argue that types of feminism usually perceived as absolutely different, even opposing, share important integrative principles. To show this I have drawn on the writing and practice of very diverse feminists, many of whom are critical of each other. Even though I highlight shared principles, I do not intend to homogenize these feminisms or suggest that their distinctions are meaningless. In fact, I would argue that to benefit from their diversity and its promise we must explore these differences in more challenging and systematic debates than we are used to in North America. Recognizing shared integrative intentions and visions should help cut through the absolute dismissals that often subsume real issues and hamper real dialogue.

One of my aims in this book is to contribute to the creation of multicentered, women-affirming, and transformative politics by drawing attention to the ways in which the project of creating such politics is very much alive and well around the world. My emphasis on the promise of integrative feminisms is not intended to downplay the racism, homophobia, class prejudice, and other weaknesses that mar our movement. I hope to show how essential and how difficult it is to build politics that acknowledge and attack these divisions of power. And I hope that the examples of feminist practice worldwide will help increase awareness in North America of multicentered, global politics both in this region and elsewhere.

ANALYSIS AND ANALYTICAL TERMS

The analysis here distinguishes between assimilationist or equality-frame feminisms and integrative or transformative feminisms. The defining value of *assimilationist* or *equality-frame feminisms* is equality, which may be understood in liberal, socialist, or other terms; change needed to achieve it may be understood in more or less radical terms. These diverse politics all advocate equal participation and rights for women in society. Their practice is essentially a pressure-group practice for women. *Integrative* or *transformative feminisms*, by contrast, are committed to specifically feminist, women-associated values as well as to equality. Since they propose these values as alternatives to the dominant ones, they can challenge not just women's exclusion from social structures and rewards but the very nature of these structures and rewards. Theirs are *full politics* that go beyond pressure for a single group and address the whole of society.

Almost all liberal reform feminists are assimilationist in approach. However, there are both assimilationist and integrative feminists in all the radical categories of feminism.[5] Black, radical, socialist, Third World, lesbian, and ecofeminists may be found on both sides of this important but little recognized divide.

The alternative value core of integrative feminisms in all their variety is the holistic, egalitarian, life-centered rejection of dominant androcentric, dualistic, hierarchical, profit-centered ideology and social structures. These feminisms refuse the oppositions that patriarchal relations presume and structure between the personal and the political, public and private, means and ends, reason and emotion, psychological and social, knower and known, production and repro-duction, individual and community, society and nature. Committed to develop-ing new political forms that reflect their holistic values, they attempt to integrate these oppositions as part of their struggles to build a new world.

Articulating integrative values involves affirming the work, characteristics, and concerns that are relegated to women, marginalized, and trivialized in industrial, patriarchal society. These feminisms not only name and resist diverse women's oppression but also name and affirm diverse women's strengths and worth. Integrative feminists believe that women should be relieved of their unequal share of responsibility for the reproduction of life and society not only so women can engage in what are currently male-associated activities but so that women's life-oriented work and concerns can become the organizing principles of the whole of society and its numerous and varied communities.

To move beyond challenging not only women's condition but general social structures and values, diverse women acknowledge their specificity as women (their differences from men) as a major resource in their politics. Integrative feminisms affirm both women's equality with men and their differences from men, that is, both *women's equality* and *women's specificity*. These characteris-tics, so often understood as static opposites, become dynamic contradictions to be lived and transformed in practice.

When diverse women's specificity is named as a strength as well as a source of oppression, differences among women can be understood not only as divisions to be overcome but as resources to be celebrated and used in struggle. The apparently contradictory facts of women's commonality and women's diversity thus also become necessary aspects of each other—to be affirmed and trans-formed together.

I call these transformative feminisms "integrative feminisms" because (1) they are essentially antidualistic, refusing the fragmentation of industrial, patriarchal society; (2) they integrate resistance to all dominations as essential aspects of women-centered and women-defined feminist politics; (3) the life-centered values they endorse in opposition to dominant separative values are integrative ones such as community, sharing, nurturing, and cooperation; and, most important, (4) these are *dialectical politics* in which the apparently opposed principles of women's equality and specificity, their commonality and diversity become dynamic contradictions that, far from being mutually exclu-sive, are mutually constitutive, each transformed by the other. For instance, equality is understood differently when it coexists with specificity and differ-ence. When equality no longer necessarily implies sameness, difference need no longer imply inequality.

Dialectical politics neither passively accept nor avoid nor propose easy reso-lutions to contradictions. They attempt, instead, to *transcend* them. That is, they strive in their struggles to shift the lived relations of contradictory terms in ways that open up new possibilities. This is not easy to do and is a continuous process, for contradictions will never be fully overcome. But the commitment of integrative feminists to address tensions creatively and constructively in political struggle is neither naive nor simplistic. It must be at the heart of any transformative project.

Dialectical politics can appear paradoxical to those who work in linear terms. Integrative feminists, for instance, seek to transcend the dualistic gender system initially by affirming one side—the female side—of the dichotomy as a necessary moment of this struggle. They affirm as they resist the category "women." Moreover, the integrative articulation of diverse women's *particular* needs and interests lies at the core of *general* politics in which opposition to all systems of domination is an essential component of feminist struggle. Far from denying women's diversity or homogenizing women as a group, the affirmation of women's shared specificity as women makes it possible for feminism to appeal to groups of women beyond the often male-identified urban, educated middle class. As women of color and workingclass and rural women with stronger women identification become more active in defining feminism, the affirmation strengthens. Articulating their specificity as women and their connection with all women does not take women away from their particular communities. It supports a more active role for women in defining their own cultures and communities. For integrative feminists, the affirmation of women's specificity and women's particular racial and ethnic identities are necessary parts of the same process. Despite the tendency for academic theorists to construct gender and race or ethnicity as opposing pulls, in actual practice they reinforce each other.

These feminisms, therefore, have the potential to speak to and unite women across divisions of race, class, and sexual orientation. They provide the necessary basis for a *multi-centered women's movement* in which all diverse women in their particularity are equally central and in which the particular conditions of all women's lives are equally representative of the general condition of women —a movement in which diversity truly is a resource. They represent the hope (locally and globally) of building a women's movement and a world that are neither ethnocentric nor decentered.

CHAPTER OUTLINE

Early feminist radicals were almost all committed to integrating the personal and the political as well as *means and ends* in the creation and practice of new politics. They knew that these politics could never be fully realized until a new society had been built. Nevertheless, they sought this synthesis in their practice because they believed that freedom can never be won by unfree means and that one's values should shape the struggle as well as its goals. Radical, nonintegrative positions soon emerged, however, that separated ends from means and/or reduced the personal to the political or the political to the personal. By the mid-1970s these *reductionist* positions (which reduced complex feminist analyses and strategies to overly simplistic positions and practices) dominated feminist published work, with the result that it began to look, in the literature at least, as if feminism's early integrative project had been abandoned (Chapter 1).

Nonetheless, the integrative project did survive, deepening into a powerful, though largely unrecognized tendency of the women's movement. Diverse feminists retained their commitment to integrate the personal and the political and means and ends (Chapter 2), even as their understanding of the integrative project expanded over the next decade to include the articulation of specifically feminist alternative values and the dialectical affirmation of women's specificity and equality, their diversity, and commonality (Chapter 3). The impact of this integrative perspective on practice in several issue areas and on feminist identity politics is examined in Chapter 4.

Today, feminism's more developed integrative politics are generating new forms of reductionism. Dialectical and transformative politics are often rejected in the name of antiessentialism. Numerous and various critics of essentialism insist that the principles of equality and specificity, diversity and commonality are static opposites. The exciting practice of diverse dialectical feminisms is either ignored or discounted. Chapter 5 describes (1) forms of antiessentialism (most often radical or socialist-feminist) that refuse the affirmation of women's specificity on the grounds that it requires abandoning the claim of equality with men and (2) forms of antiessentialism (most often poststructuralist) that refuse the affirmation of women's commonality on the grounds that it denies women's differences from each other.

Chapter 6 illustrates the range of integrative feminisms in the "Two-Thirds World." It suggests that it is not surprising that feminisms advocating a simple equality frame are viewed with suspicion by Two-Thirds World feminists. For feminisms that do not challenge the androcentric, hierarchical, and dualistic logic of industrial patriarchy become carriers of this worldview and thus, regardless of intent, part of the colonizing "modernization" process. Integrative North American feminisms are important potential allies for Third World feminists, however, and will in turn be strengthened through global dialogue, networking, and solidarity. Chapter 7 discusses the difficulties and possibilities of building global solidarity and examines increasing North American global awareness and commitment. Chapter 8 describes the growth of global communication, networking, and organizing among feminists and examines international activism around violence against women as an example of global feminist practice. Chapter 9 presents global analyses and shared visions resulting from exchanges among feminists around the world. It looks in particular at the ways in which deeply women-centered perspectives enable multicentered movement toward a freer and more life-affirming world.

1

EARLY FEMINIST RADICALISM

EARLY INTEGRATIONS

Autonomous Feminist Radicalisms

Autonomous feminist radicalisms emerged in North America as part of the sixties' broad challenge to both established and oppositional institutions and ideologies. In this period new social movements addressed the issue of alienation as well the unequal distribution of wealth. They were concerned with qualitative as well a quantitative change and sought to integrate economic, social, political, and cultural struggle.

After reform feminists first challenged men's power, radical women inside and outside of male-dominated movements became conscious of their interests as women and began to organize autonomously to resist women's oppression.[1] They were indebted to, but not contained by, other radical social movements of the time.[2]

In the Black, Chicano, and Quebec-nationalist movements feminists of all races and ethnicities, participants or not, saw powerful and progressive affirmations of identities despised by the dominant cultures. From the Black movement, feminists received a clear message that effective struggle should be built on but not limited to one's own interests. From the New Left came a commitment to resist hierarchical separations between leaders and the led. From nonfeminist but women-identified activist women of Vietnam, Cuba, China,

1

and Algeria came confirmation of women's separate interests and of their specific, even primary role in revolutionary struggle.[3]

But women also saw that the liberation sought by these movements did not extend to them, that male-defined radicalisms were reluctant to include gender among the dominations to be challenged. This shared failure to deal with the gender of power as a central question ultimately made it impossible for the Black movement to build a fully alternative culture, for Quebec nationalism to retain its progressive agenda, and for the New Left to sustain its commitment to the liberatory vision it had articulated.

The alienation and exploitation entailed in class and race divisions and in the fragmentation between, for instance, work and leisure, public and private, production and reproduction, mental and manual, reason and emotion, individual and community, personal and political, means and ends, are expressed most basically in the division of people within themselves and in society into male and female halves of a whole. None of these divisions can be effectively countered without resisting male domination and the supremacist claim that the male half of dichotomized humanity is the truly human half and that "male" activities, concerns, and characteristics alone are defining of human society and community—something these movements never did.

In fact, male-defined radicalisms opposed the power of dominant men in the name of working class, Black, Chicano, Indian, or Quebecois *men*. In the Quiet Revolution, Quebec women faced processes of secularization and modernization that amounted also to masculinization (Dumont 1992). They learned that the (then radical) separatist Parti Québecois did not and never would have feminist priorities (Un groupe de femmes de Montréal 1971). Black feminists in the United States exposed the same failure in Black groups there. Pauli Murray, Black activist lawyer wrote at the time: "Reading through much of the current literature on the Black Revolution, one is left with the impression that for all the rhetoric about self-determination, the main thrust of black militancy is a bid of black males to share power with white males in a continuing patriarchal society in which both black and white females are relegated to a secondary status" (1970, 92).

Without tackling gender domination, the New Left could not bring the struggle home either. Its attempt to challenge oppressive relations in private as well as public life became the affirmation of white *male* youth culture in opposition to the constraints of industrial masculinity. In its most extreme version the rape of women would replace the rape of Vietnam and quantitatively more alienated heterosexual sex would substitute for war. Activist and writer Robin Morgan was not alone in raising questions about the male-defined political groups and activities she had joined: "Was it my brother who listed human beings among the *objects* which would be easily available after the Revolution: 'Free grass, free food, free women, free acid, free clothes, etc.'? . . . The epitome of exclusionism—'men will make the Revolution—and make their chicks'" (1970, 127).

Feminist radicals in all their variety criticized radical movements with instrumental relations to sex and to women as part of the articulation of larger visions of politics and change.[4] They saw that male-dominated movements did not apply the principles of equality and freedom in their own personal and political relations and identified this as a core weakness in their visions and practice (Beal 1969; Lopez 1977; Piercy 1969; Warren 1977).[5]

Feminists received some positive reaction to their criticisms and initiatives. Male radicals in general, however, responded negatively or not at all to these large feminist concerns. So feminist radicals created autonomous groups and/or organized women's caucuses to carry forward general progressive struggle as well as to escape sexist environments. Far from abandoning antiracist, anticapitalist, anti-imperialist struggle for the expression of sectional interests, they defended and developed more encompassing politics than any other liberatory movements could sustain.[6] Feminist radicals' willingness to challenge male power enabled them to more successfully and consistently bring together the personal and the political and means and ends and to lay the basis for the visionary integrative politics whose development I trace in future chapters.

The Personal Is Political and Means and Ends

The understanding that the personal is political politicized masses of women never before active and enabled many who were already active to develop more independent and self-defined relationships to politics. Feminists realized that the sphere of personal and private life was not just subject to the intrusion of power relations from outside but was political *in itself*—structured to institutionalize male power over women. This insight forms the core of such early theoretical writing as Kate Millett's *Sexual Politics* (1970) and Celestine Ware's *Woman Power: The Movement for Women's Liberation* (1970), and was insisted upon in the statements of autonomous groups.[7] Marriage, the family, motherhood, love, sexuality, definitions of beauty were identified as political institutions, forms of male dominance. The political meanings of such practices as rape, prostitution, birth control, abortion, and heterosexuality were explored.

This recognition of the political importance of private life and personal relations made it possible for feminist radicals to pursue personal and political integration and cultural transformation in more sustained and concrete ways than could male-dominated radicalisms: "In this struggle, separations that have frustrated previous movements—separations between analysis and program and between personal and political life—are breaking down. Ending sexism means destroying oppressive institutions and ideologies and creating new structures and images to replace them. There is no private domain of a person's life that is not political and there is no political issue that is not ultimately personal" (Bunch 1970, 168).

Because women's oppression and exploitation are embedded in the minute details of everyday life, the personal is immediately political in a *concrete* sense. Personal transformation *has to be* central to feminist radicalism. Crippling passivity, self-hatred, and self-sacrifice born of millennia of oppression have to be overcome in the positive affirmation of female identity and sisterhood. In their much anthologized collective statement, the Combahee River Collective, a Black feminist activist group founded in Boston in 1974, testified to the power of women sharing and analyzing their experiences:

> We have spent a great deal of energy delving into the cultural and experiential nature of our oppression out of necessity because none of these matters has ever been looked at before. No one before has ever examined the multilayered texture of Black women's lives. An example of this kind of revelation/conceptualization occurred at a meeting as we discussed the ways in which our early intellectual interests had been attacked by our peers, particularly Black males. We discovered that all of us, because we were "smart" had also been considered "ugly" i.e., "smart-ugly." "Smart-ugly" crystallized the way in which most of us had been forced to develop our intellects at great cost to our "social" lives. (Combahee River Collective 1977, 364)

This collective process of self-reflection and self-affirmation stands at the core of integrative feminist practice. Since it takes place on the immediate ground of women's oppression, it involves direct confrontation with and resistance to power. Even the smallest movement toward change and autonomy for a woman brings her forcefully up against the unequal power on which "normal" interaction between the sexes is based. Therefore, the development of positive female identity is necessarily a political process that can only proceed as women act collectively to give each other support and to confront the relations of domination that their new identities challenge.

Consciousness-raising groups,[8] established by the thousands in the early period of the women's liberation movement, embodied this process. The groups were small, leaderless, nonhierarchical. They rooted their development of theory directly in experience. Intellectual understanding emerged from careful analytical attention to expressed emotions and feelings.[9] These groups represented the self-organization of women for the political purpose of achieving personal and social transformation. Contrary to later charges, far from presuming homogeneity, early consciousness raising was explicitly valued for the opportunity it provided for diverse women to share diverse experiences. Feminists understood that this opportunity had to be consciously and politically created against a backdrop of divisive social structures. C.R. groups provided the space for women in different conditions with apparently different needs and interests to explore their experiences together; to identify the patterns of control they were all (differentially) subject to; to understand the ways that women are divided and used against each other; and to resist these divisions as they built a common struggle.

In fact, when women used their own diverse experiences to analyze society, the process frequently did reveal the ways the system masked real power, made them threats to each other, and offered false individual "solutions" that reinforced women's dependence and vulnerability, like marriage and dieting. Participants often did see that no woman is free and no woman can be free until all women are free, that social change is needed to free women, and that they need each other to do it.

Far from being therapy, as is sometimes thought, consciousness raising at its best unites individual activity and change with collective theorizing and social action. As a form, these groups embody the concrete integrative attempt in early feminist politics to overcome divisions between the personal and the political, means and ends, theory and practice, process and product, subject and object, reason and emotion. They gave all participants, not just the specialist "feminist theorists" who emerged later, direct access to the creation of original and autonomous theory.

Women's Specificity, Equality, Commonality, and Diversity

Growing awareness of the oppression structured into private life enabled diverse women to understand their personal problems and dissatisfactions as political. This political understanding became the basis of conscious women identification on the part of increasing numbers of heterosexual and lesbian feminists of all ethnicities, who asserted a pride in femaleness and a growing sense of women's potential power even as they named their oppression and the ways they were divided as women.

In this process they named their commonality as women and claimed their equality with men. This dual gesture did not imply sameness among women and did not supplant other important aspects of women's identities, such as class and race. Black feminists, for instance, insisted with activist politician Shirley Chisholm, "I am both Black and a woman" (1969, 40).[10] However, it did stress women's sameness with men. Statements of women's strength in these early years of feminist struggle tended to focus on women's possession of what were culturally perceived to be male competencies and strengths. Feminists' main defense against dominant presumptions of women's inadequacies was not to deny the inadequacies but to point out that they were the result of exclusion and oppression rather than inherent. Feminists worked to overcome their sense of themselves as always secondary to men, to develop a sense of self and self-worth, to see themselves in other women, and to discover, support, even love each other as the basis for solidarity:

We women must begin to unabashedly learn to use the word "love" for one another. We must stop the petty jealousies, the violence that we Black women have for so long perpetrated on one another about fighting over this man or the other.... We must turn to ourselves and one another for strength and solace....

We do not have to look at ourselves as someone's personal sex objects, maids, baby sitters, domestics and the like in exchange for a man's attention. (Weathers 1970, 305–306)

It is the primacy of women relating to women, of women creating a new consciousness of and with each other, which is at the heart of women's liberation.... As we confirm in each other that struggling incipient sense of pride and strength, the divisive barriers begin to melt, we feel this growing solidarity with our sisters. We see ourselves as prime, find our centers inside of ourselves. (Radicalesbians 1970, 84)

The association of powerful images with women, the development of pride as women, and love and respect for women are essential and exciting aspects of feminism. The transformative power of this process for all women in a misogynist society is enormous. It forms the revolutionary core of women's recognition of their commonalities and of their demand for equality. But it did not in the early days systematically challenge the androcentric overvaluation of men and undervaluation of women. White feminists especially, many of them young, urban, educated women, tended to accept the sexist myth of female weakness and parasitism.

Much feminist theory reflected this unconscious androcentrism. Simone de Beauvoir, whose 1953 book *The Second Sex* was widely influential in Quebec, English-speaking Canada, and the United States in this period, accepted that "women on the whole *are* inferior to men" ([1953] 1974, xxviii). She argued that women [through their subordination and not by nature] have "remained doomed to immanence, incarnating only the static aspect of society" (68). Women's involvement in birth, child care, and housework has kept her tied to her body, mired in nature. "War, hunting, and fishing represented an expansion of existence, its projection toward the world. The male alone [is] the incarnation of transcendence" (68). De Beauvoir's apparent endorsement of male contempt for women and women's work and her belief that only male activities can be truly human are echoed in the early theory of all tendencies of the women's movement.

Like de Beauvoir, radical feminist Shulamith Firestone argued that "pregnancy is barbaric ... the temporary deformation of the body of the individual for the sake of the species!" (1970, 198). She wanted women freed from "the tyranny of ... biology" (193). Women's liberation required that we leave birth behind for male activities. Similarly, the socialist feminist Juliet Mitchell argued that women, confined to the family, are "largely separated off from social human activity.... They must provide sexual gratification for their partners and give birth to children and rear them. All three roles man [*sic*] shares with animals" (1967, 82). For the liberal feminist Betty Friedan, too, women's equality and personhood would be won by their entry into the skilled, adult, productive world of the labor force. In *The Feminine Mystique* she saw housework as the "ludicrous consignment of millions of women to work that could easily be done by an eight year old" (1963, 245).

Thus in this early period the structures of male power were recognized and attacked, but the androcentric definitions and values that embodied male power were left relatively unscathed. Feminists' developing sense of identity and connection as women was built more on the recognition of common oppression and the shared demand for equality than on any specifically feminist values.

Naming and challenging divisions among women and women's common oppression was a striking achievement of this early period. It enabled diverse feminist radicals to claim women's equal rights within as well as access to male-defined humanity and the world and to sustain the difficult project of integrating the personal and the political and means and ends in this struggle. In later chapters we will see that in subsequent years this integrative project is broadened and deepened by a positive recognition of women's differences from men (specificity) and from each other (diversity), which enables feminists also (1) to see women's lives as potential sources of alternative integrative values and (2) to see differences among women not only as divisions to be overcome but also as resources in a transformative struggle. Not all feminist radicalisms are integrative, however. So we will first examine early reductionisms that abandoned integrative commitments.

EARLY REDUCTIONS

Soon after autonomous feminist radicalisms emerged, distinct categories of these politics were named and claimed as, among others, socialist, radical, and lesbian feminisms.[11] All these categories include both feminists with reductionist and with integrative politics: there are self-defined lesbian, socialist and radical feminists who recognize all oppressions and are committed to integrating the personal and the political and means and ends in their practice, and there are feminists with each of these self-definitions who do not. In the mid-1970s, reductionist positions tended to dominate feminist published debate to the extent that the literature gave the impression that feminism's early integrative commitments had been entirely eclipsed.

As an activist at that time I was working with others who were committed to resisting easy "solutions" to contradictions that would require abandoning our integrative aims and means. I thought it was unlikely that Toronto was unique in this and traveled to other cities in 1976 to find and interview English-speaking integrative feminists. I have continued to interview integrative feminists of all kinds whenever the opportunity has arisen, including a second North American trip for that purpose in 1986 and numerous interviews with Third World feminists during their visits here and at international gatherings. None of the women interviewed required anonymity, so I have not felt the need to alter quotations to disguise identities. However, since the interviews were done over decades and respondents may have changed their views, I have identified some only by a pseudonymous first name.

Return to Social Class

Some socialist feminists, while asserting the importance of male domination in their analysis of personal life, returned to the view of male power as derivative of capitalism and social class. The integrative feminists I interviewed mentioned this tendency of some to privilege class analysis:

> I think that some feminists have gotten so far into class analysis that they no longer have a feminist analysis. It's important to deal with racism and classism and the effects of American imperialism on women around the world. It's complex, and I think people don't want to deal with complexity. They want a simple truth. For a lot of feminists what happened was that they got so excited (in that very real way that you can get politically excited when you realize something that you haven't before—"Oh my God, yes, class really is an issue, even if the male left calls it an issue") that they began to feel class was an issue; feminism in and of itself wasn't. (Karen Lindsey)

Charlene identified the growing containment of feminist insights within a preexisting class framework as one of the reasons why numbers of Toronto feminists decided in 1969 to leave the originally all-encompassing group called the Women's Liberation Movement to found a more explicitly feminist group called the New Feminists.

Nancy noted that the shift to a predominantly class-focused analysis was often accompanied by an increasing acceptance of hierarchical forms of organization: "Certainly both to the right [reform feminism] and left [nonintegrative feminist radicalism] of the central women's movement [integrative feminism] we're talking about, leaders came back in. They have the usual hierarchies." The development of uniquely feminist practice and visions was thus abandoned by nonintegrative socialist feminists. Even when they were organized autonomously, these feminists became essentially a female pressure group within politics defined by men.[12]

Socialist feminists were not alone in retreating from feminist integrations. Practices developed among some self-defined lesbian and radical feminists that claimed a mechanical identity between the personal and the political instead of seeing their dynamic integration as a value to be realized. One tendency reduced the political to the personal in a lifestyle politics that collapsed means and ends. Another downplayed the importance of personal change and the development of new practice and accepted the separation of means and ends in practice.

The Political Reduced to the Personal

In 1972 the "Furies" collective, a lesbian-feminist group based in Washington, D.C.,[13] systematized earlier arguments that lesbianism is the ultimate expression of women identification into an explicitly vanguardist and separatist position that only lesbians can be feminists (Myron and Bunch 1975). The aim was not only to organize to have the issue of lesbianism and its political significance recognized and debated within the wider feminist movement but to win over the movement to lesbian feminism and its members to lesbianism.

The Furies developed their position in response to the reactionary failure of many heterosexual feminists to deal seriously with lesbian oppression in society and in the women's movement. Although they argued that a certain sexual orientation was *necessary* to feminism, they did not argue that it was *sufficient*: "Lesbians must become feminists and fight against women's oppression, just as feminists must become lesbians if they hope to end male supremacy" (Myron & Bunch, eds., 1975, 31). The political offensive they launched from a separate organizational base helped foreground for all feminist radicals (1) the depth of domination in personal life, (2) the nature of social controls used to limit people's sexuality and sexual expression, (3) the degree of social persecution of gays and lesbians, (4) the prevalence of homophobia in the women's liberation movement, and (5) the contradictions heterosexual feminists face in relations with a man or men. The Furies forced all feminist radicals to deal with the issue of lesbianism and its importance to feminism.

The vanguardism of the argument that *all* women should be lesbian became, however, for some a spontanist and reductionist lifestyle politics. Charlotte Bunch, a founding member of the Furies explained to me:

I was a lesbian separatist for two years and then I decided that that was not enough. . . . I have since learned that [the Furies'] notion of what that separatism meant and other people's have not necessarily been the same. . . . Our use of separatism was a strategy that we felt had been used effectively in other movements as well to force a group of people that you basically want to work with to understand the importance of what you are saying. So we were always oriented to the feminist movement. We were never oriented to lesbians only. We were always oriented to bringing together feminism and lesbianism. There are lesbian separatists today who talk about a lesbian nation; who talk about separatism as a final goal and a kind of geographical, physical, separate space.

The important argument of the Furies that lesbianism was necessary to feminism became for some though by no means all, separatists an argument that lesbianism is a sufficient expression of feminism. The political separation within feminism that the Furies advocated became for some a politics of life-style whose correctness was determined by the degree of contact with "straight society." Politics was reduced to the personal and the integrative project abandoned in a dichotomization of humanity into male and female.

As the Furies were developing their lesbian-feminist position, other groups used feminists' increasing knowledge of women's culture and history ("her-story") to cultivate ancient powers and skills. Women's historical responsibility for health care and men's appropriation of that field were uncovered. From this came awareness of the importance of witchcraft in women's history (Ehrenreich and English 1973; Dworkin 1974) and theories of prehistorical matriarchal societies (Davis 1972).

These researchers and practitioners contributed to a growing sense of power among women, and many added a spiritual aspect to the exploration of women's skills and work (Alpert 1973). For some (few) individuals and groups, however, the new historical and spiritual sense of female activity, values, and characteristics displaced rather than enriched the political struggle. Female ways of being came to be seen as aspects of a biologically ascribed female essence and a purely women's society became the means and end of their feminism. The integrative notion of a fuller humanity for all and the integrative aim of transforming the entire world were abandoned.

Although much current criticism of lesbian feminism, cultural feminism, and feminist separatism implies that this reductionism predominates in these politics, it does not. Most feminist separatism, spiritual practice, and interest in the craft of the wise, matriarchies, and women-centered ritual enriches political struggle. The view that attention to these elements of feminist culture is necessarily antipolitical presumes an absolute contradiction between things spiritual and things political—a classic nonintegrative reduction in its own right.

The difficulty of maintaining feminism's integrative project leads to other distortions. The attempt to ground theory in personal experience that had spawned consciousness raising became for some an anti-intellectualism, and a licence to reduce political discussion to a recitation of personal problems. In some groups the attempt to devise nonhierarchical structures and relationships led to resistance to individual initiative among members and suspicion, if not refusal, of all structure. Commitment to develop the initiative, autonomy, and strength of all became in a few cases a tyranny of mediocrity and/or sameness, reducing all participants to the lowest common denominator. In these (rare) cases, the measure of feminism was a simple moralism that demanded adherence to rigid patterns of personal behavior—a reduction of the political to the personal, and ends to means.

By far the most widespread personal reductionism is found in reform feminism, which is always vulnerable to the pull of the dominant culture to individualize, psychologize, and personalize women's suffering and its "solutions." The struggle between feminist radicals over integrative or nonintegrative definitions of feminism occurs in a context of extremely powerful forces of opposition and co-optation that threaten constantly to crush and/or depoliticize women's struggle. For instance, the collective radical practice of consciousness raising is vulnerable to co-optation as therapy for individual women. Feminists I interviewed spoke with regret and some anger of this distortion:

> Just at this time last year [1975] we got a notice about a meeting that was being held here at YWCA to look at consciousness raising. I came into the meeting late and ... there were twenty-four or twenty-five women there. And I would say ... nineteen of them were people who were doing groups with women through colleges, Y's, that kind of thing. And they had absolutely no comprehension of what was meant by consciousness raising and where it was going. . . . It's really being co-opted by the T-Group phenomenon and just done in something awful. (Cynthia)

The Personal Reduced to the Political

Other feminists resisted personal reductionism in the name of its opposite, reducing the personal to the political. They denied the importance of the spiritual, cultural, and personal moment of struggle, and their analysis of domination and control in personal life led to a defense of political struggle in its traditional and narrow sense. In this tendency, best exemplified by reductionist socialist feminism and such groups as Redstockings[14] and Wages for Housework,[15] the problems of attempting to create new integrated practice led not to personal and moral reductionism but to the avoidance of questions of process and personal transformation.

The traditional political approach of some socialist feminist groups attracted women who felt that the political definition of their struggle had been lost with the development of feminist cultural activity and lesbian separatism. Some, like Marlene Dixon, an early and important feminist radical, went so far as to renounce the women's movement altogether in favor of sectarian Marxist-Leninist positions (1975, 6).

Others, such as the group Redstockings, who did not reject the women's liberation movement, outright nevertheless opposed the integrative-transformative project, narrowly defining politics to explicitly reject conscious personal transformation. Redstockings coined the term "consciousness raising" and contributed to early feminist analysis rooted in shared experiences and feelings. The group was also instrumental in developing the "pro-woman line" that stressed power differences between men and women and not women's *attitudes* as the basis of sex roles and therefore of women's oppression. They argued that psychological and sex-role theories "shift the burden of blame from men to women, obscuring the power differences between men and women, and preventing us from clearly seeing just what the barriers are that have to be overcome—barriers that exist not in our heads but in the real world" (Leon 1975, 54–55).

Insisting that radical-feminist analysis keep front and center the *power relation* between men and women challenged the vague and sloppy thinking that led reformist feminists to view women as the cause of their own oppression—a perspective that results in the substitution of group therapy and affirmative action for consciousness raising and political action. The Redstockings, however, drew extremely limiting conclusions from this important insight. They pronounced that women have no need of personal transformation in the process of struggle: "Women's submission is not the result of brainwashing, stupidity or mental illness but of continual, daily pressure from men. We do not need to change ourselves" (Redstockings 1969, 534).

On this basis they denounced not only groups that reduced their political project to a moralistic concern with lifestyle but all groups concerned to integrate personal change with social change and develop a politics in which the dynamic integration of the social, economic, cultural, spiritual, and personal is consciously fostered. Reacting against the personal reductionism that robs feminism of its political moment, they drew an absolute and artificial dichotomy between developing political understanding and changing personally, pitting the former against the later, for instance, in the following statement about consciousness raising: "The importance of listening to a woman's feelings was collectively to analyze the situation of women, not to analyze *her*. The idea was not to change women, was not to make 'internal changes' except in the sense of knowing more. It was and is the conditions women face, it's male supremacy, we want to change" (Sarachild 1975a, 135). On this basis too, they decried all concern with the development of alternative institutions and denounced the cultural and spiritual aspects of feminist struggle and values as counterrevolutionary mystification (Brooke 1975).

Nevertheless, the insistence that women's behavior is tactical-survival behavior, not self-destructive behavior causing our own oppression, poses an important challenge to a misogynist culture that devalues and blames women in general and encourages individual women to gain self-respect by distancing themselves from other women. Redstocking's principled refusal to women-blame was an essential aspect of feminism's challenge to the devaluation of women and the divisions among women.

The Wages for Housework group also helped prevent active feminists from separating themselves from other women by showing that responsibility for housework is shared by *all* women and is basic to society's definition of all women. They argued convincingly that a childless, unmarried, career, or lesbian woman was no less defined by the fact of female domestic service than a housewife at home with children.

> (Once) housework is totally naturalized and sexualized ... all women are expected to do [it] and even like doing [it]—even those who due to their social position, could escape some of that work or most of it.... We might not serve one man but are all in a servant relation with respect to the whole male world. (Federici 1975: 8)

Wages for Housework expanded the early feminist critique of marriage and the family by asserting the claims of reproduction and women's work against their invisible, derivative, and subordinate status and structure. Originally they demanded wages for housework with the aim of ultimately refusing housework and the subordination of human needs and relationships to production for profit. The demand was advanced as an alternative to the only other route through which women could gain money and some degree of independence, namely, by joining the paid labor force: "Getting a second job does not change that [housewife] role, as years and years of female work outside the house still witness. The second job not only increases our exploitation, but simply reproduces our role in different forms" (Federici 1975, 6–7).

The demand for wages for housework originally challenged the structures of people's lives at their deepest level and defined women's role in reproduction as an essential ground of struggle. As their practice developed, however, the group ignored the experiential and personal aspect of early feminist analysis in favor of a purely economic analysis. They refused to see their analysis of women's domestic labor as the consciousness-raising and self-transforming force it could be. They based their demand for wages for housework on women's sameness with men, claiming that "women are workers too" and emphasizing the *similarity* of reproductive labor to paid labor, not their *differences* as a basis for women's struggle and a transformed class struggle.

The group insisted that the *only* focus of struggle now must be to win wages for housework. Any notion of feminist politics that includes attention to the development of new women and the assertion of feminist values through alternative feminist institutions, cultures and communities was rejected. Feminists who questioned the economism of the group were told that the time to consider spiritual and personal questions was *after* wages for housework are won. In fact, the group soon ceased to call itself feminist or to speak of itself as part of the women's liberation movement, referring instead to the "Wages for Housework Movement." Like some lesbian-separatist groups that also consider themselves outside feminism, Wages for Housework represents a nonfeminist-defined departure from early integrative feminist radicalism.

Means and Ends

Redstockings, Wages for Housework, and reductionist socialist feminists and lesbian separatists all in their own way rejected a dynamic, synthesizing politics and subscribed to artificial either/or choices: either personal change or political action; either cultural development or radical opposition; a focus on either economic or noneconomic factors, on means or on ends. Despite their important contributions to feminist analysis, they imposed false dichotomies between what are actually necessary and complementary aspects of feminist politics and are clearly recognized as such by integrative feminists.

Their narrow conceptions of politics left them all immune from any sense of the importance of variety for political development and synthesis. So they saw no need to foster a dynamic and vigorous but nonsectarian process of debate. All adopted vanguardist and sectarian positions, denouncing any activity that was not identical to their own. They made political assessments in terms of different sets of political dogma that nevertheless had the same limiting effect. For a time it looked as if the early integrative politics of feminist radicals had been lost in these forms of reductionism. Each tendency's response to the other drove it further into its reductionist position, until published movement literature was dominated by a debate *between* the personal and the political (in the name always of "the personal is political," which all tendencies of the movement continued to proclaim).

In the heat of this debate, both personal and political reductionisms predicted and bemoaned the demise of a feminism that each side felt was in the stranglehold of its opposite number. By 1975 even the articles expressing integrative feminist views often did so from what their authors presumed was an isolated and minority position. At the time, much of the feminist thought of the early 1970s that remained true to feminism's early synthesizing vision and politics appeared in the form of critiques of reductionist developments in the movement. In the literature of the period the political reductionism of *some* socialist feminists, lesbian feminists, cultural feminists, political feminists, radical feminists, and feminist therapists appeared, together, to have overwhelmed the original feminist impetus toward radical synthesis.

The published feminist writing did not fully represent, however, the women's liberation movement as it was being lived and built at the grass roots. Reductionist positions were held in their many variations by women in all categories of feminist radicalism. But none of the categories has been appropriated entirely by reductionist feminists. Many women have resisted all forms of reductionism in their practice. We will see that despite the confusing variety of self-definitions and the diversity of their politics, these feminists together constitute an important tendency of the women's movement that has remained true to and continued to develop early feminism's synthesizing politics.

2

THE PERSONAL IS POLITICAL; MEANS AND ENDS

Alain Touraine has argued that the principles of Identity, Opposition, and Totality are essential to the development of any social movement: "A social movement is an expression of a conflict between social forces for the control of social change. In more analytic terms, it is the combination of three elements: the defense of unity of action—what we call the principle of *Identity*; the struggle against a social adversary—the principle of *Opposition*; the reference to the whole of society—principle of *Totality*" (Touraine 1971, 132; emphasis added). Reference to the whole of society distinguishes a social movement from a pressure group or other limited protest politics. To be a full politics, that is, a politics that speaks to social organization in general, a movement must espouse a set of values representing an alternative to the dominant ones. Touraine has called this the movement's "alternative rationality." Mass activism, no matter how large, determined, and angry, that does not articulate an alternative set of values cannot create alternative social arrangements. It is thus limited to a politics of assimilation rather than transformation.

Integrative feminisms are full politics in Touraine's sense. They resist patriarchal domination by affirming alternative, specifically feminist values (an alternative rationality). The mutually transforming integration of the personal and the political, means and ends, and women's equality, specificity, commonality, and diversity are all key elements of these politics; they all shape and are shaped by its women-centered vision.

15

IDENTITY: WOMEN'S COMMONALITY AND DEFENDING UNITY OF ACTION

Feminism requires and at the same time enables diverse women to claim their womanhood and their connection with other women[1] in the face of society's sexism and their own internalization of misogynist and antiwomen views. To recognize themselves as women, women must see that "man" has never included them; that the affirmation of "brotherhood" and "manhood" (by white, Black, native, Chicano, Quebecois, and other men) excludes them and is in most cases built on their negation; that, for men's purposes, they serve largely instrumental functions, as nature does; and that they are defined in these terms. The "Statement of Purpose" of the National Black Feminist Organization, one of the first national Black feminist groups in the United States, puts this very clearly: "We have been called 'matriarchs' by white racists and black nationalists; we have virtually no positive self-images to validate our existence. Black women want to be proud, dignified, and free from all these false definitions of beauty and womanhood that are unrealistic and unnatural. We, not white men or black men, must define our own self-image as black women" (National Black Feminist Organization 1974, 99). Quebec feminists express the same demand for autonomous self-definition in their militant refusal of the religious and nationalist matriarchal images imposed on women (Jean et Théoret 1976; *Des luttes et des rires de femmes* 1979; *La vie en Rose* 1984).

In order to resist male definitions, women must also resist their own self-hatred and despising of their sisters through continuous consciousness raising, an integrated process of thought and activity not limited to consciousness-raising groups. This process involves a woman recognizing her own strength *even though she is a woman,* and/or recognizing that she is a woman *even though she is strong,* and understanding that her strength does not separate her from other women or jeopardize her female status. It is a woman's revaluing of women and her own womanness that brings together her sense of personhood and womanhood and heals the schizophrenia endemic to the female condition in misogynist, male-dominated communities.

For women of oppressed or minority groups consciousness raising necessarily involves affirming class and ethnic as well as gender identities as central, positive, and inseparable aspects of self and of feminist struggle (Alarcon 1983; Cardinal 1992; Tynes 1987).[2] Nationalist feminists in Quebec articulated this in the early seventies with their slogan: "Pas de Québec libre sans libération des femmes! Pas de femmes libres sans libération du Québec!" ("No Free Quebec without freedom for women! No free women without freedom for Quebec!"). Chicana feminist Mirta Vidal makes the same connection between struggles and insists on women's central role in making the links:

In the spirit of Las Adelitas, Las Hijas de Cuahtemoc, and all the unrecognized Mexican women who fought valiantly for their rights, who formed their own feminist organizations, and who fought and died in the Mexican revolution, Chicanas in this country will take the center stage in the advance of La Raza.

The struggle for women's liberation is the Chicana's struggle, and only a strong independent Chicana movement, as part of the general women's liberation movement and as part of the movement of La Raza, can ensure its success (1972, 57).

Far from abandoning their culture and community, feminists insist on a more active and determining role in defining them. Their fight is against both sexism and racism, in their own communities and the wider society. Toronto's Black Women's Collective insists on this double struggle in their statement "Building a Global Movement": "We fight in our own community to put an end to sexism and recognize that Black men are no less sexist than other men just because we share the oppression of racism. Though we stand in solidarity with them against racism we stand in struggle against sexism. For Black women racism and sexism are inextricable. We can't fight one and not the other, we can't win one and lose the other" (Black Women's Collective 1988, 10). It is women's assertion of power and autonomy within their communities as well as the larger society that the men of their own cultures most resist and fear, not the abandonment of community and culture of which feminists are so often accused.

An increasingly powerful, more positive and integrated sense of self sustains feminists in all communities who, in questioning established roles and limited identities, confront the necessity of defining their own lives against the resistance of those who hold the power to do the defining. The struggle to do this is both an existential and a political battle against the structures that have given a crippling and false "security" to some but by no means all women. Women's attempts to move beyond assigned roles and meanings to create themselves through collective struggle may involve the loss of job, husband, friends, and/or social/community approval. The limiting but familiar feminine status awarded to "good women" may give way to such put-downs as "battleaxe," "ball breaker," "manhater," "matriarch," "castrating bitch," "agringada" (like a white woman), "too haole" (a Hawaiian epithet meaning "too white"). Celestine Ware writes about the fear that feminists face in this process: "One of the greatest impediments to full equality for women is their fear of being ostracized and of losing their feminine qualities if they assert themselves. Women reason that if they are not "women," that is, beings defined by their relation to men, they are nothing. Fear of the radical extension of self to achieve an unknown identity is one of the major inhibitions that feminism must overcome" (1970, 116).

Questioning established meanings and definitions involves claiming the right to name and define one's own reality—that is, claiming the right to speak humanly, asserting one's own value. Both joyful and difficult, this claim involves recognizing women's devalued strengths as well as facing fears and changing weaknesses. The challenges are to society's definitions, and structures, as well as to women's own internalized definitions: "I learned about Black feminism from the women in my family—not just from their strengths, but from their failings, from witnessing daily how they were humiliated and crushed because they had made the 'mistake' of being born Black and female in a white man's country. I inherited fear and shame from them as well as hope. These conflicting feelings about being a Black woman still do battle inside of me. It is this conflict, my constantly 'seeing . . . and touching / Both sides of things' that makes my commitment real" (Smith 1983, xxii).

Integrative feminists emphasize individual personal transformation as part of the collective political process of resisting men's power. It is the claiming of full personhood by over half the human population who have been denied this status and involves building the collective power to overturn entrenched inequality. It is a struggle that for many includes an explicit cultural and spiritual component.

OPPOSITION: STRUGGLE AGAINST A SOCIAL ADVERSARY

Individual Resistance

Personal transformation, no matter how central to feminist struggle, will not alone bring women equality or freedom—a point stressed by the radical-feminist writer and activist Andrea Dworkin when I interviewed her:

> You see we have this notion that we're very powerful individuals, and we can be very powerful individuals, but we're still utterly powerless in society. That's the first thing that has to be understood—the frame in which we have to talk about personal transformation. . . . The more one actualizes one's strength, the more one is in conflict with the institutions of society which totally restrain any woman from using those capacities in a way consonant with the strength that she has. So . . . no peace is possible, no internal peace is possible for any strong self-actualizing woman as long as institutions and power relations stay what they are. And any movement that such a woman makes in society will be directly in conflict with things as they are.

Feminists' new worldview and self-understanding demand an active and (as far as possible) transforming relation to the world. Feminists on family benefits resist demeaning definitions as well as controlling requirements. On the job they refuse to make and serve the boss coffee; they notice and object to sexual and racial harassment and discrimination in pay, hiring, and promotion; and they seek alliances with other women workers across established divisions. In day-care struggles they insist on nonsexist, nonracist education. At home and in their communities feminists begin to refuse their servant's role and resist the tendency to—and people's expectations that they will—live through others. They demand attention to women's issues in the groups to which they belong and activities in which they participate.

The logic of the structures that oppress women and the reaction that even the smallest attempt at self-expression engenders mean that *if women are not crushed,* their resistance grows as their strength develops and their strength develops as their resistance grows. But they face immediate opposition in the most private and vulnerable spheres of life as well as in public contexts. Families and communities demand that women fulfill all the petty requirements of the roles of daughter, wife, and mother as well as the large obligations of service and submission. Movement men also demand compliance with their definitions of the female and with their prescriptions for her behavior:

> Black women are being asked by militant black brothers not to practice birth control because it's a form of whitey's committing genocide on black people. . . . For us, birth control is the freedom to *fight* genocide of black women and children (Black Women's Liberation Group 1970, 360).

> If you do not play the game, the role, you are not a woman and they [leftist men] will NOT be attracted. You will be sexless, and worse, unnatural and threatening (Densmore 1971, 266–67).

> The issues of birth control, abortions, information on sex and the pill are considered "white" women's lib issues and should be rejected by Chicanas according to the Chicano philosophy which believes that the Chicana woman's place is in the home and that her role is that of a mother with a large family. Women who do not accept this philosophy are charged with betrayal of "our culture and heritage," OUR CULTURE, HELL! (Frances Flores in *Regeneracion,* cited in Vidal 1972, 54).

Collective Organization and Support

Decisions made by women of all ethnicities to define and to claim full human status and power are political decisions that require collective organization if they are to be sustained. Providing an alternative to the hostile world "out there," groups can reinforce individual resistance through approval, through shared suffering and joy, through opportunities to develop new skills and analyses, and through concrete forms of support for personal change such as babysitting, providing a place for a woman who wants to leave her husband to stay, lending money, helping each other job hunt, and supporting a woman's decision to come out as a lesbian.[3] They also make possible collective questioning and refusal, and the collective renaming of reality, thus providing a basis for political action. Betsy Warrior, a founding member of the early Boston-based group Cell 16 and the journal *No More Fun and Games*, spoke to me about the strength she found in meeting other women who shared her views:

> I saw this ad in the paper that said, anybody who feels suffocated by the patriarchy or who has never been able to breathe under this system should meet with this women's group. "We plan to abolish all phallic institutions. We plan to institute free twenty-four-hour child care and free abortions on demand," and things like that. Me and my girlfriend [one a battered ex-wife on welfare and the other a housewife] said, "Wow, that sounds nice doesn't it?" We decided to go to this meeting, just check it out, see what was happening.
>
> We thought we probably wouldn't want to belong to it, because we weren't the types that joined groups. We were very isolated and shy. We figured, well, they're probably college types too and we'd have nothing in common with them.
>
> I really liked some of the women there. They started talking about some of the things that I had always been reading about, and thought about, but thought I was the only one that thought about them. For the first time in my life (and I was twenty-eight then, I had been married for seven years before that and divorced for six or seven years), I had people to relate to, that thought about the same things. We weren't crazy anymore. After that we kept going back.
>
> We started writing right away. I had never written anything, I was really intimidated even by the thought. I started doing it because we all encouraged each other. We had only started meeting in July and by the end of the summer we had all written enough to make a book, and we put out our first journal.

Sisterhood/Solidarity

"Sisterhood" is the name given to the commitment of diverse women to a common struggle based on feminist analysis and values. For integrative feminists it was never, as some suppose today, simply a claim of shared oppression or a naive expression of belief in any "natural" or inevitable affinity among women. It is instead a basic *political* principle of support entailing a vision of solidarity to be built and lived consciously by women across the divisions of racist industrial patriarchal society. Frances Beal, author of an influential statement circulated in 1969 by the Black Women's Liberation Committee of the Student Nonviolent Coordinating Committee (SNCC) wrote in a later article:

> There is a lot of money to be made on the social and economic exploitation of the black woman, often with her cooperation. This holds true for all women in

this society. So long as women can be paid less they can be used as surplus labour and as a source of cheap labour when necessary. In the home they are used as a free labour source.

The task before us is to develop a sisterhood which stretches across all countries. A sisterhood that finds within itself the resolve and strength to actively participate in all phases of the liberation struggles, while at the same time making sure that the role of women in the new society will be one which will not be oppressive and will not be a continuation of the stunting attitudes which are still in mode today, even among the most revolutionary of men. (Beal 1981, 23)

This notion of sisterhood is revolutionary precisely because women's differences are so much more obvious than the shared oppression and potential solidarity that feminist analysis reveals.

As Black feminist Mary Ann Weathers makes clear, having "female oppression in common" is not to share a homogeneous condition and is not a guarantee of automatic solidarity. It is, rather, the basis from which women can forge political links:

> *All* women suffer oppression, even white women, particularly poor white women, and especially, Indian, Mexican, Puerto Rican, oriental and Black American women whose oppression is tripled by any of the above mentioned. But we do have female oppression in common. This means that we can begin to talk to other women with this common factor and start building links with them and thereby build and transform the revolutionary force we are now beginning to amass. (1970, 306)

As integrative feminists affirm sisterhood, they explicitly recognize and resist the uses of difference by the powerful. They assert each woman's own struggle as part of the wider struggle of all women, and offer mutual support. Theirs is very far from a struggle on behalf of others who are weaker, but it clearly includes a commitment to the least among us and a recognition that no woman is free unless we are all free. The Redstockings Manifesto, for instance, stated:

> We define the best interests of women as the best interests of the poorest, most insulted, most despised, most abused woman on earth. Her lot, her suffering and abuse is the threat that men use against all of us to keep us in line. She is what all women fear being called, fear being treated as and yet what we all really are in the eyes of men. She is Everywoman: ugly, dumb, (dumb broad, dumb cunt), bitch, nag, hag, whore, fucking and breeding machine, mother of us all. Until Everywoman is free, no woman will be free. When her beauty and knowledge is revealed and seen, the new day will be at hand. (Redstockings 1969, 535)

This vision of sisterhood directly challenges not only structured divisions among women but divisive class and race and patriarchal evaluations and definitions that have kept us apart—"good women" and "bad women," old and young, housewives and welfare mothers, Black and white, middle-class and working-class, rural and urban, heterosexual and lesbian. It requires that relatively privileged women see their connection with "other" women; abandon false self-respect, false security, and derived and dependent privilege, all of which are conditional on their separation from other women (Rich 1979b); and see, for instance, that most of them are one man away from welfare and that the marriage relationship has much in common with prostitution. It also depends on women on the less powerful side of divisions being willing to risk seizing the resulting fragile opportunities for solidarity (Asian Women 1971; Murray 1970, 102).

Clearly, only feminisms opposed to all oppressions, with visions broad enough to encompass the interests of all women, can support this women-identification—a point that feminists of color and working-class feminists see most clearly. The development of these politics and of women-identification is extremely difficult in a racist, capitalist, mysogynist, and homophobic world. Nevertheless, integrative feminists take up this challenge. As Glenda Simms, a Black feminist and president of the Canadian Advisory Council on the Status of Women, asserts, "I would say that *we cannot now lay claim to 'global sisterhood.'* However, we can state definitively that our survival as a social force for change lies in our belief that sisterhood has the potential for becoming a global phenomenon" (Simms 1993, 190).

Commitment to this goal does not, of course, mean that working in mixed groups is always or even often an immediate priority for women of color, Jewish, working-class, or lesbian women, or for French-speaking women in Quebec. Integrative feminists who share the ultimate aim of a broad, racially diverse, cross-class international movement differ on the vexed question of whether, when, and how to work with women from more powerful groups, and their decisions will vary with particular circumstances. They all agree, however, that where it becomes possible, this developing sisterhood/solidarity represents a major and necessary resource in the struggle against race and class and colo-nial as well as male domination.

The sisterhood/solidarity of women "working together to achieve their common humanity" is a political requirement for a feminist movement that can "sustain unity of action against a social adversary," that is, the dynamic realization of Touraine's (1971) principles of Identity and Opposition. It must be both a personal and a political commitment and achievement. The existential courage to face nonbeing has as its necessary correlative the courage to take responsibility for being and to create—through confrontation and theory, culture, and community building—the necessary conditions for this struggle. This can neither be reduced to a narrow activism that ignores personal and spiritual transformation and expression nor limited to a false interior freedom that avoids the question of objective conditions and participation in history. It requires a recognition of the personal that enriches the notion of the political.

TOTALITY: INTEGRATIVE FEMINIST VALUES

Over time, integrative feminists began to recognize women's strength and values as well as to refuse women's oppression. Even before feminists had articulated a full theoretical critique of maleness and the male world, when they tended to see their project as one of aspiring to male-associated strengths and status and tasks, conflicting insights flourished. As we have seen, Simone de Beauvoir, Shulamith Firestone, Betty Friedan, Juliet Mitchell, with most feminists in the early period, failed to fully challenge androcentric values and to articulate women-centered alternatives. They nevertheless loudly and insistently denounced what men did to women. Since maleness was the shape not only of the humanity that feminists aspired to but also of the oppressor they resisted, activists came more and more to question men's behavior, men's evaluation of themselves, and men's standards for evaluation. Male aggression, for instance, was named and attempts were made to explain it. When men in every community reacted to these critiques, and to the demands that they participate in more human-centered, less destructive activities such as housework and child care, their belittling of women's concerns and women's work made it clear that their standards and values were political. Feminists responded by asserting their supposedly trivial and apolitical concerns, around housework for instance, more explicitly and consciously (Benston 1969; Mainardi 1970; Powell 1979; Le Théâtre de Cuisine 1976; Warrior 1970).

Feminist reasssessment of male and female activities robbed men of much ego gratification, and when men revealed their deep dependence on the exaggerated ego support of women, feminists identified this need as a handicap. They began to question the presumption that male-female differences were all female deficiencies and to see many of the differences as male deficiencies. One of the earliest explicit political articulations of this viewpoint appeared in the controversial "Fourth World Manifesto": "All female culture traits are defined as negatives by the dominant world culture. We do not believe them to be so (except those that keep us subservient, such as passivity, self-sacrifice, etc.).

We are proud of the female culture of emotion, intuition, love, personal relationships, etc., as the most essential human characteristics. It is our male colonizers—it is the male culture—who have defined essential humanity out of their identity and who are 'culturally deprived'" (Burris 1971, 118).

Feminists originally met apart from men to avoid their intimidating presence and active opposition and to build the confidence and skills they felt they lacked. But soon women's caucuses and autonomous women's organizations founded partly from a sense of women's weakness became a celebration of women together. Mutual support and collective action led to increasing appreciation of each other's strengths and sensibilities. In political groups, consciousness-raising groups, and alternative cultural and service institutions, feminists created contexts in which women could discover things about themselves and each other that are very different from the dominant stereotypes.

Although women's groups are not always successful, many women seem to be less dependent on individual glory, more sensitive to the needs of others, and less anxious for leadership roles than men. They seem more willing to do the necessary humdrum tasks and to avoid time-consuming discussions whose only point appears to be for participants to hear their own voices. Feminists who had overcome in themselves the tendency to automatically privilege what men did and said, frequently discovered that women could speak more sense than men, were more fun to be with, and were more radical. They came to see women-only groups as the preferred way to work—expressions of women's autonomous strength rather than refuges for underdeveloped women.

At the same time, lesbian feminists insisted that their lesbianism was not only an escape from men but an affirmation of love for women (Radicalesbians 1970). Native women, organizing within the Indian movement, began to challenge the notion of humanity as male through the reaffirmation of traditional views of a human balance between male and female. Black feminists questioned the stereotype that women are weak and produce nothing. They wrote proudly of their mothers' female culture and the significance of its lessons of resistance to both racial and patriarchal power; and they showed that Black women are productive, strong, and loving as well as oppressed.[4]

Historical and anthropological research, continuing consciousness raising, and women's growing struggle around housework revealed that the majority of all the world's women, however oppressed, are productive and strong. The economic contribution of indigenous women, pioneer women, women religious, slave women, Third World women, women workers, and housewives was revealed as disproportionate to men's. The human value as well as the economic value of women's work was affirmed. Motherhood and nurturing were no longer seen merely as the burdens of the oppressed (which they are) but also as quintessentially human activity confined, distorted, and exploited by male, class, and race power.

Black feminists' connection to more intact female subcultures and their understanding of the political importance of affirming Black pride against racist devaluation meant that Black feminists were among the most consistent in refusing the devaluation of women, naming women's specificity as a resource in struggle, and recognizing women's personal struggle to revalue themselves as a risky but necessary political effort:

Black people have freed themselves from the dead weight of the albatross of blackness that once hung around their neck. They have done it by picking it up in their arms and holding it out with pride for all the world to see. . . .

Women must come to realize that the superficial symbols that surround us are negative only when we ourselves perceive and accept them as negative. We must begin to replace the old negative thoughts about our femininity with positive thoughts and positive actions, affirming it and more. (Chisholm 1969, 42–43)

Quebec feminists, whose society had undergone "modernization" relatively recently, also drew on surviving women's subcultures and existing women's mass organizations to build feminisms that recognize women's specific concerns and work and values (Clio Collective 1987; Cohen ed. 1981; Dumont 1992). Their experience of nationalist cultural affirmation provided them as well with models for female affirmation that white English-speaking Canadian and U.S. feminists initially lacked. They drew direct lessons about the importance of female identity, pride, and solidarity from parallels with the nationalist struggle in Quebec (Jean 1977).

Increasingly, integrative feminists of all self-definitions broke with the male as norm and began claiming women's particular life and work experience as a political resource. Radical feminist Andrea Dworkin calls on the particular courage and concerns of women who have given birth, mothered, or been raised to mother as essential resources in the struggle against patriarchy. She finds heroism in women's "nurturance and sustenance of lives other than our own," and hope in women's "resolute commitment to and faith in human life" (1976, 63/64).

Lesbian feminist Adrienne Rich (1980) identifies a continuum of women-identified, female-centered, supportive relations that have never been entirely destroyed by the "compulsory heterosexuality" enforced by patriarchy. Revealing the draconian measures used throughout history to separate women, she argues that the nurturing, creative, and courageous female relationships that have nevertheless survived embody the potential of a new society.

Socialist feminists Ann Ferguson and Nancy Folbre see women's "nurturance work" as the source of both their oppression and their "potential strength as bearers of a radical culture . . . of sharing, co-operation and collective involvement" (1981, 329).

Feminists of color particularly stress that women's connection to and valuing of life provides a necessary value frame for radical struggle: "Will we liberate ourselves so that the caring for children, the teaching, the loving, healing, person-oriented values that have always distinguished us will be revered and honored at least commensurate to the honors accorded bank managers, lieutenant colonels and the executive corporate elite? Or will we liberate ourselves so that we can militantly abandon those attributes and functions, so that we can despise our own warmth and generosity even as men have done for ages?" (Jordan 1977, 115).

Thus we find radical, lesbian, and socialist feminists of all races as well as Black and Third World feminists (1) who are committed to full autonomy and equality for women and to the overthrow of patriarchy; (2) who are convinced that these goals must be achieved by ending the socially created hierarchical dichotomizing of life by gender as well as the enforced forms of motherhood, family, and heterosexuality that institutionalize gender hierarchy; and (3) who deny the existence of any biological or essential "femaleness" yet see no contradiction in affirming women's specificity and claiming it as a political resource in the feminist struggle.

For integrative feminists the female-associated values, activities, and characteristics they affirm are not female by nature but are historically more developed in women and have come to be labeled as female. Even as they are asserted and their social association with women recognized, the long-term aim remains to end the dichotomizing and hierarchizing of human qualities and activities by sex. In this politics the human becoming of women is inseparable from the integrative redefinition of humanity through the refusal of both the politically enforced social and historical fact of gender-divided human characteristics and activities and the devaluation/subordination of the feminine-ascribed integrative ones, such as caring, nurturing, cooperation, and intuition. This displacement of the male as norm calls on values grounded in diverse women's material and physical existence, but it is not an automatic expression of essential "woman." It is a hard-won *political* achievement of power by feminists to name desires, interests, and views of the world in opposition to the dominant views in their own communities and in the wider society.

The feminist affirmation of female-associated characteristics and activities challenges the separation of "man" from nature and women and his control of both as the measure of his humanity. It affirms holistic values and activities rather than the separative claims of production and profit. It is therefore, paradoxically, an explicitly antidualistic attempt to transcend all patriarchal industrial dichotomies. Clearly, integrative feminists do not so much reject the Marxist aim to end alienation or the Black-nationalist aim of full humanity as reveal the inconsistencies of these abstract visions, which can only be concretely pursued when the stark fact of men's oppression of women is recognized.

INTEGRATING MEANS AND ENDS

Faced with women's urgent needs and desires, and with reductionist debates whose terms they could not accept, thousands of feminists in the early years took up work with their sisters on local, clearly defined projects shaped by integrative values and commitments.[5] The seventies saw (1) continuing mass campaigns around issues like rape, sexism in advertising, equal pay for work of equal value, day care, abortion law repeal, and marriage and property law reform; (2) feminist initiatives in such mainstream contexts as education, health, social services, law, and the churches, trade unions, and professions; (3) a tremendous growth of alternative feminist services; and (4) the emergence of feminist culture and communities with the explosion of feminist literature, poetry, art, film, video, theater, and dance as well as cultural spaces such as newspapers, journals, coffee bars, bookstores, art galleries, and music festivals.[6]

In all these areas integrative feminists attempted to develop new ways of working prefiguring the new society and new social relations they sought, and contributing, through both their successes and their failures, to ever clearer notions of liberation as well as to women's capacity to live freer lives. They resisted false choices between structurelessness *or* hierarchy, homogeneous leveling of participants *or* stars, personal self-transformation *or* political action, sectarianism *or* liberalism, reformism *or* revolution, cultural *or* political focus. Women's human becoming and its cultural expression were recognized, celebrated, and included within the political project.

Sectarianism and vanguardism were rejected in a celebration of variety, reflecting a sense that feminist radicalism's diverse participants and areas of activity were necessary to a broader, still emergent feminism that would never be monolithic or single-voiced.[9] An essential part of this politics was the ongoing attempt to use liberatory means for liberatory ends: "In the practice of our politics we do not believe that the end justifies the means. Many reactionary and destructive acts have been done in the name of achieving 'correct' political goals. As feminists we do not want to mess over people in the name of politics. We believe in collective process and a nonhierarchical distribution of power within our own groups and in our vision of a revolutionary society" (Combahee River Collective 1977, 372). These feminists were not only claiming power but trying to transform it. Their aim was not control over others but the empowerment of all (*Les têtes de pioche* 1977; *La vie en rose* 1981): "The bonding of women must be utterly different and for an utterly different end: not the misering of resources and power, but the release, in each other, of the yet unexplored resources and transformative power of women, so long despised, confined and wasted" (Rich 1979b, 9–10).

One difficulty integrative feminists face in sustaining this effort is the constant and powerful mainstream pull to professionalize the political issues feminists name. Consciousness raising becomes group therapy led by professional facilitators. Wife-beating becomes domestic violence or family dysfunction. "Experts" emerge who can testify to "battered woman syndrome and "premenstrual stress" in trials of women who have defended themselves physically. These practitioners act *for* rather than *with* women whom they see as patients, clients, or defendants rather than actual or potential sisters in struggle. This trend defuses, contains, and co-opts feminist resistance.

Reform feminists with liberal, individual analyses often lend themselves unwittingly to this process. Integrative feminists, however, faced with women's urgent needs and the vastly superior resources of the state and established institutions, also often find themselves working in mainstream contexts and/or in autonomous feminist projects that are constrained by mainstream requirements. Women's studies programs are subject to university regulations. Banks require that groups have officers for signing purposes. The Elizabeth Fry Society, which works in Canada to support women prisoners, must abide by prison regulations. Feminist employment agencies designed to support immigrant women looking for work can, despite the best intentions, become agents for employers. Transition houses may have to match social service hours and adopt some social service procedures to receive funding and referrals. Fund-raising takes a tremendous amount of time and distorts projects by requiring that they fit funding guidelines (i.e., emphasizing service aspects over educational and political activities, requiring hierarchical structure, setting short-term deadlines for what should be long-term projects).

The pressures on feminism's transformative politics are widely recognized. Less widely recognized is the fact that these politics persist. Co-optation and attack are continuous, but so is the increase in movement experience and resources that feminist radicals can call on in their practice.

Integrative feminists make different decisions about where and in what ways to work—inside or outside "the system," with or without government or foundation funding, for instance. All agree, however, that it is important for feminists to work everywhere. Their "utopian" goals do not absolve them of the need for pragmatism. But theirs is pragmatism in defense of integrative practice rather than reductionist abandonment. It is less about accepting necessary limits on integrative goals than about learning, often through failure, how to develop effective structures without undermining the values of equality and collectivity. Feminists I interviewed spoke of learning from their experience, for instance, that broad political agreement and stable group membership are necessary for successful consensus decision making; that it is important to maintain openness and responsiveness when initiating a project, but it is also crucial to define it clearly at the outset, and it is possible to do both; that the specialized skills of individuals are valuable, and a group may reap benefits from them even while sharing skills and working collectively.

These feminists see themselves and others as contributors to politics that will be many more years in the making and will be fully realized only with the advent of a new society. They are committed to diversity, nonsectarianism, and nonvanguardism[7] as values in themselves, but also because they recognize that there is no single correct path forward.[8] The risks and lessons and debates of dynamic and disparate practice among diverse women are the main resources for the task of figuring out "what ... make[s] society change, what, besides raised consciousness, ultimately results in a new social order" (Charlotte Bunch).

CONCLUSION

In the early phase of the women's movement, feminists' recognition of and resistance to male power enabled them to forge a dynamic unity between Touraine's principles of Identity and Opposition to achieve (1) a fuller, more concrete vision of the free and equal humanity and society that is the aim of much progressive struggle and (2) a closer integration of means and ends through their vision's direct influence on and reflection in practice. Feminism's full development as a politics, however, requires also the realization of Touraine's principle of Totality, which occurred only with the later rejection of androcentric norms and values. When feminists build the power to refuse negative patriarchal definitions of women, their claims of autonomy and humanity no longer depend on their ability to distance themselves from female-associated activities and responsibilites that have been constructed ideologically and materially as inimical to freedom. They escape the paralyzing contradiction of making politics for women while denying themselves as women.

Progressive struggle can no longer be *man*kind's alone. Integrative feminists are presuming to redefine its nature by expanding its boundaries and definitions so that not only the struggle's means and ends but the seekers (male and female) become more "womanly" and thus more fully human. Feminists of varied communities can therefore affirm their particular female histories, skills, concerns, and responsibilties as grounds for a specifically female voice in defining their own communities and as resources in the struggle for progressive change in general.

After twenty-five years of this struggle optimism is tempered by realism. Nevertheless, integrative feminists continue to refuse all reductionist solutions to the tensions they seek to transcend in their practice. Amid the enormous variety of their immediate preoccupations all integrative feminists affirm the importance of:

- preserving feminism's autonomy of organization and practice while organizing, also, within male-dominated institutions;
- continuing to develop new political structures and processes;
- accepting the tremendous personal-political strain and excitement involved in refusing to sacrifice means to ends, process to product;
- seeking always a feminist personal-political ethic of interaction that emphasizes what one women (Nancy) called "niceness" and another (Esther) referred to as "doing a good job about how to support each other";

- building the strength to recognize the lack of easy answers and yet be able to "bumble along trying to figure out things" (Lorraine) without imposing false and simplistic limits and definitions;
- developing feminism as a perspective on the whole of society rather than a series of positions on separate "women's issues";
- resisting all dominations, including those of race and class and colonialism, without subordinating women's oppression or treating it as derivative;
- pursuing the difficult political quest for solidarity and sisterhood among women not only despite but through their diversity; and
- seeking always a synthesis of all the elements of life and politics that are separated in patriarchal, capitalist, and racist society.

In this project the integration of means and ends, of the personal and the political become an important aspect of a politics that seeks ultimately to integrate the productive and reproductive, the public and private realms of society in a world organized around the central value of life lived fully and equally in autonomy and harmony. Affirming women is, thus, a key aspect of the struggle against sexual and all other dualisms, and recognizing women's particularity is the basis of a general politics.

3

SPECIFICITY, EQUALITY, COMMONALITY, AND DIVERSITY

WOMEN'S SPECIFICITY

In the mid-1970s substantial integrative feminist published work began to appear.[1] This literature was clearly a product of years of rich activist experience. Its shift from androcentric to gynocentric approaches and its articulation of alternative feminist values partly reflect the lessons learned in practice by young, educated, often originally male-identified women and partly reflect the increasing power of other groups of women.

Many scholars had clearly moved past seeking simply to *include women* in existing artistic and literary traditions and academic disciplines to questioning the very core of such knowledge:[2] "We set out to make the maps we had a little larger, a little more complete and suddenly we found ourselves needing not flat maps but a globe" (Minnich 1977). This movement beyond what came to be called an "add women and stir" approach is a major epistemological challenge to patriarchal knowledge and represents the discovery, in the scholarly realm, of feminism's transformative rather than assimilationist voice.

Feminist historians, for instance, focused on the circumstances of women's lives to "look at ages or movements of great social change in terms of their liberation or repression of woman's potential, their import for the advancement of her humanity as well as 'his,'" and they found that: "the moment one assumes women are a part of humanity in the fullest sense—the period or set of events

31

with which we deal takes on a wholly different character or meaning from the normally accepted one. Indeed, what emerges is a fairly regular pattern of relative loss of status for women in those periods of so-called progressive change" (Kelly-Gadol 1976, 810).

Students of art and literature analyzed the specifically female sensibility they found in women's work (Chicago 1975), discovering or rediscovering, for instance, the integrative values in the work of Virginia Woolf and Zora Neale Hurston—and relating these to the distinct and long invisible experience of women defined by, and resisting, their sexual and domestic service to men.

Particularly but not exclusively in Quebec, with the emergence of *l'écriture féminine* (feminine writing) and *écriture au féminin* (writing in the feminine), contemporary writers began to consciously develop and explore this sensibility. They deliberately set out to uncover distinctive female existence and to construct the revolutionary possibility, in language and in the world, for free women to claim and create women-centered and women-identified feelings, physicality,[3] and activity, that is, to name potential lives for women that do not begin or end with men but with themselves and each other (Bersianik 1976; Brossard 1977; Gagnon 1977).

Sociologists began to construct "a sociology *for* women rather than *of* women." Their research encompasses "questions which could not have been posed before" and which reveal the "extraordinary depth and extent of what remains to be discovered by women working from the perspective and experience of women" (Smith 1975, 367).

In philosophy the concern was no longer to adjust classical theory to fit women in but to challenge the premises that have excluded women. Feminist philosophy would be "like" in its need to ground its formulations in the realities of the human condition, and "unlike" in that it would be developed from the novel angle of female exprience (O'Brien 1976). This focus revealed (among other things) that all political theory "is based on a rejection of the process of reproduction as a meaningful principle of social organization. It is this assumption that reproduction as such is of no importance in the creation of a significant life for man [*sic*], that is *the* sexist assumption at the very basis of political theory, out of which everything else flows" (Clark 1976, 51–52).

In the mid-1970s, as well, the early feminist critiques of maleness, male characteristics, and male values, along with political affirmations (more consistently voiced by Black than white feminists) of women's strengths, were joined by an academic literature that explicitly and systematically challenged the androcentric presumption that male-female differences equaled female deficiencies.[4]

Jean Baker Miller's book *Toward a New Psychology of Women* (1976) is among the earliest and most influential academic treatments of women's specificity. Miller argues what many Black and white rural and working-class women knew, and urban middle-class feminists were learning,[5] that although women's abilities to express vulnerability, to experience, give voice to, and understand emotions, and to work in cooperative ways have been interpreted as weaknesses and have left women vulnerable in male-dominated society, they should not be abandoned. They are absolutely essential to human community and would be decided strengths in a more compassionate society. And she shows how revaluing these qualities could contribute to an alternative value basis for the transformation of society. Autonomy, for instance, is currently understood as separation from the influence of and affiliation with others, necessarily opposed to cooperation and connection. A definition that incorporates rather than rejects women-associated qualities would see self-determination as growing from connections with others and would challenge the necessity of any opposition between the two.

Susan Griffin in *Woman and Nature: The Roaring inside Her* (1978) documents "man's attitude that woman is inferior to him and closer to nature" (xv). But unlike de Beauvoir, Mitchell, and Firestone, who earlier rejected that proximity, Griffin embraces it as ground for resisting "all those separations which are part of the civilized male's way of thinking and living" (xvi), including the separation of thought from the emotions that enables men to claim an objectivity and universality for their worldview. She posits a "different way of seeing"(xvi) rooted in women's lived experience of the union of mind and body, thought and emotion, the spiritual and the physical, and traces the halting, *conscious, political* process in which the love of women and women together can reclaim the physical, the fleshly and the emotional in an identification with nature that gives voice to women's repressed integrative experience and vision.

In her visionary exploration of these themse she quotes feminist poet Audre Lorde:

> Out of my flesh that hungers
> and my mouth that knows
> comes that shape I am seeking
> for reason.
>
> "On a Night of the Full Moon" (Lorde 1982: 20–21)

Here Lorde and Griffin are rejecting not reason or the male-associated side of the dichotomies but the separation of reason from emotion and the body, the dichotomies themselves.

Carol Gilligan's (1982) reports of research in which she found women's moral development to be different from men's and women's sense of justice to be more affiliative and contextual have also been influential in exploring women's differences from men as something other than a disability. Gilligan argues that incorporating women's concerns into dominant definitions of justice would lead to the recognition of relationships, connections, and mutual responsibility as well as a fairness that would greatly broaden and enrich how justice is conceptualized.

Here, as with Miller, Griffin, and Lorde, the argument is integrative—not a substitution of diverse women's concerns or characteristics for men's but the transformation of narrow male-defined definitions into less separative, less dichotomous concepts, structures, and ways of being. Elizabeth Janeway expresses the spirit of this project when she says, "[This] determination among women to define and value our own goals and methods, our own world view [is not] a reverse of the masculine view, a dichotomized half-scene, but an extension of an inadequate view toward one that is fully human" (1976, 10–11).

In the mid to late seventies, too, the political literatures of diverse feminisms revealed the emergence of perspectives grounded in women's lives, particularly in their subjection to physical use and abuse, their desires, and their general responsiblity (whether biological mother or not, married or unmarried, heterosexual or lesbian) for the survival and reproduction of human life and community.

Integrative socialist feminists saw that sexual domination is not reducible to class domination and recognized the key importance of reproduction to both capitalism and patriarchy and, therefore, to cross-class women's struggles: "Women's revolutionary potential emanates from the very nature and organization of the work *as domestic work*—both in its patriarchal and in its capitalist elements. To the degree domestic labor is a sexual organization of economic existence it is a cross-class reality that affects all women. This is the feminist, political concern which is left out of the discussion of domestic labor when the preexisting analytical categories of class take priority" (Eisenstein 1979, 170). Analyzing the relations of reproduction and the power inherent there, as well as the relations of production that are the traditional focus of socialist analysis, opened the way for the articulation of explicitly integrative socialist-feminist projects that broke with Marxist limits in attempting to bring together production and reproduction, class and gender,[6] and the material and psychological.

Quebec feminists, facing still-powerful conservative Catholic forces, realized from the beginning that the issue of motherhood was central to their struggle. Integrative Quebec feminists rejected expected roles and relationships and challenged men's power to enforce these, but they did not deny their mothers or their mothers' work and concerns. They named the dependence and drudgery predominant in many women's lives but honored these lives even as they denounced women's subservience (Dumais 1983; Jean et Théoret 1976).

For most integrative feminists of color, increasing theoretical and political attention to motherhood was an organic continuation of feminisms that had from the beginning recognized Black women's relative strength and independence and Black mothers' key role in a tradition of resistance to racist oppression (Chisholm 1969; Murray 1970; Ware 1970). Black feminists drew on their experiences of strong mothers in subcultures in which individualist, patriarchal norms were less dominant and mother-daughter connections had been less damaged or devalued than they had been for more colonized, more male-identified young middle-class, educated white women. The positive naming of motherhood and "motherwork" was for feminists of color often the restatement or re-affirmation of prefeminist women-centered values and connections (Bell-Scott et al. 1991): "Among Chicanas, it is our tradition to conceive of the bond between mother and daughter as paramount and essential in our lives. It is the daughters that can be relied upon. Las hijax should remain faithful a la madre, a la madre del la madre" (Moraga 1983b, 139). But for many young white urban feminists, particularly in English-speaking Canada and the United States, affirmation of motherhood and "motherwork" required a rethinking of prefeminist and early feminist androcentric dismissals of women and women's work and connections (Morgan 1977, 8).

Feminisms that concentrate exclusively on the male world and paid work emphasize women's sameness with men in ways that leave the androcentric invisibility of reproductive work largely unchallenged. They have little appeal to the vast majority of women of color and white women for whom labor-force involvement means demanding, routine, low-status, low-paid (though not unskilled) work undertaken on top of already exhausting work at home. Attention to diverse women's shared and particular responsibility for reproductive labor, by contrast, reveals deep connections among women with very different relations to the labor force and across divisions of race, class, and culture. A widely cited United Nations survey has estimated that women worldwide do between 66 and 75 percent of the work of the world, receive 10 percent of the earned income, and own 1 percent of the property. Focusing only on women's unequal place in the paid labor force masks the extent of the exploitation, and the contribution, of women all over the world, magnifying the barriers between women globally by emphasizing activity that is largely restricted to industrial societies and varies hugely among these. It generates divisive and mystifying terminology such as "working women," which hides the fact that housewives work and that "working women" do housework, and leads to the erroneous presumption that participation in the labor force involves simple and unambiguous "progress" for women.

The increasing power of wider groups of women has exposed these mystifications and contributed to the development of more adequate frames for the articulation of women's common interests. The emergence of the "relatively unexplored" (Rich 1976, xii) question of motherhood[7] and reproduction as a "major political question" (O'Brien 1976), which has enabled this development, is a product of the hard-won ability of feminists in all communities to draw on their own experience as it is lived and not as it is represented to them by patriarchal cultures.[8]

Housewives and single mothers (Black and white) refused to be patronized, and named the work they did and the joy they found in their children; Black and white working-class women who had two jobs—at home and in the paid work force—made it clear that paid labor was no liberation in itself; working-class, rural, Black, and older women who remained part of strong women's networks refused the early characterization of women as weak and divided. The early feminist (re)creation of women's space and women's culture, which enabled the discovery of lost women connections, women identification, and women love by urban middle-class feminists, took place as other women who remained part of more intact female subcultures and were much less susceptible to individualist, competitive male values were finding their voices.

The resulting articulation of integrative feminist values made it possible to move beyond the simple refusal of women's cross-cultural and cross-historical association with reproduction to acknowledge and examine women's specific experiences of and special relation to motherhood and the world. Thus it became possible to question the dominant definition of (an essentially male) humanity by opening up new personal and political territory. Motherhood was affirmed as a uniquely important and human, specifically female activity at the same time that its necessity for all women, its instinctual basis, and its biologically "natural" association with women were denied.

One theme of the writing on motherhood is the importance of men's involvement in or integration into the tasks of child care, not only to free women from the enforced labor involved but to humanize/feminize men and change their priorities and view of the world. It is clear to feminist radicals that increasing male involvement in child rearing before or apart from real increases in women's power would simply intensify men's control of reproduction and could actually be dangerous to children. Yet the end of the segregation and sexual division of labor in reproduction is deeply related to integrative-feminist visions of a world structured around entirely different life-centered activities that are the concern of all.

The fact that the *experience* of motherhood is largely women's is considered to place women center stage in progressive politics today, even though the *institution* of motherhood enslaves them. Integrative feminists' attention to motherhood is thus an assertion of motherhood's general significance, not the biologically determined position it is sometimes taken to be. Barbara Christian (1985) makes this clear in her description of the universal and transformative values that both African American Alice Walker and Nigerian Buchi Emecheta articulate in their literary treatments of motherhood:

> (B)oth writers see that motherhood provides an important insight into the preciousness, the value of life, which is the cornerstone of the value of freedom. They are also clear about the fact that this particular way of seeing the world does not necessarily proceed from being a biological mother; rather, it is a state of mind that women can lose if biological motherhood is legislated or forced upon them as their necessary state, a state in which they are restricted by being responsible for society's children. It is the entire society that must take on that angle of seeing the world, of judging its development from the standard of the value and continuty of all life.
>
> ... Thus motherhood includes not only the bearing of children, but the resistance against that which would destroy life and the nurturance of that which would support and develop life. For the female is inseparable from the struggle

of the living to be free, and freedom cannot exist unless, women, mothers or not, are free to pursue it. (247)

This dialectical centering/revaluing (for the world) and decentering/rejecting (for women alone) of motherhood as a defining metaphor for feminist struggle is expressed by Adrienne Rich:

> The tenderness, the passion, the trust in our instincts, the evocation of a courage we did not know we owned, the detailed apprehension of another human existence, the full realization of the cost and precariousness of life. The mother's battle for her child—with sickness, with poverty, with war, with all the forces of exploitation and callousness that cheapen human life—needs to become a common human battle, waged in love and in the passion for survival. But for this to happen, the institution of motherhood must be destroyed.
>
> The changes required to make this possible reverberate into every part of the patriarchal system.(1976, 285–86)

Thus the political visions of many Black, Third World, socialist, materialist, radical, and lesbian feminists call for the end of the sexual division of labor (the structural separation and marginalization of reproductive work) through the generalization of its integrative values, concerns, and tasks throughout society:

> We refuse to remain on the margins of society, and we refuse to enter that society on its own terms. . . . The human values that women were assigned to preserve [must] become the organizing principle of society. The vision that is implicit in feminism [is that of] a society organized around human needs. . . . There are no human alternatives. The Market, with its financial abstractions, deformed science, and the obsession with dead things . . . must be pushed back to the margin. And the "womanly" values of community and caring must rise to the center as the only human principle. (Ehrenreich and English 1979, 342)

Without exception, integrative feminists name the significance of diverse women's differences from men without resorting to biological explanations. They articulate these differences not as women's essence or as the source of women's automatic essential voice but as the material and physical ground from which diverse women, through conscious political struggle, can build the power to articulate specific interests and alternative integrative values.

Many integrative feminists are strictly materialist in the classical sense of the term. They document deeply different male and female life and work experiences and, therefore, differing relationships to social structures and institutions such as war, law, nation, class, wealth, family, and birth as sources of potentially distinct interests, values, and voices (Allen 1986; Collins 1990; Juteau-Lee 1983; Ruddick 1980). Others bring together economic and psychological, individual and social factors in theories that self-consciously expand the definition of materialism (Al-Hibri 1981; Deming 1977; Dinnerstein 1977; Fisher 1979; Harding 1981; Hartsock 1983; O'Brien 1981).

Far from narrowing feminism's political vision, the integrative focus on what is specific to women facilitates the development of perspectives on the whole of society. For affirming women is essential to challenging the hierarchical and oppressive dualisms that structure gender and all other dominations. The dualism that shapes Western thought is revealed to be the male condition, not the human condition it has been presumed to be. Diverse women's more integrated life experience and relationships to their bodies, their mothers, and birth suggest ways of thinking and being that overcome the apparently inevitable dichotomies of patriarchal thought:

> Feminism presents and represents a fundamentally different experience of the relations of people and nature than that posed by male dualism. It insists, further, that the principle of integration can form the basis for a political praxis which is rational, humane and far more progressive than any generically one-sided praxis, including Marxism, can ever be. (O'Brien 1981, 166)

> [Women's] experience of continuity and relation with others, with the natural world, of mind and body—provide [*sic*] an ontological base for developing a nonproblematic social synthesis, a social synthesis that need not operate through the denial of the body, an attack on nature, or the death struggle between self and other, a social synthesis that does not depend on any of the forms taken by abstract masculinity. (Hartsock 1983, 246–47)

Thus the refusal of the hierarchical separation of production and reproduction is the core of integrative visions that refuse all the separations and fragmentations of racist, patriarchal, industrial society and, in doing so, embody and develop feminist opposition to *all* domination: "The rejection of the dualism, of the positive-negative polarities between which most of our intellectual training has taken place, has been an undercurrent of feminist thought. And rejecting them, we reaffirm the existence of all those who have through the centuries been negatively defined: not only women, but the 'untouchable,' the 'unmanly,' the 'nonwhite,' the 'illiterate': the 'invisible.' Which forces us to confront the problem of the essential dichotomy: power/powerlessness" (Rich 1976, 48).

WOMEN'S DIVERSITY

Even though identity-based groups were not as common in the earliest years as they have since become,[9] women of many communities have been active and published[10] from the beginning of this phase of feminism and have spoken clearly and unequivocally as members of the groups to which they belong. Integrative feminists refuse the false choice between their ethnic, class, national, and gender identities and struggles that is constantly put forth by antifeminists and by nonintegrative feminists.[11] They read their race, ethnic, and class identities reciprocally through their identities as women—recreating each in the light of the others: "I want to be whole, I want to claim myself to be puertorican, and U.S. american, working class and middle class, housewife and intellectual, feminist, marxist, and anti-imperialist. I want to claim my racism, especially that directed at myself, so I can struggle with it, so I can use my energy to be a woman, creative and revolutionary" (Morales 1979, 91).

For all groups of integrative feminists this claiming of identities "they taught us to despise"[12] is a wide-ranging political process that involves not only the redefinition and revaluation of women and ourselves as women but women-centered articulations of new political issues and new perspectives on old ones. It aims to transform cultures, concepts of social justice, and progressive struggle in the groups and comunities we belong to and in society at large.[13]

This depends on women not only naming their oppression by men in general and by the men of their own groups but also reclaiming/re-creating female identity, passion, and tradition in their own cultures.

> Quand des femmes parviennent à se regrouper entre elles et qu'il y a du projet et du désir, de ce que j'appelle la belle énergie des femmes pour et avec des femmes, il y a du mouvement et un mouvement qui rend possible des changements radicaux qui nous font vibrer de tout notre corps, de toute notre sueur, de toute notre tendresse, de tous nos muscles, de toute notre force vers d'autres femmes. Cela s'appelle une modification du niveau de conscience. Tout cela remue autour de nous la merde patriarcale. Ça la rend évident and invivable. Quelque chose surgit ainsi de la quotidienneté: un mouvement des femmes qui en son sens métaphorique and réel nous ramène à la vie (1978, 2).[14]

This making visible of the hidden and distorted connections, strengths, and histories of women in particular cultures and in general lies at the core of all integrative feminisms: "When we name the bond between the women of our race, from this Chicana feminism emerges. For too many years, we have acted as if we held a secret pact with one another never to acknowledge directly our commitment to one another. Never to admit the fact that we count on one another *first*. We were never to recognize this in the face of el hombre. But this is what being a Chicana feminist means—making bold and political the love of the women of our race" (Moraga 1983b, 139).

The revolutionary process of ending women's silence and apparent acceptance of male definitions and values among increasing groups of women provides the necessary basis for feminisms whose subjects are not abstract "woman" but concrete and diverse women: "We must and will have women leaders among us. Native women are going to raise the roof and decry the dirty house that patriarchy and racism has built on our backs. But first, we must see ouselves as women. Powerful, sensuous beings in need of compassion and tenderness" (Maracle 1988, 25).

The autonomous bonding within ever more diverse groups of women, many from cultures with still strong (though subordinate) women's traditions, strengthens the women identification at the heart of all integrative feminisms. Paula Gunn Allen "recovers" the feminine in American Indian traditions, which "during 500 years of Anglo-European colonization ... [have] seen the shift from gynecentric, egalitarian, ritual-based social systems to secularized structures closely imitative of the European patriachal system" (1986, 195). Barbara Smith, with other Black feminists, has made the point that "Black women's ability to function with dignity, independence, and imagination in the face of total adversity—that is, in the face of white America—points to an innate feminist potential" (Smith 1983, xxiv). And Alice Walker's term "womanism" expresses Black feminism's strong organic roots in women's culture, emphasizing the conscious affirmation of women's specificity and strength that distingish it clearly from nonintegrative feminisms. A womanist "loves other women, sexually and/or nonsexually. Appreciates and prefers women's culture, women's emotional flexibility (values tears as natural counterbalance to laughter), and women's strengths" (Walker 1983, xi).

As more women win the power to be heard, the resulting articulation of more types and levels of difference has not narrowed self-defined groups of women but revealed powerful competing identities and ever richer cross-cutting specificities. The identities of Black, Jewish, lesbian, old, working-class, or disabled women are neither exclusive nor expendable. Integrative feminists are discovering and claiming complex multiple identities and links with diverse groups who share various important aspects of self. As more of women's particular experiences and perspectives are named, the recognition of diversity necessarily involves discovering the richness of shared specificities and complex politically constructed subjectivities rather than constructing high walls between static "insider" and "outsider" groups based on single, reified characteristics or conditions.[15] The retrieval and renewal of identities, then, paradoxically becomes a militant refusal of rigid, limiting concepts of self, the conscious rejection of essential identity for the complexity of political identity.[16]

> What am I? A *third world lesbian feminist with marxist and mystic leanings*. They would chop me up into little fragments and tag each piece with a label.
>
> You say my name is ambivalence? Think of me as Shiva, a many armed and legged body with one foot on brown soil, one on white, one in straight society, one in the gay world, the man's world, the women's, one limb in the literary world, another in the working class, the social, and the occult worlds. A sort of spider woman hanging by one thin strand of web.
>
> Who, me confused? Ambivalent? Not so. Only your labels split me. (Anzaldua 1983, 205)

This integrative political articulation of difference and identity should not be confused with the reductionist, apolitical vanguardist, essentialist, or merely "tolerant" expressions of diversity and identity that abound. It is a process that, in putting personal transformation at the heart of politics as "the most essential element of feminism" (Moraga 1983c, n.p.), reaffirms women's diverse daily experience as the ground of feminist theory and practice and supports early feminist radicalism's emphasis on consciousness raising as an individual and collective process that, through both reflection and action, takes women beyond their own experience. In this politics exchange and dialogue informed by imagination, by sensitivity to oppressions not necessarily one's own, and by a shared commitment to women and to "a revolution in the hands of women" (Moraga and Anzaldúa 1983, xxiii) fuel feminist theory and vision: "Cultural identity—our right to it—is a legitimate and basic concern for all women of color. . . . But to stop there only results in the most limiting of identity politics: 'If I suffer it's real. If I don't feel it, it doesn't exist.' If politics is about feeling—which feminism has rightfully politicizied—then we need to expand our capacity to feel clear through and out of our own experience as well" (Moraga 1983c, n.p.).

The capacity to connect beyond our own experience across deep differences requires that women in all communities name and resist power differences in the women's movement as well as in their own communities and society at large. Racism, anti-Semitism, homophobia, and ablism among feminists have to be resisted individually and collectively in our theory and our practice. This struggle becomes both necessary and possible as wider groups of women find their voices and affirm their identitites. As diverse feminist voices add weight to the articulation of women's specificity (differences from men) and name the world and women's issues from different points of view, they denounce, often angrily and with pain, the limits of feminisms that claim to speak for all women before all women can speak for themselves. They condemn the idea of an abstract "everywoman" with no specified class or race or sexual orientation. This "everywoman" is invariably white, middle-class, urban, heterosexual, able-bodied, and young (or at least not old), for it is women in these groups in our racist, capitalist, heterosexist, agist, ablist society who, like men, have to learn consciously to see their own particularism and the relations of power that entrench and mask it.

In North America, lesbian feminists (of all ethnicities) were among the first to raise these issues when they challenged the early women's movement's generally assumed (though sometimes explicitly enforced) heterosexual norm, a norm that at best leaves lesbians invisible and at worst actively silences or denies them. Regardless of whether lesbian feminists believe lesbianism is inborn or chosen (and they differ on this) and whether they see a sharp distinction between lesbians and other feminists or a continuum of women-identified women, in resisting the prejudice they face in the women's movement, they identified heterosexuality itself and not just marriage as an enforced practice that institutionalizes all women's oppression. Lesbian feminists' naming of the controlling role of enforced heterosexuality and creation of alternative lesbian cultures are major challenges to and resources for the women's movement, which have transformed and deepened the analysis, theory, and practice of all integrative feminisms.

It is not by chance that lesbian feminists were among the first groups to examine the divisions of race and class among them or that lesbian feminists, particularly lesbian feminists of color, continue to play a key role in challenging power differences in the women's movement.[17] The depth of lesbian women identification, sense of commonality, and passion for connection has enabled these feminists to face painful divisions while continuing to affirm their sisterhood, or at least the potential and their desire for sisterhood. The complementary relationships here between (1) affirming women identification and articulating differences from other women, and (2) defending the interests of particular women and expanding feminism generally are defining dynamics of integrative feminist practice.

These dynamics are clearly reflected, for instance, in the "Open Letter" that the DisAbled Women's Network, D.A.W.N. Toronto, circulated to the women's movement. Its angry criticism of intolerance, prejudice, and insensitivity (backed by power) challenges able-bodied feminists to live up to their commitments to inclusivity and provides important information to help them do so. This letter names disabled women's differences from and connections to other women and, in the process of education/consciousness raising, expands feminism: "We must never, never, never shut any women out. All women are equal. All belong in the women's movment. Or its all a BIG LIE. You need to deal with your problem of excluding us. We won't go away. We are your sisters. And we are organizing around the world! Soon the spectacle of disabled women picketing inaccessible women's events will become a reality. Every minority has a point when collectively we say ENOUGH IS ENOUGH. We are no exception. *We are your sisters*" (Doucette 1986, 81).[18] This process of challenge, which emphasizes not only commonalities and strengths but divisions and weaknesses and focuses not on resources and potential but limits and dangers, is important and difficult for all feminists, because none of us are free of their effects. Both feminists who question established power in the women's movement and those who are questioned feel at risk in the intense struggle for a truly multicentered women's movement.

The contributions of feminists suffering class and/or race and/or colonial as well as sex oppression are crucial to the development of integrative politics, not because they are automatically, by virtue of biology or life circumstances, endowed with insight but because the lived experience of oppression and struggle provides direct motivation for resistance and important resources for analysis. These insights and politics are not restricted to certain groups of women. "Color and class don't define people or politics"; rather, people are defined "by their struggles against the racism, sexism, classism that they harbor and that surrounds them" (Morales 1979, 91).[19] Integrative feminists are of all classes and races and sexual orientations. There are antiracist white feminists, anticapitalist middle-class feminists, and antiheterosexist heterosexual feminists.

Women of color, Jewish, Quebecois, working-class, and lesbian women, however, are more likely to bring to feminism experiences of cultures of resistance that ground them in a political sense of things that Anglo-Saxon middle-class, heterosexual, English-speaking, North American women generally have to learn from scratch—what Beverly Smith has called "political savvyness" (Smith and Smith 1983, 114). They are more likely to be aware that identity is constructed, not given, and is the beginning, not the end, of politics—a ground to move from rather than remain on. Their sense of the need for solidarity/sisterhood is often urgent. And they know at first hand that it is elusive even among women of color, lesbian women, and working-class women—that solidarity/sisterhood requires political will as well as shared experiences of oppression (which are, in any case, never fully and simply shared).

The political articulation of diverse women's voices and the political affirmation of diverse identities among feminists thus strengthen the inclusive antiracist and anticapitalist commitment of integrative feminisms. Such efforts do not, of course, ensure perfectly antiracist, anticapitalist, antipatriarchal, anticolonial politics, but they do ensure a real struggle to create a multicentered women's movement.

Recognizing and resisting power differences within feminism is necessary for the creation of this multicentered movement, but it is not sufficient. Both more and less powerful groups of women must go beyond this resistance to create themselves as centers of their own politics with active rather than reactive practice. In order to do this white and/or middle-class and/or heterosexual feminists who are aware of the many forms of oppression to which women are subject have to resist being immobilized by liberal guilt.[20] It is important that women who have presumed that they are *the* center of the women's movement relinquish this belief. But they have to remain the active center of their own politics. They need to listen to and learn from other women while contributing as well in the more active ways required for authentic political relationships and real solidarity.[21]

It is difficult, too, for women who are in the process of claiming their own centers to fully and immediately break with the hold of the colonizing "center." They may be tempted to play the "authentic other" and/or guru/seer/accuser/ teacher opposite inadequate or guilty colonizing feminists while, paradoxically, allowing the latter to remain the defining locus of the interaction.

Developing feminist identities grounded in the naming and revaluing of our various female conditions and traditions makes it possible to struggle against power differences in feminism as one important part of autonomous processes of connection and transformation. For it privileges autonomous practices in which women create themselves as the centers of their own politics,[22] as the necessary building blocks of multicentered movement.

The editors of *This Bridge Called My Back* describe how their book "began as a reaction to the racism of white feminists [but] soon became a positive affirmation of the commitment of women of color to our *own* feminism" (Moraga and Anzaldúa 1983, xxiii). And Toni Cade Bambara in her foreword to the book describes how this shift awakened the contributors "to new tasks"

and a new connection	us
a new set of recognitions	us
a new site of accountability	us
a new source of power	us

Two years later, in 1983, the guest editorial collective of the special "Women of Colour" issue of *Fireweed* prioritized connections among the latter from the beginning of their project and stated their dual and related goals as "first to reach out to women of colour and second, to educate white feminists" (Gupta and Silvera 1989).

With these nonessentialist, nonreductionist, identity-based politics new forms of nonhomogenizing solidarity become possible and the meaning of difference can be transformed from "divide and conquer ... [to] define and empower" (Lorde 1984, 112). Feminists have always recognized and refused to be divided by patriarchally constructed and defined differences among women. Today, the growing activism and power of many groups of women has made it possible for feminists to recognize some of women's differences from men and from each other also as resources in a common, though not monolithic struggle against male power and other forms of oppression. This alternative, positive understanding of differences lies at the core of the creation and celebration of multicentered movement. It does not mean the end of universal values or visions but promises that any woman's particular experience can illustrate and inform the universal. As Sonia Sanchez says, "I've always known that if you write from a black experience, you're writing from a universal experience as well. ... I know you don't have to whitewash yourself to be universal" (1983, 142).[23] This is not the denial but the transformative redefinition of center, in a politics that aims to be truly the product of all women and to be deep and broad enough to represent the interests of all women.[24]

Women's affirmation of specificity in our claim to human status "as women" has challenged dominant dualistic conceptions of humanity dependent on the construction of marginal and deficient "others." The resulting break with homogeneous concepts of universal (masculine) humanity has contributed to new visions of shared humanity no longer based on sameness, and to new concepts of equality and justice constructed upon rather than at the expense of human particularities.

In integrative politics, therefore, the apparently irreconcilable principles of equality, specificity, commonality, and diversity are essential to each other. They function in dynamic relation. The transformative dialectic among them is a rich source of creative new thought and practice essential to politics that aim beyond assimilation to such radically new integrative concepts and relationships as *unity without sameness* and *difference without domination*.

4

INTEGRATIVE PRACTICE

The theoretical affirmation of women's equality, specificity, commonality, and diversity has both contributed to and benefited from developing integrative practice among diverse feminists. Over the years feminists with many different self-definitions clearly identified the sharp distinctions between their own politics and that of reductionist feminists who categorize themselves similarly. Integrative lesbian feminists rejected narrow lesbian separatism (Bunch 1975a, Clarke 1983b); integrative socialist feminists criticized socialist feminists who "refuse to understand how patriarchy defines our private lives and that this is as crucial to understanding society as capitalist class relations" (Eisenstein 1979, 351); integrative radical feminists criticized others who accept male values uncritically and for whom the "image of the person . . . sought for the woman is a masculine one" (Lewin 1977, 85). Integrative feminists of color criticized those for whom identity politics is "a racial/cultural separatism . . . where we dig in our heels against working with groups outside our own particular race/ethnicity" (Moraga 1983c, n.p.). Integrative anticapitalist Quebecois feminists committed to sovereignty criticized those who failed to recast nationalist and/or Marxist frames: "Indépendiste, marxiste, syndicaliste, les femmes actives et politisées travaillent présentement dans un encadrement fait et pensé par des hommes, c'est-à-dire, pour le salut futur de générations d'hommes (de mâles) à venir" (Brossard 1976a, 2).[1]

45

Explicitly integrative political perspectives have been delineated under a variety of names, including nonaligned feminism (Bunch 1976), radical feminism (Brossard 1978; Rich 1978a), Black feminism (Combahee River Collective 1977), metaphysical feminism (Morgan 1977), socialist feminism (Eisenstein 1979; Jaggar 1983), ecofeminism (King 1981), materialist feminism (Juteau-Lee 1983), Third World feminism (Moraga and Anzaldúa 1983; Sandoval 1991), womanism (Walker 1983), all-inclusive feminisms (Dill 1983), féminisme libertaire (Sève 1985).

These integrative positions are often self-consciously synthetic. For instance, socialist feminists characterize their politics as a synthesis of feminism and Marxism (Petchesky 1979). Black feminists emphasize integrating the struggles against race, class, and sex oppression (Combahee River Collective 1977). When Bonnie Thornton Dill (1983) wrote about the importance of integrative feminisms, she called them "all-inclusive feminisms."

Integrative perspectives are also sometimes presented as a way of transcending inadequate options. Ecofeminists seek to "transcend the radical feminist/ socialist feminist debate" (King 1981, 14). Charlotte Bunch (1976) argues for "nonaligned feminism" as a way beyond the imposed choices between support and opposition for the Left and between political and cultural feminisms. Chela Sandoval (1991) identifies as characteristic of Third World feminism a "differential consciousnes ... [that] kaleidoscopes together" equal rights and revolutionary, supremacist and separatist forms of oppositional consciousness to constitute "a new paradigm" (16). Adrienne Rich (1976) describes dialectical politics and holistic visions that create alternatives to false and limiting patriarchal polarizations. She writes about the feminist necessity to live the "dialectic between change and continuity; to reintegrate the mother (care) and daughter (free spirit) in ourselves that patriarchal attitudes have encouraged us to split and to polarize" (257); to find the strength to refuse to either become our bodies or try to exist without them (291); to queston the division between "man/culture/consciousness and woman/nature/unconsciousness" (82).

These are not, of course, identical feminisms. Nevertheless, they share all the integrative-feminist commitments. The fact of their diversity is an important potential resource in sustaining many pressing concerns in the face of competing demands for time, energy, and attention. When their common commitments are recognized and dialogue is fostered, integrative lesbian, Black, Third World, radical, socialist and ecofeminisms can all strengthen important and potentially underdeveloped aspects of each other's politics. Feminists in each tendency can and do (often bitterly) call others to account for failures in areas of special concern. Together, these diverse feminisms keep present and available to all, the various necessary components of what is and must remain an imperfectly synthesized politics.

I don't want to imply that these are all simply parts of a single overarching politics. There are very real differences of analysis among them, aspects of which are not compatible. When only differences and not shared values are recognized, however, misrepresentations and misunderstandings are widespread, debates are less productive than they could be, integrative feminists gain less from their diversity, the broad integrative tendency of feminism remains invisible, and the qualitatively much deeper division between integrative and nonintegrative feminisms is obscured.

LEGAL REFORM AND EQUALITY

As women have put "women's issues" on the agenda of courts and legislatures, feminists have observed the limited and in many cases negative impact of reform framed only in terms of the classic notion of individual equality:

- No-fault divorce laws and property law reforms give equal rights to husband and wife without acknowledging the economic vulnerability of women and children or the enormous and particular contribution/needs of children's prime caretaker, thereby greatly enhancing men's chances of custody and women's of poverty (Brown 1981).
- The legal renaming of rape as sexual assault in Canada (in a vain attempt to rid the charge of the misogynist cultural presumptions so damaging to the woman victim in court) has served to hide the fact that the crime is not gender-neutral but an attack by men on women (Cohen and Backhouse 1980).
- Court rulings in the United States acknowledge women's individual right to abortion as a right to privacy without recognizing that the private realm is not a realm of freedom and self-determination for women but actually institutionalizes men's power over women (MacKinnon 1983).
- Simple equal-pay laws can be used to redress wage discrimination only for the relatively few women who do exactly the same work as men.

In a society structured by gender women's main problem is not that irrelevant differences between the sexes are used by individuals and organizations to exploit women (which they are) but that the system is structured in such a way that sex differences of condition are real and therefore often a relevant category of distinction. On the one hand, limiting the requirement of equal treatment by law to circumstances where the female condition approaches that of the male restricts the principle to application to very few areas of life or to very few exceptional individuals. It does not, for instance, allow discriminatory treatment of pregnant workers to be questioned. On the other hand, requiring equal treatment of unequals tends, as some of the examples above show, to disadvantage the disadvantaged and further entrench inequality.[2]

Integrative feminists involved in struggles for legal reform have increasingly realized that it is not the recognition of women's specificity in law that disadvantages women, but men's power to define and enforce this specificity to male advantage with the androcentric presumption of the male as norm. In fact, escaping from the dilemma posed by the two different inadequate equality approaches requires building the power to displace the male as norm—that is, to achieve legal reform that constitutes diverse women in law *as women* and not as either "different from men" or "would-be men."

Therefore, integrative-feminist legal initiatives have developed that do not abandon but rather defend, extend, and redefine the concept of equality while recognizing also specificity and diversity. Integrative feminists seek to end "enforced inferiority by sex rather than sex differential treatment" (MacKinnon 1979, 115)—to achieve equal outcomes rather than equal treatment—and they realize that minor adjustments of laws or the extension of existing rights to women will not achieve this outcome. Such an outcome will require major social restructuring, reconceptualization of rights, redistribution of power, work, and wealth, and the revaluation of women's work and activities.

Men's rights, like their sexual freedoms, property rights, and right to privacy, have developed historically as rights *over* women's bodies and women's (and other men's) work. Therefore, integrative feminists' struggle for full person-hood and equality in law is not simply for access to men's rights: it challenges these rights and the male dominance they institutionalize. Women's resistance to the oppressive sex, class, and race divisions of rights and of labor requires naming in law specific female harms (such as sexual harassment), needs (such as pregnancy leave), and contributions (such as primary care of children) that breach patriarchal silences. Since the integrative vision includes ending the sexual division itself as well as the sexual disadvantage of women, these specificities are named in ways that do not institutionalize them as female.

Examples of these initiatives, undertaken in the legal arena as elsewhere by feminists with diverse self-definitions, include the groundbreaking legal charac-terization of sexual harassment as sexual discrimination (MacKinnon 1979); the development of a legal statute that defines pornography as a gendered practice that degrades and injures women or men and children treated as women and lists specific actionable harms not before named in law (Dworkin 1989); arguments that earning power and professional qualifications must be recognized as assets in property settlements in the event of divorce (Dulude 1984), that primary care provision to a child should entail presumptive rights of custody (Brown 1981), that pregnancy is not a disease and that rights for pregnant women should be argued on their own terms and not on disease or disability models (Finley 1986), and that the wages of women doing "female" jobs should be compared with those of "male" jobs of comparable skill and working conditions, though not necessar-ily in content, and adjusted accordingly.[3]

Among integrative feminists involved in legal theory and legal reform, there are vehement ongoing debates. Nevertheless, without institutionalizing activ-ities as female, they all recognize diverse women's specific conditions and activities and advocate reform that speaks to specifically female needs. They all directly challenge male power in their attempts to constitute diverse women in law as other than deficient departures from the male norm. They make visible whole areas of life that have remained invisible and undervalued in a system of law that recognizes only male needs and rights. They also contribute to the slow process of eroding racial and sexual (if not class) divisions of labor and power.

Although legal reforms alone cannot achieve social transformation, law reform guided by integrative principles and a clear analysis of class and race and patriarchal power is contributing to social change and to the further development of practical feminist activism guided by transformative visions.

SEXUALITY AND EQUALITY

Simple equality principles have also proven inadequate for feminist practice in the area of sexuality. Here, too, specific female oppression and interests as well as specific feminist values and visions are articulated as a ground for practice. Much of the original motivation for young radical women of all kinds to form separate women's caucuses and groups and develop their own politics came from their sexual treatment at the hands of radical male "comrades" and from their dissatisfaction with the failure of male-defined radicalisms to question instrumental and exploitative sexualities.

Feminists in the 1960s at first criticized the prohibition of female sexual expression. Black feminists, for instance, refused male-defined Black-nationalist prescriptions for the politically correct good Black woman: "The men are black and proud; the women are black and pregnant" (Ware 1970, 164). And they, with others, criticized the "sexual revolution" for its hypocritical failure to recognize women equally as sexual beings and to give women equal access to its "freedoms" (Koedt 1968). It is not just women's exclusion from sexual activity, however, but also their exploitative and differential inclusion that is the problem (Densmore 1971; Un groupe de femmes de Montréal 1971). Black feminists analyzed the racist and sexist influences that shaped even some radical and nationalist Black men's apparent sexual preference for white women (Morrison 1971; Sizemore 1973). The feminist agenda expanded to incorporate not only demands for equal sexual self-determination for women but also critiques of patriarchal sexuality and sexual relations, and commitments to tranform these:

> There is no *freedom* or *justice* in exchanging the female role for the male role. . . .
> There is no *freedom* or *justice* or common sense in developing a male sexual sensibility—a sexual sensibility which is aggressive, competitive, objectifying, quantity oriented. There is only equality. . . . Commitment to sexual equality with males . . . is a commitment to becoming the rich instead of the poor, the rapist

> instead of the raped, the murderer instead of the murdered. I want to ask you to make a different commitment—a commitment to the abolition of poverty, rape, and murder; that is, a commitment to ending the system of oppression called patriarchy; to ending the male sexual model itself. (Dworkin 1976, 12)

Integrative feminist challenges to the "male sexual model" involved both (1) a critique of patriarchal sex as competitive, aggressive, exploitative activity shaped by racism as well as sexism and proscribed and/or enforced for women by men, and (2) the exploration/creation of autonomous women's desires and/or relationships as an alternative to patriarchal prescriptions. This two-sided project entails the complex articulation of women's points of view as both victim and actor: "From a Black feminist standpoint sexuality encompasses the both/and nature of human existence, the potential for a sexuality that simultaneously oppresses and empowers" (Collins 1990, 66).

Enforced heterosexuality, the mystification of romantic love, restricted reproductive freedom, prohibited abortion, enforced sterilization, exploitative reproductive technologies, marriage as an institution, prostitution, pornography, rape, and incest divide and degrade women and mandate their sexual service to men. But they are criticized by women who are not entirely contained/defined/shaped by patriarchal power, women who envisage alternatives and seek to build less exploitative relationships that celebrate women's connections and desires rather than deny them. Both lesbian and heterosexual integrative feminists of all ethnicities explore what women want sexually and what feminists want to want: "The fear of our desires keeps them suspect and indiscriminately powerful, for to suppress any truth is to give it strength beyond endurance. The fear that we cannot grow beyond whatever distortions we may find within ourselves keeps us docile and loyal and obedient, externally defined, and leads us to accept many facets of our oppression as women" (Lorde 1978, 58). They struggle with the contradictions of their current desires and relationships, as they envision and move toward new ways of loving and being in community; and they live the tensions as challenges and resources in political movement: "Lesbian feminism was a movement based on the power of a 'we,' not on individual women's fantasy or self-expression. This was a movement that had a politics—that realized that prostitution, pornography, and sexual violence would not be redefined as therapeutic, economic, or sexy to fit any individual woman's whim in the name of free choice. It was a movement that recognized the complexities of choice and how so-called choices for women are politically constructed" (Raymond 1989, 153).

Integrative feminists differ widely in the relative importance they give to the use and abuse of women's sexuality and of women's labor in our oppression, though all agree that both are significant. Not all integrative feminists emphasize struggles around sexuality or sexual exploitation. Those who do vary enormously in the relative weight they place on resisting women's sexual exploitation/degradation and/or on exploring sexual alternatives. They are deeply divided over what tactics are appropriate in the struggle, over what role, for instance, the state can play in liberatory reform; whether the struggle against pornography represents an opportunity to reach traditional women with feminist messages or a danger of co-optation by the right or both; how the impacts of race and class as well as patriarchal oppressions are constructed sexually; what kinds of sexual exploration and creation are possible in a society structured by the sexual exploitation of women; how to name the nature and extent of women's sexual exploitation in ways that add to women's sense of agency rather than victimization.

All integrative feminists recognize, however, that although women as well as men are shaped and damaged by prevailing sexual relations and values, women do not define and enforce them. Part of the struggle for the power to re-create ourselves and our world therefore involves enabling women's autonomous sexual voices. These voices potentially sound very different from the part(s) we speak in the patriarchal sexual scenario. They question the whore-madonna divide, name the sexual fear of women and the harms done to women, speak of women's passion for women, and name the powerful desires for caring, communication, reciprocity, security, excitement, and community that appear, if at all, only in contained and distorted forms in female fantasies endorsed by the dominant culture.

Integrative feminists agree that these alternative women-defined descriptions of reality express not an essential/ biological women's sexuality immune from social structuring but the insights of an exploited group with sexual interests and needs very different from those of the dominant group. Forced pregnancy, rape, pornography, and prostitution look more dangerous and more threatening, and marriage and sexual purity more limiting and more necessary to most women than to most men. Women across our differences share an interest in opposing these institutions. From their distinct interests as women feminists can build resistance to patriarchal sexuality/sexual oppression.

Integrative feminists disagree about the extent to which women's sexual desires today are different from and less separative than men's and, therefore, about the degree to which women's autonomous expression and creation of sexual values can prove an immediate resource in feminism's struggle for new, less exploitative sexualities. They all accept, however, that women's desires cannot be read from the dominant sexual culture or practices and that liberatory sexuality will have to be consciously created against these.

Despite their wide differences in emphasis and tactics, integrative feminists agree that sexuality/sexual desire is a social construct currently shaped by and shaping patriarchal relations of domination. Sexual behavior is not separable and cannot be understood apart from the political context of patriarchal, race, and class power. Therefore sex is not a "private" but a political concern. Both lesbian and heterosexual feminist practices around sex are necessarily collective as well as individual struggles about social and personal transformation:

> I am reflecting on the erotic as our embodied yearning for mutuality. As such I am interested not merely in a "theology of sexuality"—examining sexuality through theological lenses; but rather in probing the Sacred—exploring divine terrain—through sexual experience. . . .
>
> I am attempting to give voice to an embodied—sensual—relational movement among women and men who experience our sexualities as a liberating resource and who, at least in part through this experience, have been strengthened in the struggle for justice for all. (Heyward 1989, 3)

> Resisting patriarchy ultimately meant that I had to reconstruct myself as a heterosexual, desiring subject in a manner that would make it possible for me to be fully aroused by male behaviour that was not phallocratic. In basic terms, I had to learn how to be sexual with a man where his pleasure and/or his hard-on is decentered, and mutual pleasure is centered. That meant learning how to enjoy being with a male partner who could be sexual without viewing coitus as the ultimate expression of desire. (hooks 1993, 21)

This is a struggle not only to end sexual exploitation or sexual repression but to create new sexualities and a new world. For both heterosexual and lesbian integrative feminists of all ethnicities and classes, whether they emphasize the spiritual or the material aspects of their struggle, or women's oppression or agency, this process requires collective, self-reflective, open practice in which both critique/resistance and exploration/creation are guided by integrative values and visions and both personal and social practices are open to question and reform.

INTEGRATIVE IDENTITY-BASED POLITICS

In North America more activist women are becoming aware of the gender aspects of their struggles and are organizing *as women*;[4] and more long-time feminists are choosing to organize around a variety of identities.[5] The resulting growth of identity-based activism has involved an increase in exclusive, apolitical expressions of identity as well as transformative ones. Nevertheless, in the women's movement in the 1990s (at least outside academic women's studies programs) it is increasingly the case that:

- the definition of issues and struggles comes from women closely involved;
- any group of women can presume to make contributions to general feminist analysis and struggle on the basis of their particular experience;

• diverse identity-based and other groups are consciously building feminist politics.

In this context integrative feminist groups such as those described below, are emerging in which shared identity becomes the basis for organizing across diversity and articulating universal values; the articulation of a shared identity helps women both find and celebrate each other, become present to other feminists, and participate in the wider women's movement. These groups provide bases to reach out from, not to hide behind. They strengthen the many voices that are necessary components of a multicentered women's movement (Albrecht and Brewer 1990; Anzaldúa 1990; Cardinal 1992; Peters and Samuels 1976; Telling It Collective 1990).

The National Black Women's Health Project, Women Hurt in Systems of Prostitution Engaged in Revolt (WHISPER), and Welfare Warriors are inspiring, women-positive, women-defined groups with large and inclusive visions of social change, providing a focus of organization and identity for specific yet diverse groups of women. They enable their members to find each other, name and act on their own needs and concerns, and become the center of their own practice; and they provide powerful evidence of the significant ways this contributes to general understanding and empowers all women.

For these three integrative-feminist groups, organizing around specific yet broad identities (in these cases as poor mothers, prostitutes, and Black women) is a basis for consciously including far more diverse women than would otherwise be possible. The groups foster communication and inclusion among their members and break down divisions imposed and enforced by structures of power.

Shared identity is a political achievement for these groups, not a given condition. They use feminist principles stressing women identification, support, and affirmation as a frame for respectful sharing and connection across differences, combined consciousness raising and activism, and the development of original women-centered analyses that situate their members' own oppression in global structures of domination. Group members understand their own organizing to have global significance and use it to link with and learn from women around the world.

Welfare Warriors,[6] founded in 1986 in the United States, is a group of poor mothers concerned to:

> put an end to stereotypes immobilizing us. . . . Welfare myths not only serve to justify sexist, racist and classist abuse of women, they also work to keep us divided and conquered. Poor mums distrust each other, fearing that the other mothers really fit the stereotypes of dependent, lazy, loose, lying, child abusing and drug addicted. Working and middle class people are conned into using us as scapegoats for society's failures. Thus the myths serve to keep people from uniting to fight for justice in their community and developing effective strategies in this war of the rich against everybody else. (Gowens 1993, 33)

The group insists that *all* people are dependent on each other and society, not just mothers of children who depend on community child support (welfare). These mothers are, in fact, among the most independent mothers in the nation, but they *should not have to be:* "As long as dependence is a dirty word, all groups of dependent people will continue to be oppressed. As a nation we must once again strive for a society based on interdependence" (33).

This alternative vision of a cooperative and caring community that respects, supports, and provides resources for children and others is the ground from which the Welfare Warriors reach out "to forge global connections with other poor mothers—and to develop alliances with other feminist groups" (Welfare Warriors 1991, 20). They articulate the specific needs and terrors of mothers "living poverty"[7] around the world as extreme instances that illuminate all women's condition.[8]

They draw attention to poor women's particular possibilities of solidarity around the world and to their potentially major contribution to all women's struggle: "Impoverished mothers are the largest group of women in the WORLD—and possibly the most multi-racial, multi-cultural, multi-able group of women that exists. We have great differences but one thing in common: *we are MOTHERS raising children in systems that do NOT work for mothers and our children and which are very HOSTILE to us*" (Welfare Warriors 1991, 20).

The [U.S.] National Black Women's Health Project[9] was founded by Byllye Avery in 1983 after many years of involvement in feminist health activism and two years of discussions and planning with African American sisters. The First National Conference on Black Women's Health Issues that year, cosponsored by the National Women's Health Network, drew two thousand women to Spelman College and began a process of networking and organizing that has resulted in 150 chapters in thirty-one states in the United States and numerous groups in the Caribbean and Africa (six groups in Kenya and one each in Barbados and Belize in 1990).

The group's newsletter, *Vital Signs,* radically challenges the sexist and racist ideology and structures of the dominant culture and society while putting Black women at the center of an alternative, inclusive, caring, sisterly, cultural, spiritual, political, and Afracentric yet universal perspective. Angela Davis, long-time Black activist and member of the Project's board of directors, stresses the power of this frame for working across diversity:

> Our work focuses on physical, mental and spiritual health needs of Black women. Until recently, the emphasis has been on "self-help," as adapted from the larger feminist health movement, but geared to the particular needs of Black women. The most exciting aspect of this organization is its ability to unify Black women beyond the limitations of age, social class, occupation and geographical origin. A typical gathering includes girls as young as thirteen and women as old as seventy-five, rural women on welfare and women who are lawyers or univer-

sity professors, women from the most rural areas of the South and women from urban centres like New York. (Bhavnani 1989, 77–78)

The National Black Women's Health Project is built around a core process of Black women sharing their lives and experiences, naming their own health needs, and providing for them through self-help groups. Mutual support and validation are stressed. Love and nurture are affirmed; Black women are urged to love themselves first, a radical spiritual as well as political message. The group's developing analysis recognizes social inequality and oppression along with personal power and responsibility. Their practice is designed to help Black women value themselves, to recognize the ways that adversity has built them up as well as worn them down, and to become active agents in their own lives and in social change.

The National Black Women's Health Project organizes and supports local groups, promotes public education, runs large and innovative health projects, and participates in protests aimed at policy change. The group strives to empower Black women to define and meet Black women's health needs while articulating an analysis of the class, race, and gender oppressions that put their health at risk: "Our analysis, which will be put into practice around effective coalition building, must always be done around the sisters who are forced to function at the bottom of the society—that is, the sisters who have the lowest income, who have the least access to services, who have the hardest time. They are who we need to hear from" (Avery 1990b, 308).

The group's practice is built on the premise that a culturally specific rather than abstract approach is needed for success. But the group is not isolationist. The National Black Women's Health Project grew out of both the limitations and the strengths of the National Women's Health Movement and has become a powerful force shaping a more inclusive, racially aware, and multicentered feminist health politics in general. This politics has been further enriched by the subsequent founding of the National Latina Health Organization in 1986 and the Native American Women's Health Education Resource Center in 1988;[10] and by increased global networking. Members of the National Black Women's Health Project, for instance, attended the International Conference on Women in Africa and the African Diaspora in July 1991, networking with Women in Nigeria (WIN) and WAND (the Women and Development Unit of the University of the West Indies).

Women Hurt in Systems of Prostitution Engaged in Revolt[11] was founded in 1985 in Minnesota. "WHISPER is an organization of women who have survived systems of prostitution and women who are committed to ending this form of violence. We are women of diverse, racial, ethnic, and economic backgrounds, and all affectional orienations. Together we are creating change in our personal lives and our communities" (*When...* n.d., n.p.) Systems of prostitution are defined broadly by the group as "any industry in which women's and

children's bodies are bought, sold, or traded for sexual use and abuse,...
[including] pornography, live sex shows, peep shows, international sexual slavery, and prostitution as it is commonly defined" (*WHISPER* 1985/8b, 1).
Members' common experiences and identities as survivors of various aspects of
the sex industry provide an inclusive frame for participation by otherwise
extremely diverse women. The identity basis of membership in this group, as
with those described above, enables it to reach out and build support among
women across deep divisions: "For every real difference between women (like
culture, religion, race, class, sexual orientation, disability), prostitution exists to
erase our diversity, distinction and accomplishment while reducing all of us to
meat; to be bought, sold, traded, used, discarded, degraded, ridiculed, humiliated, maimed, tortured and too often murdered for sex." (ibid.).

The acronym WHISPER is used to highlight the fact that women in systems
of prostitution do name and share their experiences, although their knowledge
is drowned out by the dominant myths "shouted out in pornography, in mainstream media and by self-appointed experts" (ibid.). The group supports and
empowers prostitutes and ex-prostitutes in their efforts toward individual and
social change. It is also concerned to link with other women's groups, educate
other women and the wider public, and contribute its members' particular
knowledge to the development of general feminist analyses and practice.

In addition to producing its newsletter, the group coordinates an oral-history
project with prostitutes and ex-prostitutes; runs Radical Education Groups,
"where women can examine the impact of prostitution on their lives, explore
new ideas and together create change in both our personal lives and communities" (*Before...* n.d., frontispiece); produces educational and informational
material for prostitutes; organizes and participates in educational forums
across North America; pressures for legislative change; advocates increased
services for survivors; and participates in local, national, and, increasingly,
international consultations.

WHISPER intends the voices and presence of survivors of systems of prostitution to influence wider feminist struggle. The group analyzes prostitution in
the context of all women's dependence and vulnerability to patriarchal power,
attending to the particular vulnerability of women subject also to race and
class power. Members bring a "blend of passion, personal experience, commitment to feminism, and a history of organizing against violence against
women" (*Before...* n.d., 9) to their claims that systems of prostitution can best
be understood as forms of violence against women. Through their own experience of prostitution and their research, members document prostitution as a
particular form of rape and reveal the significant parallels between the situation of prostitutes and trapped and battered wives. Members of WHISPER,
like feminists everywhere, are refusing the definitions of experts and taking
power into their own hands to name and change their lives. They provide new

understandings not only of prostitution but of wife beating, rape, and the structures and processes of male power generally. Their work has helped activists in the battered women's movement develop more radical, inclusive analyses and encouraged them to extend services to survivors of prostitution as well as marriage.

WHISPER is convinced that only feminisms that speak to the experience of its members are worthy of the name. In developing the *particular* voices of prostitutes they contribute to the *general* development of feminism as the inclusive, multicentered movement it must be. The group provides a place from which prostitutes can reach out to both their peers and other women as centers of their own politics and struggle. Increasingly, their outreach efforts include a global component. The newsletter carries information about global structures of prostitution, their relationship to international economic and military arrangements, and the growing resistance of women around the world.[12] And group members participate in international dialogue, learning from and contributing to the ways these struggles are understood and defined for legal, policy, and political purposes. For instance, WHISPER joined the sixteenth session of the United Nations Working Group on Contemporary Forms of Slavery in Geneva in 1991 (reports in *WHISPER* 6, nos. 1–2 [winter/spring 1992]).

Welfare Warriors, the National Black Women's Health Project, and WHISPER are just a few of the North American feminist groups that presume to speak for particular groups of women in voices with universal significance and to be central in a movement with many centers. In naming their own experience they expect to deepen our understanding of all women's reality and to contribute to shaping feminism generally: not because all women's experience is the same, but because the reality is shared and must be named, understood, and attacked in its entirety by us all. They insist on the importance of their particular perspectives and practices without being vanguardist or sectarian; they actively support and celebrate the coming to voice of other groups of women everywhere.

SOLIDARITY ACROSS DIVERSITY

At the same time as feminists are naming their specific and various identities more consciously, and more diverse women are becoming feminists, many feminists in both identity-based and non-identity-based groups are attempting to recognize and honor differences among women more explicitly in their practice. They are responding not just to the fact of diversity but to the often angry demands that lesbians, women of color, older women, disabled women, poor women, prostitutes, and others have made over many, many years. The active insistence of many less powerful women that power differences must be recognized in feminist politics is fueling attempts to develop more inclusive practice (Ignani et al. 1988; Matthews 1989).

Feminist conferences, festivals, publications, demonstrations, and projects often try (with greater or lesser success) to represent, reflect on, contribute to, and grow from the increasing breadth of women's movement. This is evident in the changing content of such Journals as *Canadian Woman Studies, Fireweed, Healthsharing, Ms., Off Our Backs, Sinister Wisdom, Sojourner,* and *Woman of Power* and in the proliferation of workshops, events, dialogues and conferences designed to explore the question of working together across diversity.[13] International Women's Days, Take Back the Night Marches, lecture series, music festivals, art and photography exhibitions,[14] women's studies, health, psychology, spirituality, peace, and other conferences, even when not explicitly focused on themes of racism and/or diversity, increasingly reflect the richness and heterogeneity of women's movement. Groups and projects attempt as well to build on the new possibilities of and requirements for authentic political relationships and dialogue that emerge with the development of autonomous practice among wider groups of women. Angela Davis commented in an interview on the progress being made and the distance still to travel:

> Previously white women used to be quite anxious and quite defensive, they expressed feelings of guilt when the issue of racism was raised, now they reflect more seriously on the problem. I recently spoke at a conference in Milwaukee organized by ... the National Association of Women's Centers. The member groups are community women's centres and campus women's centres. Their mission statement was very good. It pointed out the need to develop multiracial, multi-ethnic women's centres and to structure the services in such a way that they reflected the experiences and the needs of women of colour. But then the problem was that while there were some women of colour present at that conference, it was a majority white conference. So I raised the issue there of what they were going to do in order to translate this understanding into strategy and tactics. It is exciting that we can now talk about strategic and tactical approaches. (Bhavnani 1989, 73–74)

In a plenary address to the "Making the Links: Anti-Racism and Feminism Conference," in Toronto in November 1992, Black feminist poet Dionne Brand talked about her need, both personal and political, not just for coalitions around lowest-common-denominator agreements but for new and exciting groups and spaces, and for a women's movement in general in which we could all, in all our diversity, be fully and unapologetically, even joyously, everything we are.[15] Each of us, being more fully who we are would at the same time strengthen our unity.

The Latinamerican Coaliton to End Violence against Women and Children (LACEV) in Toronto is one example of a strategic coalition based on shared visions rather than lowest common denominators. It is feminist defined, though not restricted to feminists, and brings together community members, victims of violence, and members of and workers with over thirty English- and Spanish-speaking grassroots groups and social agencies "to eradicate violence against women and children in the Hispanic community within the context of the family and society at large" (Latinamerican Coalition 1992, 3).[16]

The Coalition defines violence broadly and politically in ways that take into account class and race and gender power. It fosters new forms of dialogue and organization in engaging the strengths of diverse women to collectively seek women-centered alternatives to professional definitions and practice. Participants have no doubt that their culturally specific work is a "contribution to the eradication of violence, not only from the Spanish-speaking community, but from the Canadian society at large" (Latinamerican Coalition 1992, 2). They are claiming one of the many centers of Canadian feminism as their own.

Our attempts to create new political and cultural structures have not always met with success, however, and are often fraught with tensions, anger, resentment, and guilt. To devise ways of working together and forms of solidarity that can emphasize and affirm both our commonality and our diverse conditions, feminists must tackle in our movement the deep divisions of power that structure the very society in which we are embedded. We cannot hope to fully overcome these divisions in our movement until we have a new society. But we can make real progress, and the success of our struggle depends on this. It is a challenge that must be faced.

IDENTITY AND SUBJECTIVITY:
THE POLITICAL BASIS OF MULTICENTERED MOVEMENT

In the 1980s and '90s integrative political expressions of identity have emerged alongside reductionist (sometimes even essentialist) expressions of identity that undermine solidarity and sisterhood among women. Moreover, feminist practice that recognizes power differences among women and is consciously designed to build on women's diversity coexists with practice that remains narrow and ethnocentric, oblivious to differences of power among women. These tensions provide rich ground for theoretical reflection on both the potentials and the risks of "identity politics." As in the 1970s, the existence of reductionisms in a period of creative practice has fueled thoughtful articulations of integrative positions.

In numerous articles and books feminists examine the importance of the political articulation of women-centered identity and diversity to the development of analyses that incorporate attention to all oppressions, and practices that build sisterhood on the basis of difference.[17] As Charlotte Bunch said in a 1991 interview,

> I believe that only as we take seriously the differences among women, the different forms that our oppression manifests itself in, will we begin to feel a solidarity not based on denying anyone's experiences, but that fully embraces all women. . . .
>
> As you look at all the diversities, you can then ask, "What seems to be common to all these different writings?" or, "What are the ways in which all these different women talk about some common experience?"
>
> You arrive at the commonality after seeing diversity. (Goldberg 1991, 24)

The approach Bunch describes is both more obviously necessary and increasingly possible as more varied groups of women articulate cross-cutting identities and subjectivities, name their varied realities, struggle together (though on occasion impatiently and with no immediate success) around questions of women identification and sisterhood, and create themselves as multifarious *female* centers of their own politics in a movement with many centers of equal general significance.

Integrative feminists both inside and outside identity-based groups understand that they are what bell hooks calls "a stage in the construction of radical black [or other] subjectivity" (1990, 20) and are key to building the political relationships essential to broad and inclusive, though not homogeneous women's solidarity. Integrative feminists are vocal in their criticisms of "identity" politics that reduce the political to the personal; proclaim a tolerance of "difference" that displaces concern with structures of power; and/or impose sectarian, separatist, essentialist, moralist, or vanguardist limits on the political process.

Janice Raymond (1989), for instance, contrasts "lesbianism as a political movement to lesbianism as a lifestyle" and decries the fact that "in the name of tolerance, difference, and lesbian community, many lesbians are dissuaded from making judgments." She argues that "a tyranny of tolerance that passes for difference" (154) reduces "lesbian liberation [to] ... lesbian libertarianism" (149) and argues instead for lesbian feminism grounded in community and lesbians' radical "difference from what hetero-society wants us to be" (155). Hazel Carby makes a related point in criticizing "'politics of difference' ... in which the politics of race is actually being avoided, displaced, and even abandoned, ... because [it] works with concepts of diversity rather than structures of dominance" (1990, 84–85). Pratibha Parmar (1989), while recognizing the importance of collective identities, warns that differences among women can be exploited if identities are used to compete in hierarchies of oppression. Barbara Smith and Merle Woo (hinden 1991) and June Jordan (Christakos 1992) insist, with all integrative feminists, that it is, after all, shared political visions and shared struggles, and not just shared identities, that make allies.

5

NONINTEGRATIVE ANTIESSENTIALIST REDUCTIONISMS

REDUCTIONIST DEPOLITICIZATION OF FEMINISM

The emergence in the 1980s of feminisms with visions encompassing the dialectical integration of women's equality, specificity, diversity, and commonality has prompted new, more sophisticated reductionisms that repudiate these integrations, just as those discussed in Chapter 1 repudiate personal-political and means-ends integration.

Mainstream North America's deeply apolitical and individualistic culture leaves feminism's transformative political project particularly vulnerable to both essentialist and antiessentialist reductionisms. These include (1) reductionist affirmations of female identities presumed to be determined by birth or condition and in turn to determine one's political perspective and possibilities and (2) opposing reductionisms that absolutely reject "identity politics" and/or the affirmation of women's specificity as always and necessarily determinist and essentialist. According to these nondialectical approaches, diverse and complex women-centered identities, far from being resources in the struggle to create new politics and a new world, stand in absolute contradiction to women's equality and solidarity. They are either rejected or claimed on these grounds by nonintegrative feminists and antifeminists respectively.

Diversity and Solidarity

Feminism's early success in naming the shared conditions and experiences of diverse women is a political triumph, won despite enforced divisions of class, race, and sexual orientation. It is not, even in its most inadequate articulations, simple capitulation to dominant myths regarding "natural" or essential gender, but progressive political resistance to divisive myths and facts of difference. In fact, this political articulation of women's shared interests provides the necessary frame for the affirmation of women's diversity.

With the articulation, also, of women's specificity it becomes possible to explore their diversity outside male imposed terms, be they liberal, socialist, nationalist, environmental, or conservative. Radical, socialist, or poststructuralist feminist rejections of women's specificity therefore remove the basis for the creative and women-affirming explorations of differences as well as commonalities so crucial for the creation of a multicentered nonuniform feminist solidarity.

To see integrative-feminist affirmations of women's diversity as rejecting women's specificity or commonality is not only to appropriate but to decontextualize and depoliticize key aspects of feminist struggle. As we have seen, the need to resist racism among feminists, and sexism in communities of color, has meant that feminists of color affirm *both* diversity among women *and* women's specificity more consciously, explicitly, and persistently than many other feminists: "Our times and our children's lives demand that black women live with a double consciousness and sing a double song—of gender and race" (Prettyman 1980, 240). Only grievous ethnocentric and apolitical misreadings could mistake the militant integrative "refus[al] to make a choice between our cultural identity and sexual identity, between our race and our femaleness" (Moraga and Anzaldúa 1983, 106) for a rejection of the category "women."

These misreadings are ethnocentric on numerous counts. One obvious one is their failure to honor the integrity of the positions of integrative feminists of color by recognizing only part of their arguments. This failure is related to a tendency on the part of reductionist feminists, one that bell hooks has commented on (1990, 21), to hear what feminists of color have to say only about race and racism. Full and visionary theoretical and strategic analyses by feminists of color, their insistence that power differences among women are significant and that general feminist struggle must be built through the affirmation and activism of all women, are often read reductively as simple refusals of feminist solidarity and struggle on the grounds of race![1] These readings are then used by reductionists to buttress their arguments that recognizing women's specificity is incompatible with recognizing their diversity and that the search for commonalities, connections, and solidarity is necessarily ethnocentric. This plays on the liberal guilt of some and the fear and anger of others, inhibiting rather than supporting the exploration of differences in the construction of social movement. It undermines the women identification that is the source of both the need and the courage to engage in the daring political process that Cherríe Moraga calls for when she says:

> It is essential that radical feminists confront their fear of and resistance to each other, because without this, there *will* be no bread on the table. Simply, we will not survive. If we could make this connection in our heart to hearts, that if we are serious about a revolution—better—if we seriously believe there should be joy in our lives (real joy not just "good times"), then we need one another. We women need each other. Because my/your solidarity, self-asserting "go-for-the-throat-of-fear" power is not enough. The real power as you and I well know, is collective. I can't afford to be afraid of you, nor you of me. If it takes head-on collisions, let's do it: this polite timidity is killing us. (1983a, 34)

This powerful quotation recalls us to the spirit of a feminist activism deeply aware of power relations, highlighting the need to affirm and love women and to recognize both commonalities and differences in a life-and-death struggle against male, class, and race interests that seek always to divide us.[2] In racist, homophobic, and class-divided societies, it is always easier to see differences than commonalities among women. False ethnocentric presumptions of sameness among women are damaging to the feminist project because they undermine the recognition of, and the resistance to, power differences between women that is the only possible basis for solidarity. Nevertheless, if we don't pursue our connections politically as we also name our differences, we are simply naming and replicating power-based divisions.

Feminists who address differences of power and privilege among women without also recognizing women's shared, though not identical, specificity and vulnerability fail to see this. They have lost sight of the importance and fragility of feminism's main vision and task, which is to build solidarity/sisterhood across deeply structured and heavily enforced separations.

Visions and Values

To suggest that women's specificity must be denied in order to claim women's equality and humanity and/or to recognize women's diversity leaves no basis for transformative politics. As we have seen in previous chapters, affirming integrative values such as cooperation, nurturing, connection, and reciprocity, which are trivialized and relegated to women and the margins of society, has provided the alternative rationality allowing feminisms to move beyond pressure for assimilation to transformative visions and practice. The affirmation of diverse women's specific work, characteristics, and concerns is the necessary basis for a deep challenge to the patriarchal power that institutionalizes oppressive dualisms and dominations. It makes possible dialectical redefinitions of universality/diversity, individuality/community, autonomy/dependence, justice/compassion, equality/heterogeneity and supports new visions of life-centered nonhierarchical nonuniform social arrangements, and new forms of multicentered (rather than either monolithic or decentred) political unity and struggle. Antiessentialist denial of women's specificity is a refusal of this alternative value frame and therefore limits feminism to a politics of either redress (equality) or reaction (deconstruction) rather than transformation.

The Integrative Challenge

It is a risky business for feminists to move from simply denying to recognizing and attempting to redefine the hitherto male-defined differences between genders, races, and classes that have institutionalized and justified not only women's subordination but all systems of domination. Women's special historical identification with reproduction, caring, sharing, nurturing, and nature has in the past been inseparable from our oppression—has been, in fact, its very structure. The redefinition of women's difference by diverse feminists is inseparable from the arduous task of restructuring our fragmented and alienated world in which relations of domination are built from the hierarchical separation of reproduction and production, nature and society, leisure and work, and in which what is associated with the female is marginalized and devalued.

The *liberatory* revaluation of the traditionally devalued female-associated aspects of life that is crucial to progressive change requires a critical dialectical approach that enacts transformation at the very moment of affirmation. Integrative feminists have to create politics that acknowledge and affirm women's specific histories as diverse women, even as they challenge sex differences, their essentialist articulation, and the oppression that is justified and structured through them. They must affirm one side of patriarchal gender dualism as part of the process of undermining that dualism and name diversity as part of the process of undermining the hierarchies built on it.

It is a measure of feminism's growing strength that the androcentrism and male power that have defined and enforced gender dualism to women's disadvantage can be challenged and that diversity can begin to be claimed as a resource in a common feminist struggle. Feminist practice increasingly grounded in autonomous explorations and analyses of women's diverse lives and experiences has enabled us to envision the project of personal/political transformation in female-centered integrative terms.

Yet a sense of danger remains. Many feminists suspect that any articulation of women's specificity is an unwitting capitulation to patriarchal myths, right-wing values, and/or biological reductionism. This fear is heightened when women's "special" nature and "special" subordinate responsibilities are glorified and called women's nature by a resurgent right wing. It is aggravated also by tendencies to read all feminist treatments of diverse women's specificity as essentializing and homogenizing. Feminist essentialism is rare.[3] Very few feminist radicals understand biology apart from the social, regard it as absolutely determining of social possibilities, or deny women's diversity in naming their difference from men. Nevertheless, the common unfounded belief that essentialism is widespread adds to many feminists' reluctance to deal theoretically with women's specificity.

LIBERAL REDUCTIONISMS: SPECIFICITY DISPLACES EQUALITY

Suspicion of feminisms that name women's specificity and criticize the limits of a simple equality frame is fed by the obvious limits of some nonintegrative work in which insistence on the importance of women's work and women's sphere and/or attention to reproduction and its values tend to displace rather than enrich the feminist project (Elshtain 1979; Friedan 1981).

Betty Friedan, for instance, in her book *The Second Stage* (1981), argues that if the important equality struggles of feminism are to be "the beginning of something more basic than a few women getting good [men's] jobs" (127), the "either/or" (246, 263) choice between work *and* family, posited by the right and accepted by some feminists, must be refused. In contrast to her earlier minimization of women's work, she acknowledges the "the real value of 'woman's work' to life and to society, whether it is done by women or men inside the home or out" (247); and she urges recognition of the importance of both work and love in "both/and thinking" (246) that affirms women's particular concerns and ways of being in a "new kind of . . . generative [political] power" (257).

But Friedan's is not an integrative transcendence of the principles of specificity and equality in a deeper antidualistic women-centered critique of fragmented industrial patriarchal society. She proposes instead a "transcendence of sex role polarization" (261), potentially fueled by the capitalist search for profit (329), protected by "guaranteed rights of privacy" (214), and possibly led by "men [who] may be the cutting edge" (35) today.

Friedan's critique of her own earlier brand of equality-defined feminism (which, she argues, substitutes for the feminine mystique an equally narrow "feminist mystique" that denies "women's own needs to give and get love and nurture, tender loving care" (28) and appeals to women only as individualists) is accompanied by a rejection of feminism's analysis of and resistance to male power. Friedan's refusal to countenance issues of male power means that despite her denunciation of "obsolete liberalism and simplistic conservatism" (248), her discussion of the limits of a simple equality frame, and her apparently integrative sentiments, hers is ultimately a pluralistic rather than integrative position. Sex role transformation and "equality and choice" (322) remain the defining aims. Although this may now be a choice *for* as well as against motherhood and/or family, it remains an individual choice in the context of a dichotomous society. In integrative feminisms the principles of equality and specificity are each transformed in the other's presence, contributing to deeper and broader and more radical visions of change. Since a liberal frame cannot, in fact, encompass this transformative integration, Friedan's recognition of women's specificity involves abandoning equality and, with it, feminism.

RADICAL AND SOCIALIST FEMINIST REDUCTIONISMS: EQUALITY DISPLACES SPECIFICITY

Anti-integrative Theoretical Critiques

The essentialism of the right wing and of the few feminists who may presume a dual-species humanity and/or homogeneous womanhood and the abandonment of the struggle against male power by some liberal feminists who affirm women's specificity have tended to obscure the possibility of affirming women's specificity as part of a deeply radical integrative politics. As a result many feminist radicals adamantly oppose *all* feminist discussion of women's particular characteristics on the grounds (1) that such discussion necessarily implies a biologically given "women's nature" and distracts attention from structures of power and (2) that acknowledgment of difference always unavoidably validates inequality. A position paper of the Radical Feminist Organizing Committee argues, for instance, that

> to our way of thinking, the notion that "women's qualities" are somehow better than "men's qualities" is in basic opposition to the theory of feminism. Feminist theory states that the potential for all qualities—from aggressiveness to nurturing—exists within each person. But under a system of male supremacy, certain traits are deemed "masculine" and others "feminine." Since gender is not innate but is socially constructed the goal of feminism is to eradicate the categories of "masculine" and "feminine." An appeal to women's distinctive characteristics only reinforces these categories.... Focusing as it does on men's and women's character traits, the movement ignores the structural aspects of male supremacy. ... Historically, the notion of women's difference has been one source of our oppression, and, in the current context, extolling it traps us once again in the male supremacist system. (Mehlman, Swanner, and Quant 1984, 16)

The issues here are real ones and are raised by a radical-feminist network that has made important contributions to feminist analysis and practice.[4] But their position fails to distinguish between recognizing socially constructed male-female differences and believing in essential differences that determine social possibilities. They accept the reductionist either-or choice between the principles of specificity and equality and so are forced to urge that male-female differences be denied or at least ignored in feminist theorizing. "The categories 'masculine' and 'feminine'" can thus only be "eradicated" through assimilating women to men's humanity, for the male norm cannot be challenged. The larger vision of transforming men and the world in accordance with alternative integrative values cannot be articulated, and the ground for an alternative feminist rationality and transformative politics is lost in a politics trapped within an equality frame.

"Antiessentialist" critiques of the recognition of women's specificity are made by both radical and socialist feminists in the name of defending a politics of equality.[5] Nonintegrative radical feminists charge radical feminists who affirm women's specificity, whom they usually call cultural feminists, with abandoning politics and the struggle for equality amid essentialist celebrations of women and women's culture (Echols 1989; Redstockings 1975). Alice Echols (1989), for instance, traces what she considers to be feminism's downfall as a radical politics to the early lesbian-feminist arguments that autonomously defined female sexuality is or could be different from objectifying, exploitative male sexuality and male-enforced sexual relations and could serve as a resource in the struggle toward a more equal and human society. Echols sees this argument as abandoning feminism's claim to women's equality, not only because it is, in her terms, "essentialist" but also because it departs from libertarian openness by advocating nonexploitative mutuality in sexual relations.

In fact, almost all radical feminists, whether they acknowledge or deny women's specificity, are committed to ending oppressive sex-role systems, which they insist are the product of unequal exploitative social relations rather than nature (Douglas 1990). Yet many socialist feminists characterize all or almost all radical feminisms, including those that reject the specificity of women, as grounded in a belief in the natural superiority of women and dismiss them on that ground (Segal 1987). Alison Jaggar, for instance, argues that "by accepting sex differences as biologically given, many radical feminists in the United States have turned away from the traditional task of feminism" (1983, 98). Hester Eisenstein sees in the work of diverse radical feminists "a feminist version of the eternal female" (1983, 106).

Andrea Dworkin, who has vehemently and eloquently rejected biological reductionism as "ideological rot" (1977, 43), is nevertheless widely criticized as "essentialist." She expressed her absolute opposition to essentialism on a panel for Gay Pride Week in New York in 1977:

> Pulled toward an ideology based on the moral and social significance of a distinct female biology because of its emotional and philosophical familiarity, drawn to the spiritual dignity inherent in a "female principle" ... women have increasingly tried to transform the very ideology that has enslaved us into a dynamic religious,

> psychologically compelling celebration of female biological potential. This attempted transformation may have survival value. . . . But the price we pay is that we become the carriers of the disease we must cure. (1977, 115)

Even so, she is frequently accused of believing that "'men oppress women' because they are men" and "implicitly assuming biologically deterministic views of sex, gender, and sexuality which offer few possiblities for change" (Collins 1990, 173). Ann Snitow acknowledges that "Andrea Dworkin is not a biological determinist in [her book] *Intercourse*" (1989, 222) and yet reads her as arguing that "in sex women are immolated as a matter of course, in the nature of things" (207).

Patricia Collins and Ann Snitow both mistakenly read their disagreement with Andrea Dworkin over the nature and depth of sexual oppression conceived as a social relationship as a disagreement over biological determinism. Ironically, it is not uncommon for the extreme social constructionism of radical feminists such as Andrea Dworkin and Catharine MacKinnon to be criticized as essentialist. In fact, both reject the analytical distinction between biological sex and social gender, because, they argue, it masks the deep social construction of sex and sexuality as well as gender, not because they deny social construction.[6]

Socialist feminists who reject radical feminism as by definition biologically determinist are nonetheless divided over whether to acknowledge women's specificity or utterly reject it. Lynne Segal sees all feminist theorizing about difference as a "search for a female biological essence or psychic experience which is unchanging and universal" (1987, 214). Linda Gordon associates the recognition of women's specificity with "an assumption that some eternal female principle defines our destiny beyond our control" (1986, 30).

However, as we have seen, an increasing number of integrative socialist as well as integrative radical, Black, Third World, native, and Quebecois feminists believe that the "specific social or class position of women gives them a specific standpoint" (Jaggar 1983, 368).[7] Quebecois feminist Micheline de Sève counterposes to the "egalitarian feminism of Simone de Beauvoir" a

> feminism which places "value" on women's experience. . . . To value the culture of women does not mean perpetuating their political invisibility and their confinement to the sphere of family relations. Rather, it entails the application of their experience to all human activity, both public and private: the women who have camped for years at the gates of the Greenham Common military base in Great Britain embody both a break with the dominant social order and affirmation of an alternative lifestyle. They intervene as women and as autonomous political beings, defending their quality of life and the environment without violence but not without firmness. (1989, 180–81)

Patricia Hill Collins examines Black feminist thought as "a specialized knowledge created by African-American women which clarifies a standpoint of and for Black women, ... thought [that] encompasses theoretical interpretations of Black women's reality by those who live it" (1990, 22).

Political Debates: The Case of Sexuality

The development of integrative-feminist perspectives has provoked noninte-grative critiques in many areas of practice. The resulting debates have been particularly harsh around issues of sexuality. These issues consequently provide a good example of the differences between integrative and nonintegrative femi-nist approaches.

Continentwide grassroots activism concerning such issues as sexual harass-ment, pornography, rape, rape in marriage, incest, prostitution, and pornography includes public education, provision of alternatives for victims, demonstrations, speak-outs, direct action, film and slide shows, letter-writing campaigns, self-defense classes, tours of red-light districts, support for sex-industry workers, economic pressure, pressure on government for legislative reform and enforce-ment, and the creative exploration of alternative nonexploitative, nondependent sexual and sensual relationships.

Integrative-feminist participants in and supporters of these activities vary greatly in their positions despite their shared values. They put varying emphases on public education, direct action, economic pressure, legal reme-dies, and the creation of alternatives; and they disagree, for instance, over:

- whether even the transformative attempt of Catharine MacKinnon and Andrea Dworkin's Minneapolis Ordinance to put women into law with specific harms and rights can successfully use the patriarchal courts to women's advantage against pornography;
- whether in a pornographic and sexually hierarchical society, *any* sexual rep-resentation can escape its context and be read unproblematically apart from exploitation—that is, whether the category of erotica can be a real one;
- whether direct action (against pornography outlets for instance) discredits the struggle;
- whether one can use the law to create conditions that will undermine the institution of prostitution while supporting and empowering prostitutes.

Despite differences in emphasis and strategy, however, integrative feminists share a perspective that, as noted earlier, includes:

- political analyses of sexuality as structured by and structuring male power;
- integrative values that involve a commitment not only to ending sexual domination and exploitation but also to creating, in the personal/political process of struggle, a nondependent, nonobjectifying, and empowering sexuality.

Integrative analyses and visions have been vociferously and angrily criticized on a number of counts by reductionist feminists working within a libertarian or liberal frame. These feminists, for instance, reject any self-reflective critique of sexuality as an unacceptable restriction of individual freedom. For them, practice around sexuality is not a collective personal/political effort to realize certain still evolving values individually and in society but a struggle for the greatest freedom of individual choice in this area. Both resistance to such social institutions as pornography and prostitution and critical discussion of our own sexual practices and desires[8] are rejected as "a gallop back to Victorian sentimentality" (Echols 1989, 153).

Such critics dismiss as essentialist feminist arguments that current sexual arrangements do not reflect women's interests or desires and feminist attempts to explore what women's desires would be/are apart from patriarchal shaping and enforcement. For they believe these arguments invoke a female sexuality that is in some deep and presocial sense different from men's. They also reject analyses of the exploitative nature of sexual structures on the grounds that these analyses undermine women's agency, and reinforce rather than challenge women's victim status (Willis 1992). Alice Echols says of the "anti-pornography crusade," for instance, that it "functions [by] ... reinforcing and validating women's traditional sexual conservatism and manipulating women's sense of themselves as the culture's victims and its moral guardians" (1983, 455).

Because some of the concerns these reductionist feminists raise are echoed by integrative feminists who accept the importance of a political analysis of sexuality and a value frame for feminist practice, debates in the area of sexuality can be confusing. The shared integrative frame of diverse feminist positions on sexuality can remain hidden, and their underlying differences from nonintegrative positions fail to emerge. For instance, feminist positions with respect to pornography have been characterized as antipornography *or* anticensorship, although many feminists are opposed to both. This kind of labeling reflects reductionist presumptions and hides integrative possibilities, thus weakening integrative politics. Another example of labeling that masks integrative feminist politics and possibilties is the use of the terms "antisex" and "pro-sex" to refer, respectively, to feminists who are committed to changing current sexual practices and those who are not. These labels deny the possibility that sexual relations can be criticized from a deep commitment to an empowering sexuality, that holding out for nonexploitative sex is a pro-sex position. There is a close political parallel here to the use of the term "pro-life" to refer to an antiabortion position. Implying that those who argue for women's access to abortion are antilife masks the fact that abstract commitment to all or any life puts less value on life than concern with its quality and dignity.

In resisting both integrative feminisms' political analyses of sexuality and their value content, reductionist positions paradoxically become both liberal and essentialist. Without an integrative frame they are unable to avoid these reductionisms. Their insistence on treating sexuality apart from questions of power leaves them to deal with desire as if it were not socially constructed but a given force or instinct. Since collective values and process are rejected as oppressive, their notion of freedom is exclusively one of liberal or libertarian individual freedom from social constraint or repression of the sexual drive.[9]

Equality and Specificity in the Academic Literature

The fact that increasing numbers of diverse feminists affirm women's specificity as well as women's equality, while others reject attention to women's specificity as necessarily reactionary, has given rise to an academic literature explicitly addressing the question of equality and difference within feminism. This literature documents the uneasy historical and current coexistence of the two strands in feminism for which I have used the terms "specificity" and "equality." "Difference" and "equality" are more frequently used in the academic literature, however (Benhabib and Cornell 1987; Eisenstein and Jardine 1980; Lamoureaux 1986; Snitow 1989). The two strands are also distinguished by such terms as "maximilist" and "minimalist" (McFadden 1984), "sorority" and "equality/liberty" (Bartlett 1986), "romanticism" and "rationalism" (Vogel 1986), "feminine antirationalism" and "feminist rationalism" (Di Stefano 1988), "relational" and "individualist" (Offen 1988), "nature" and "social" (Riley 1988), or "essentialism" and "social constructionism" (Juteau 1990).

All these authors argue that both sides of the coin are by definition part of feminism and that neither can displace the other to claim the whole. Some go beyond this to assert that any resolution of the resulting tension is impossible and should not therefore be the aim of feminist practice. They suggest that the tension, "far from being our enemy, is a dynamic force that links very different women" (Snitow 1989, 216) and should therefore be embraced rather than regretted. Even these authors tend, however, to see the contradiction as a relatively static one and to present the tension as one *between* different feminist politics rather than also *within* integrative feminist politics.

Although there are feminisms that displace equality in the affirmation of "difference," we have seen that these are rare. The main divide among feminisms is not between those which affirm "difference" and those which affirm "equality." It lies between those which insist on a single principle of equality and those which refuse the obvious limits of this frame and attempt to integrate the principles of equality and specificity. The academic literature tends to mask the existence of this diverse integrative tendency of feminism by constructing falsely parallel "equality" and "difference" feminisms.

Maggie McFadden, for instance, categorizes feminisms according to their treatment of women's difference from men: "The *minimizers* opt for structures which unite the female with human enterprises from which she has too often been excluded, and the *maximizers* articulate patterns expressive of the unique perspective of the female" (1984, 495). She notes some cases that link these two positions but fails to recognize how broad and diverse is this tendency of feminisms whose transformative dynamic is grounded in the creative tension between the principles she names. Christine Di Stefano identifies a partial and inadequate feminist rationalism that "commits us to equality and to the elimination of gender differences, but . . . is constituted within a set of terms that disparage things female and feminine," which she opposes to an equally inadequate feminine antirationalism that "attempts to revalorize the feminine, with the nasty effect of failing to criticize it," hence tending to "slide into antifeminism" (1988, 13).[10].

Unlike those who posit separate categories of "difference" and "equality" politics, Ann Snitow sees the divide "between the need to build the identity 'woman' and give it solid political meaning and the need to tear down the very category 'woman'" (1989, 205)[11] as constantly forming and reforming inside categories of feminism. She shows that feminism cannot do without either of these essential moments. But she argues that knowing this does not absolve feminists from having "to choose a position on the divide" (216), because "there is no transcendence, no third course. The urgent contradiction women constantly experience between the pressure to be a woman and the pressure not to be one will change only through a historical process; it cannot be dissolved through thought alone" (209). This is true, but to say that this contradiction cannot be resolved today is not to say that there can be no politics that consciously embrace both requirements and work with this dynamic tension as a dialectic rather than a static contradiction.[12]

Some writers realize this and advocate refusing the specious choice between equality/freedom and specificity (Bartlett 1986; Miles 1985; Saint-Jean 1983; Sève 1989; Tardy et al. 1986/87). However, the academic feminist literature dealing with "equality and difference" feminisms generally leaves the wide range of North American integrative-feminist political theory and practice invisible.

POSTSTRUCTURALIST REDUCTIONISMS: DIVERSITY DISPLACES COMMONALITY AND SPECIFICITY[13]

Poststructuralist feminist reductionisms are rendered largely as a defense of women's diversity against affirmations of women's commonality and specificity. They have emerged in North American academic circles partly in response to the challenges of an increasingly diverse women's movement and the development of dialectical politics that incorporate the principles of equality, specificity, commonality, and diversity. There is no counterpart to poststructuralist theory in grassroots practice, but feminists in the academy are attracted by its attention to fragmentation, subjectivity, and diversity. Post-structuralist responses to these pressing issues differ markedly from integrative approaches. Despite the valuable insights some feminists find in this writing, its underlying presumptions invalidate the integrative project.

Ironically, poststructuralist feminists criticize as essentialist not only radical, socialist, and other feminists who recognize women's specificity but also those who criticize this recognition as essentialist. They reject not only the biological essentialism mistakenly presumed by many to be prevalent in the women's movement but any use of gender as a basic analytical/political category.[14] "A feminist frame of reference . . . cannot be either 'man' or 'woman,' for both of these are constructs of a male-centered discourse, both are products of the 'straight mind'" (Lauretis 1987, 13).

For poststructuralist feminists resistance to the false and oppressive dualistic "universal" theories of white male Euro-Americans—who have named their own interests as general interests and defined themselves as central to "marginal," devalued "others"—requires that the resulting oppressive "binary oppositions" be deconstructed/deferred/reversed/displaced rather than affirmed/transformed/transcended. In this view the current struggles of marginal groups ("others") such as women, colonized peoples, ethnic and racial groups, and gays and lesbians to claim their own centers and articulate their own identities, interests, and values in voices of their own represent not so much resistance as unconscious capitulation. Identities need to be deconstructed, not affirmed, and struggles need to be decentered rather than become multicentered. According to this position, naming women as a social group reinforces divisions by gender and so feeds gender oppression rather than women's ability to resist: "Notions of gender are not the point of our liberation but rather the grounding of our continuing oppression" (Nicholson 1990, 16).

The limiting presumption here is that the only alternative to essentializing and entrenching binary oppositions is "deconstructing" them. Only "reversing and displacing" prevents sexual difference from being accepted "as real or self-evident in the nature of things" (Scott 1986, 1066); therefore, all feminists attempting to name the world and to speak *as women* have been "engaged in . . . a hunt for the generic woman" (Spelman 1988, 187), a "search and claim for an essential female/ethnic identity—difference, . . . [which] can never be anything more than a move within the male-is-norm divide-and-conquer trap" (Trinh 1989, 101).

Treating women as a social category is presumed to involve a search for or imputation of some (immutable) essence of gender, cultural or social if not biological. So "theories do not have to be explicitly essentialist in their arguments . . . to be effectively essentialist in their narrative strategies" (Butler 1990, 329–30). The fact that the hallmark of almost all feminisms is the unmasking of gender as a social construct—the de-naturing of gender—does not inhibit these critics. Their all-encompassing concept of essentialism conflates analyses of women as a social class with the rare approaches that treat women as a biological category.[14] As a result, they read almost all nonpoststructuralist feminist theory and practice as a surrender to essential gender rather than a resistance to and transformation of gender.[15]

Gender Read against Race and Class

Since claiming voice/identity "as women" is presumed by poststructuralist feminists to require the "construction of the category 'woman' and social group 'women' as a unified totalizable whole," it is assumed to leave "no structural room for race (or for much else) in theory" (Haraway 1990, 202). The personal/political individual and collective struggles of diverse women described in preceding chapters to create themselves as autonomous, connected, effective political subjects are construed as simply misguided essentialist searches for nonexistent "originary wholeness." Feminists' transformative engagement with the fragmentation of their own lives and selves is seen as an ignorant and totalizing failure to recognize the very fragmentation that is actually the focus of their practice.

According to this view, the fact that "the category of women is internally fragmented by class, color, age and ethnic lines" (Butler 1990, 327) invalidates the category as anything other than the perpetuation of an ahistorical, homogenizing, totalizing, authoritarian, and exclusive fiction:[16] "the fixity of gender identification . . . is built upon the denial of a decidedly more complex cultural identity—or non-identity as the case may be" (Butler 1990, 339).

Elizabeth Spelman, for instance, argues that we could only consider women to be of the same gender "if what it meant to be a 'woman' was the same for all of them no matter what their race or class or nationality—and if all women were subject to sexism in the same way" (1988, 81). For her the category "gender" implies the existence of "one who is all and only woman, who by some miracle of abstraction has no particular identity in terms of race, class, ethnicity, sexual orientation, language, religions, nationality" (187).

In this view of gender and political subjectivity, women's commonality and specificity are necessarily articulated in opposition to women's diversity. Principles that for integrative feminists are essential to one another become static contradictions. The decision to act *as women* is read as a failure to see that "the ambiguities, conflicts, and paradoxes that distinguish and differentiate women from men and from themselves . . . [are] . . . interwoven strands of a tension, a condition of contradiction that, for the time being at least, will not be reconciled" (Lauretis 1986, 15).[17] To see oneself as part of the group "women" is presumed to involve denying one's race/class/nationality. On these grounds integrative feminists' ongoing—necessarily always incomplete—political struggles for coherent articulations of diverse women's specificity/subjectivity/commonality are repudiated (though, as we will see later, they are sometimes reclaimed in complex theoretical formulations).

Integrative feminists name the margins as privileged places, and "others" as privileged identities of resistance, even as they struggle to transmute them into diverse centers of visionary, nontotalizing, but nevertheless shared politics. Their affirmations of diverse women's skills, cultures, and values establish women's agency as well as the fact of their oppression. Since women have been denied subjectivity/voice/centrality/reason/ humanity, to claim these things *as women* is to subvert the dualisms that create them as silence, passivity, emotion, matter, margin, "other," "nature." Therefore, paradoxically, to speak *as women* in the struggle for equality is to challenge the "natural" category "women" as constitutive of dominant and oppressive dualisms. If poststructuralists notice that the "essentialism" they have been uncovering is not so simple after all but includes both an affirmation of and a challenge to gender and "women," this duality is read as an unconscious contradiction: "Feminist discourse is full of contradictory and irreconcilable conceptions of the nature of our social relations, of men and women and the worth and character of stereotypically masculine and feminine activities" (Flax 1990, 52).

Diversity Read against Specificity

Feminists of color and lesbian feminists with especially articulate and creative integrative positions have been particularly noticed and particularly misread. Some poststructuralists, like Biddy Martin and Chandra Talpede Mohanty (1986), Diana Fuss (1989), Trinh T. Minh-ha (1989), and Gayatri Spivak (1990) criticize "women of color" and "lesbian" identity as no less essentialist than the identity "women." Others (more often white), such as Elizabeth Spelman (1988), Donna Haraway (1990), and Teresa de Lauretis (1986), treat the articulation of these diverse identities as legitimate expressions of differences that invalidate the homogenizing categories of "women" and "gender."

Feminists of color and lesbian feminists have angrily and poetically named and criticized ethnocentrism, racism, and heterosexism among feminists. They have rejected false generalizing about women from urban white middle-class heterosexual experience and warned of the dangers of too easily assuming sameness/sisterhood/solidarity. As we have seen, for integrative feminists this is very far from rejecting movement as "women." Racism and heterosexism are challenged and diverse autonomous identities articulated in the spirit of building "wimmin's movement that is more international in scope and universal in application" (davenport 1983, 90), not to deconstruct women's movement.

Yet the often angry and despairing denunciations of "white feminists [who] have appointed themselves ... official spokespersons [for] the entire movement" (Radford-Hill 1986, 163), of analyses based on ethnocentric, heterosexist, and class-bound generalizations, and of nonintegrative "sisterhood" built on flawed presumptions of sameness are taken by some poststructuralist feminists to support positions that deny the possibility of all generalizations about gender and "women" and of shared visions and struggles. For instance, despite their deep women identification and commitment to the political significance of both identity and solidarity, "writers like bell hooks, Audre Lorde, Maria Lugones[, who] have unmasked the implicit reference to white Anglo women in many classic feminist texts, ... [and] Adrienne Rich and Marilyn Frye[, who] have exposed the heterosexist bias of much mainstream feminist theory," are read by Linda Nicholson and Nancy Fraser to support the poststructuralist call that feminism leave behind the "essentialist vestiges [that] persist in the continued use of ahistorical categories like gender identity" (1990, 33).

Elizabeth Spelman (1988) opens her book with a quotation from Audre Lorde to the effect that "there is a pretense of homogeneity of experience covered by the word *sisterhood* that does not in fact exist," using it to support her own argument that the idea of sisterhood is necessarily totalizing, must presume homogeneity, and therefore must be rejected. This view is not shared by Lorde, however, (1984, 1988), who is celebrated for her contribution to a feminist understanding of diversity as a potential resource in the common feminist struggle. Lorde's criticism of racism in the women's movement reflects her commitment to building authentic nonhomogenizing sisterhood/solidarity: "The failure of academic feminists to recognize difference as a crucial strength is a failure to reach beyond the first patriarchal lesson. In our world, divide and conquer must become define and empower" (Lorde 1984, 112). Spelman also cites Berenice Reagan and bell hooks in support of her critique of the notion of a common oppression of women. Yet both these activists/authors, although frequently critical of white feminists' presumptions of shared conditions, recognize that all women are subject to patriarchal power. They are committed to the difficult struggle of building broad revolutionary solidarity among women across race and class to resist all dominations. Bell hooks, for example, calls for "the strength of a diverse feminist struggle and movement, one that is oriented toward becoming a mass-based political movement" (1990, 221).

Diversity Read as Deconstruction

Integrative feminist politics are complex enough to be easily misread as either essentialist or deconstructionist by those who reject dialectical possibilities. The women-centered experimental *écriture féminine* of Quebecois feminists challenges traditional definitions of women, and power relations between men and women, as it affirms and creates women's specific desires, experiences, values, and connections in new language forms and new visions. The dynamic transformative project at the heart of this work has been hailed as deconstructionist by some and rejected as essentialist by others, although its subversive and visionary intent is also widely recognized and shared.[18]

Adrienne Rich's (1978b) powerful "dream of a common language" puts front and center differences and divisions among women and articulates a longing that we might recognize and hear ourselves in each other. This "dream" she represents as requiring a conscious political naming of connection and a claiming of identity by diverse women—a celebration of womanhood and community in diversity and adversity. It is a far cry from presuming "natural" identity, or centralizing and imposing identity and meaning. Yet Haraway suggests that what is required is "a dream not of a common language, but a powerful infidel heteroglossia" (1990, 223). The crucial feminist struggle to communicate across our differences, to hear and understand each other, to discover our commonalities against all the powers that divide us is assumed to rule out a diversity of voices and is read as being a desire for sameness or a centralized imposition of meaning. Therefore, for poststructuralist feminists recognizing diversity requires a rejection of the feminist desire/struggle for effective communication among women. Haraway, for instance, advocates a "cyborg politics [that] is the struggle against perfect communication, against the one code that translates all meaning perfectly" (1990, 218).

Nancy Miller, (1986) by contrast, finds Rich's nuanced personal/political exploration "of dispersal and fragmentation" and her struggle within political community to overcome them, an abundant resource in the attempt to develop a deconstructionist understanding of women's particular relationship to integrity and textuality, desire and authority. And Nicholson and Fraser claim Rich for poststructuralism because of her interest in "modes of theorizing that are attentive to differences and to cultural and historical specificity" (1990, 33).

The integrative politics of Barbara Smith are also subject to both essentialist and deconstructionist interpretation when their dialectic is not recognized. She says, for instance:

> As Black women we have an identity and therefore a politics that requires faith in the humanness of Blackness and femaleness. We are flying in the face of white male conceptions of what humanness is and proving that it is not them, but us" (unpublished paper cited by Moraga 1983b, 131).

Here she refers to a self-identity won against all the dominant definitions of women and Black people, not to a "natural" or given identity. She says "an identity and therefore a politics" because without a politics there can be no oppositional/alternative identity; both identity and politics require an alternative set of values and an alternative definition of the world. Yet this powerful articulation of the active interdependence of achieved identity and alternative values and vision—each requiring and creating the other—is cited by Diana Fuss (1989, 99) as reflecting an essentialist belief that "identity necessarily determines a particular kind of politics"! The dynamic notion of an oppositional/ transformative identity and politics consciously, reciprocally, and continuously shaping one another is judged to be a unilinear, "naturalistic" determinism.

Other poststructuralists, however, hail Smith as one of their own. Donna Haraway quite rightly sees that in *Home Girls* Smith "subverts naturalized identities ... while constructing a place from which to speak called home" (1990, 227). The "home" Smith names/claims is won through a process of redefining and revaluing herself and other Black women through her empowerment in feminist and Black movement. Her construction of home, as of identity, is both product and producer of political struggle, an empowering dynamic grounded in a reclaiming of her lived experience as an embodied Black woman, a rediscovering and honoring of her Black female connections and female relations, an expression of her love for (unromanticized) Black women. It is profoundly women-centered in a way that Haraway would mistake as essentialist in most feminists. Because she can see that Smith's is not an essentialist politics, she presumes that her invocation of "home" is ironic. For Haraway "irony is about contradictions that do not resolve into larger wholes, even dialectically, about the tension of holding incompatible things together because both or all are necessary and true" (1990, 190). But for Smith, "home" is a theme she chooses to make sense of, represent, and ground a dialectical process. She has no need of irony or of deconstruction to resist and transform gender and the world.[19]

Haraway does not appreciate that the nonessentialist affirmation of complex identity by many feminists is dialectical rather than deconstructionist or that it is part of a broad and diverse tendency of the women's movement. Instead, she credits some feminists with the creation of a unique "cyborg identity" (1990, 216) that "marks out space that cannot affirm the capacity to act on the basis of natural identification, but only on the basis of conscious coalition, of affinity, of political kinship" (198) and contrasts this creative gesture to what she presumes to be the "naturalization" (198) of identity carried out by most feminists. She interprets Cherríe Moraga's "retelling of the story of the indigenous woman Malinche" (Haraway 1990, 217) in *Loving in the War Years* (1983b) as deconstructionist, even though the kind of reclaiming/redefining of history, culture, and ideology by women from women's point of view that Moraga celebrates affirms women identification and connection in ways that Haraway usually considers essentialist. She recognizes that the "retold stories" of these "cyborg authors" are "versions that reverse and displace the hierarchical dualisms of naturalized identities" (217) without reconsidering her dismissal of most of this kind of reversal as an essentialism that reinforces rather than challenges heirarchical dualisms. Since she reads most integrative feminists as essentialist and claims others for poststructuralism,[20] her analysis renders dialectical feminist politics invisible.

Integrative Deconstruction

Some poststructuralist feminists not only recognize but also subscribe to the integrative-feminist explorations of identity that they analyze. For instance, Biddy Martin and Chandra Talpede Mohanty's deconstructionist reading of Minnie Bruce Pratt's article "Identity: Skin Blood Heart" ([1984] 1988) focuses on its questioning of identity. Martin and Mohanty note that this "unusual text" questions "the all-too-common conflation of experience, identity, and political perspective" (1986, 192). They acknowledge, however, that community, connection, and experience remain central to her vision. For Pratt, they say:

> Community . . . is the product of work, of struggle; it is inherently unstable, contextual; it has to be constantly reevaluated in relation to critical political priorities; and it is the product of interpretation based on an attention to history, to the concrete, to what Foucault has called subjugated knowledges. There is also, however, a strong suggestion that community is related to experience, to history. For if identity and community are not the product of essential connections, neither are they merely the product of political urgency or necessity. For Pratt, they are a constant recontextualizing of the relationship between personal/group history and political priorities. (Martin and Mohanty 1986, 209)

Paradoxically, this analysis both describes and denies integrative-feminist politics. Despite these critics, few if any feminists believe in simple "natural" identities. In fact, most feminist practice is concerned to build political subjectivities and connections notwithstanding the personal fragmentation and political divisions endemic to patriarchy, capitalism, and colonialism. Nor do many feminists see the category of experience as transparent or conflate experience, identity, and politics.[21] The "slogan" that "the personal is political," among other things, rejects this mistaken notion. The core practice of consciousness raising is nothing if not a commitment to the collective work necessary to build political understandings of common systems of oppression from diverse experience. Much feminist theory, literature, and practice deals with and describes the difficult but necessary political struggle to build coherent and autonomous *female* subjectivities and communities in the face of the complexities of women's lives and loyalties and the cultural refusal of powerful and positive identity to women.

Nevertheless, Minnie Bruce Pratt's feminist treatment of identity is presented as atypical by Martin and Mohanty, who also imply that careful reading is necessary to reveal even this "unique" text as nonessentialist. Their suggestions that Pratt's meaning is obscure and her integrative approach unique serve to mask the existence of a widespread tendency of the women's movement that shares with Pratt an approach described by Martin and Mohanty as "reconceptualizing power [identity and gender] without giving up the possibility of conceiving power [identity and gender]" (1986, 209).[22] Sadly, "actual existing" integrative feminisms thus remain invisible even to would-be "integrative poststructuralists."

Numerous feminist poststructuralists are incipiently and conflictedly integrative. They see that feminist struggle cannot be waged without "women" and are unwilling to give up this struggle; yet they consider the recognition of "women" and gender to be unavoidably essentialist.[23] In this, they face a dilemma they have created for themselves:[24] "How can feminist theory base itself upon the uniqueness of the female experience without reifying thereby one single definition of femaleness as the paradigmatic one—without succumbing, that is, to an essentialist discourse on gender?" (Benhabib and Cornell 1987, 13).

The imaginary essentialism of gender that poststructuralists believe is inescapable creates falsely static contradictions to which they offer elaborate theoretical solutions that point in the direction of integrative feminism without being fully dialectical. Diana Fuss, for instance, finds that Luce "Irigaray both *is and is not* an essentialist" (1989, 70) and argues for a replication of this "double gesture" in a controlled essentialism balanced and kept in check by deconstructionism.

Linda Alcoff in her article "Cultural Feminism versus Post-Structuralism" calls for a nonessentialist gender politics: "If we combine the concept of identity politics with a conception of the subject as positionality, we can conceive of the subject as nonessentialized and emergent from a historical experience and yet retain our political ability to take gender as an important departure. Thus we can say at one and the same time that gender is not natural, biological, universal, ahistorical, or essential and yet still claim that gender is relevant because we are taking gender as a position from which to act politically" (1988, 433). This is a complicated rendering of rather obvious understandings that form the basis of much feminist practice. "Taking gender as a position from which to act politically" is unavoidable in feminist politics. Alcoff, however, presents her position as a unique "third way" offered in the face of a crisis in feminism caused by widespread feminist essentialism opposed only by equally inadequate deconstructionist insistence that "'women' do not exist and demands in their name simply reinforce the myth that they do" (420).

In a parallel argument Drucilla Cornell insists, against many deconstructionists, that "feminine sexual difference must find expression if feminism is not to find itself in collaboration against its own ends" (1991, 21). But her view that only a feminist alliance with deconstruction will enable "the elaboration of the specificity of Woman or women as constructed by a particular context" without "essentialist or naturalist accounts" (3–4) discounts the diverse dialectical expressions of women's difference and equality, commonality, and diversity that abound, and are in fact required, in actual practice.

Poststructuralist feminists thus invent immobile, nondynamic contradictions that cannot be transformed/transcended. They presume that all contradictions are of this order and dismiss dialectical feminist politics as misguided illusion—or worse. The belief that "dialectics is [necessarily] a dream language longing [unrealistically] to resolve contradiction" (Haraway 1990, 215) leaves those poststructuralists not prepared to abandon "women" in an untenable position. They criticize integrative feminists for what can only be to them the irrational practice of "simultaneously naturalizing and denaturing the category 'woman'" (Haraway 1990, 199) while, themselves, developing tortuous ways of doing just this. They dismiss nonessentialist dialectical practice as essentialist while arguing for a nondialectical "strategic use of positivist essentialism" (Spivak 1987, 210).[25]

Thus even the poststructuralist theorists most committed to women's struggle and most aware that *women* must make this struggle ultimately undermine it. They resist the integrative practice they realize is necessary by postulating its nonexistence and theorizing its impossibility (and sometimes also its undesirablity). They remain nonintegrative despite their integrative insights.

Conclusion

Poststructuralist feminists range from those who propose deconstructionist theory as a superior alternative to what is perceived to be an almost total lack of feminist theory (Weedon 1987) to those who detect or want to add deconstructionist sensibility in feminist theorizing (Lauretis 1986). Nevertheless, they all ultimately reject the recognition of women's specificity, the use of such concepts as "women," gender, identity, and subjectivity, and the desire for clearer understandings of the world as essentializing and totalizing practices that replicate and reinforce rather than challenge structures of power.

The incredibly demanding individual and collective struggles to create oneself as an autonomous social actor, to develop coherent women-centered approaches to the world, to understand social relations from women's points of view, to see the world and envision the future in new ways are dismissed by poststructuralist feminists as naive at best and authoritarian at worst. Claims are made instead that truly sophisticated understanding and liberatory practice lie in recognizing the incoherence, fragmentation, and inadequacy of individual subjectivity, of political unity, and of theoretical understanding and in accepting this condition as insurmountable.

Poststructuralist-feminist perspectives substitute reactive politics for the transformative project of creating new political processes, new possibilities, and a new world. They also reconstitute/reconstruct/reinforce the divide between theory and practice that integrative feminisms consciously resist. Far from being a guide to practice, deconstructionist theory consists primarily of criticism of and resistance to both practice and theory. The theoretical project of clarifying one's understanding of social relations of domination in order to change them is largely rejected as impossible and in any case undesirable: "Clarity is a means of subjection, a quality both of official, taught language and of correct writing, two old mates of power: together they flow, together they flower, vertically, to impose order" (Trinh 1989, 16).[26] The expectation that practice will both contribute to and benefit from increasing (though never, of course, complete or assured) analytical clarity is suspected to reveal authoritarian aspirations toward a "hegemonic global theory of feminism" (Spivak 1987, 84) and "the production of universal, totalizing theory" (Haraway 1990, 223). For poststructuralist feminists "this image of a homogeneous, monolithic Feminism ... must be resisted" (deLauretis 1986, 15) through the clear representation of the absolute and severe limits of practice and theory.

A homogeneous, monolithic feminism is, of course, not a real threat in practice, since practice, as we have seen, is enormously varied. Any centralized imposition of formal programs or theoretical orthodoxy is absolutely out of the question, except perhaps in academic settings. Such a danger is, in any case, far better resisted by paying attention to real, diverse practice, participating in it, and making it the subject of one's theorizing/strategizing than by spending one's time theorizing the limits of practice and theory.

Today, it is not hard to find exciting kinds of feminist practice among ever wider groups of women who consciously and collectively claim the right to define themselves, to speak for themselves, and to name their world; who articulate their own values and visions; and who build solidarity as they articulate their differences. Yet poststructuralist feminists fail to see the new dialectical possibilities these types of practice reveal and create. Their theory remains impervious to the lessons as well as the imperatives of practice. Rather than comment on/critique/contribute to the particular nature of the identities, voices, analyses, visions that feminists are articulating, poststructuralist feminists question the very possibility of identity, voice, analysis, and vision. It is particularly disturbing—poststructuralists might say "ironic"—that these feminists are refusing identities and voices that women have never had just as it is becoming possible for us (and "others") to claim them.

In the resulting avoidance of politically substantive discussion, poststructuralist theorists set themselves apart from feminism as a social movement and a political practice. They define poststructuralism as theory and feminism as practice and situate themselves resolutely on the sidelines, from which vantage point they can comment, without activist engagement or responsibility, on either the hopeful signs of emerging deconstruction in feminism (Lauretis 1986,

9; Haraway 1990; Martin and Mohanty 1986) or the baleful influence of essentialism in feminism (Spelman 1988; Trinh 1989) or both (Nicholson 1990).

The separation of theory and practice is particularly evident in the work of those integrative poststructuralist feminists who recognize that in feminist practice "there must be a sense of identity even though it would be fictitious" (Marks 1984, 110) and that analysis, vision, and voice are also necessary, and yet continue to focus on the impossibility/undesirability or at least "untheorizability" of all these. Gayatri Spivak notes the irrelevance of deconstructive theory to practice: "Certain peoples have always been asked to cathect the margins so others can be defined as central. . . . In that kind of situation the only strategic thing to do is to absolutely present oneself at the center. And this is theoretically incorrect" (1990, 40). Poststructuralists present their acceptance of severe theoretical limits as crucial resistance to the totalizing claims and consequences of all other theory. But this disarming theoretical humility is, of course, only comprehensible within the realm of an essentially elitist theory deeply separate from practice.

Their principled opposition to totalizing theory and their belief that the possibility of theoretical understanding is extremely limited mean that poststructuralist theorists feel no need to articulate alternative or more adequate structural analyses of the world than those they critique. This abstention compounds the implicit elitism of the poststructuralist approach, for it leaves much of the literature little more than "typologizing, defining, and branding various 'feminisms' along an ascending scale of theoretico-political sophistication where 'essentialism' weighs heavy at the lower end" (deLauretis 1989, 4).

Antiessentialist elitisms and reductionisms of all kinds—radical- and socialist-feminist as well as poststructuralist—tend to overlook real structures of power; presume to separate theory from real questions of practice; undervalue and jeopardize the struggle for solidarity, clarity, and subjectivity; separate feminism from "women"; and exclude the development of alternative values from practice. They thus serve not only to depoliticize feminism in general but to discipline and suppress its antidualistic vision and its most radical dialectical theory and practice.

6

INTEGRATIVE FEMINISMS IN THE "TWO-THIRDS" WORLD

THIRD WORLD FEMINISMS[1]

The same conditions that underlie women's increasing activism in North America are operative in aggravated form in Third World countries, where processes of "modernization" and "development" are intensifying dependence on Western industrial nations and the transnational capitalist economy, dividing and impoverishing whole communities, and degrading environments. Women in particular are being marginalized, losing even minimal traditional securities and powers at the same time as their work load increases to inhuman proportions. Militarism and war fostered by poverty, dependence, and exploitation affect women disproportionately. Growing fundamentalist and communalist responses to Western domination and loosening traditional constraints are, all over the world, resulting in the imposition on women of the most patriarchal readings of tradition. All these developments leave women increasingly vulnerable to already extensive, in some cases endemic violence against them and enforce their relative, in some cases almost absolute exclusion from decision making at all levels.

These conditions make the urgency of resistance acute, and their particular impact on women calls for women to respond *as women*. Thus they foster not only the necessity but also the possibility of new forms of action for women. And many Third World women can call on important resources in their action

85

that we in North America often lack. They frequently have more intact women's subcultures, identities, and organizations; less mystified and romantic notions of male-female relations; and clearer understandings of male power as well as imperialist, class, and race power. And they may have access to alternative indigenous and tribal values and/or more active and radical political cultures than we know in North America.

Although "Two-Thirds" World[2] women have always been involved in community and national struggles, the period since the mid-1970s has seen an enormous and continuing increase in the autonomous activism of women around issues and aims defined by and for women, whether or not they are self-defined as feminist. Women are using separate women's events and organizations to redefine and add issues to community struggles. In campaigns for land redistribution, for instance, women name the potentially negative consequences for their relative power in their own communities if land is redistributed only to men. They demand, often against the opposition of men in their families, to be included in the redistribution. A national conference of women in India including many rural women, for instance, passed the following motion: "When land is won as a result of people's struggle, or distributed by the government, it should not be given in the name of a male head of household but in equal shares to adult men and women of the family. Houses and homestead land given by the state should be given in the name of women only" (Omvedt, Gala, and Kelkar 1988, 81–82). Access to redistributed land is an issue as well for El Salvadoran women seeking a voice in negotiations between liberation forces and the government (Alemán, Miranda, and Montenegro 1993).

Continuous economic, environmental, legal, military, cultural, and physical threats to women underlie widespread and growing resistance to dictatorship, militarism, fundamentalism, economic dependence and exploitation, and violence against women. The last few years have witnessed protests from women in Saudi Arabia demanding the right to drive; from Croatian, Bosnian and Serbian, Irish, Somali, Sinhalese and Tamil, and Israeli and Palestinian women against the violence of occupation and civil war; from women in Kenya against the death of nineteen girls and rape of seventy-one others by male classmates in their rural boarding school; from women in Turkey against virginity checks on schoolgirls; from women in Thailand against police involvement in sex tourism and child prostitution; from women in Guatemala opposing forced conscription of mainly indigenous young people into the army; and from women in Andrha Pradesh resisting Arrack (alcohol) trade in their villages.

All over the world women are responding to deteriorating or crisis conditions by founding, and defining in their own terms, sustained environmental, economic, health, housing, social-justice, antidebt, pro-democracy, antiviolence, and peace movements of such major proportions as the Green Belt Movement in Kenya,[3] the Chipko Movement in the mountain regions of the

Himalayas,[4] the Self-Employed Women's Association in India,[5] and Mothers of the Disappeared movements in Latin America and Sri Lanka.[6]

Since these local, regional, and national groupings are firmly rooted in community struggle and wider women's movement, and since respect and mutual support are strong among women-centered groups, the line between feminist and nonfeminist groups is indistinct and shifting. However, a significant and increasing proportion of the activism among women in the Two-Thirds World is explicitly feminist-defined.[7] Such groups as Kali for Women Press in India, Gabriela Mindinao in the Philippines (Angeles 1989), the Third World Women's Movement against the Exploitation of Women (Perpiñan 1986), Yewwu-Yewwi PLF in Senegal, the Tanzania Media Women's Association (TAMWA), the Centro de la Mujer Peruana Flora Tristan (Flora Tristan Center for Peruvian Women) (Carillo 1990), Sistren in Jamaica (Ford-Smith 1986), the Women and Development Unit (WAND) of the University of the West Indies (Yudelman 1987), Women in Nigeria (WIN), the Sudanese Women's Union (Ibrahim 1992), Nijeri Kori in Bangladesh, Emang Basadi in Botswana (Molokomme 1991), the Association for the Advancement of Feminism (AAF) in Hong Kong (Ho 1990), and Casa Sophia in Chile (Lehmann 1987) are just a few of the hugely varied groups whose contributions to global feminist movement are grounded in indigenous traditions of women's struggle and definitions of feminism.

Third World feminisms, like North American feminisms, have been forged against powerful opposition. Many of their general statements stand partly as correctives to ridicule, misrepresentation, and critique—charges of being antimale, individualist/careerist, divisive, responsible for the breakdown of family and community, and so on. Feminists in the Two-Thirds World are also subjected to patronizing charges of being duped by middle-class white/Western women into betraying their own communities and cultures.[8] South Asian feminists note that these attacks come from many sources:

> Feminists have been called western, bourgeois, anti-men at various times. We have watched with amazement and often a feeling of regret at the strange alliance of bourgeois controlled press, right wing fundamentalists and sections of the progressive forces in our countries as they mocked, ridiculed and attacked the assertions of women's autonomy from capitalist/patriarchal controls. We see this labelling as a deliberate blindness and refusal to acknowledge the issues which have been taken up by the feminist movement in our countries. (South Asian Feminist Declaration 1989, 11)

Diverse feminists in the Two-Thirds World categorically reject these attacks as reflecting a politically self-serving double standard. "'Feminism' or 'women liberation' is branded an imperialist, cultural-domination ploy and therefore anti-African. Of course, this is clearly an African sexist view, a mechanism of scape-goating women as traitors to African values" (Anonymous 1985, 7). They refuse both the view that Western origins necessarily make an idea irrelevant and the suggestion that women's resistance is a Western import. "The Dakar Declaration on Another Development with Women" claims feminism as part of centuries-old traditions of struggle around the world: "Feminism provides the basis for new consciousness and for cultural resistance to all forms of domination. Such resistance by women to domination has been present in many countries throughout the centuries, and has provided the women's movement with continuity in its active struggle for equality" (Dakar 1982, 15). Asian feminists point to specifically Asian traditions of debate and resistance: "the issue of whether women could join the order and become nuns was debated by the Buddha and his followers in the 6th century B.C. There has been a continuing debate on women's right to education in many countries in Asia" (Bhasin and Khan 1986, 4). Muslim feminists insist that "we Muslim women can walk into the modern world with pride knowing that the quest for dignity, democracy and human rights, for full participation in the political social affairs of our country, stems not from imported Western values, but is a true part of the Muslim tradition" (Mernissi 1987, viii). Feminists in Mauritius insist that "women [here] have never taken their oppression sitting down. The struggle is perpetual. From the times of the Dutch settlement in the 17th century, women have tried to voice their demands" (Muvman Liberasyon Fam 1983, 186). African feminists are impatient that

in spite of evidences [of African women's traditional power] which are supported by oral tradition and social structures, present attempts by African women to recover equality and freedom are ridiculed by male power and interpreted as a mere "mechanistic mimesis" and as contamination from the West. The rationale behind this is as absurd as asserting that black slaves who were exploited in the 19th century in America had never been free people in their own societies and that in trying to free themselves from slavery they were merely identifying themselves with white people. (Baffoun 1985, 4).

Creating and defending intrinsic Third World feminisms involves resisting not only antifeminist caricatures of feminism and charges that women's resistance is a Western import but also the actual insistence of some nonintegrative feminists that "legitimate" feminisms should focus exclusively on "women's issues" narrowly defined:

On the one hand, there are those who dismiss [Third World feminists] as not being truly "feminist" because of their unwillingness to separate the struggle against gender subordination from that against other oppressions. On the other hand, there are those who accuse them of dividing class or national struggles and sometimes, of uncritically following women's liberation movements from outside. This is why we need to affirm that feminism strives for the broadest and deepest development of society and human beings free of all systems of domination. (Sen and Grown 1987, 13)

Third World feminisms are as diverse as First World feminisms. The lack of attention in the next section of this chapter to analytical and strategic debates should not be read to imply either that these feminisms are monolithic or that all Third World feminisms are integrative. Political debates among feminists in the Two-Thirds World vary in both form and content in each nation, region, and even locality—reflecting not only diverse conditions and struggles but also diverse political histories and contexts—but they are ubiquitous.

Issues of feminist autonomy and solidarity are debated with emphasis on women's ethnic and class diversity and feminism's relation to the Left and other progressive movements, to nationalism, to religious and other traditions, to state and/or "development" funding, to government-appointed and sanctioned women's groups, or any number of other institutions, depending on the context. The relative weight of educational and legislative reform activity is debated with respect to early marriage, pornography, polygamy, clitoridectomy, prostitution, dowry, amniocentesis. Among others, differences over whether to stress the importance of ideological/religious factors or material conditions or both in institutionalizing and reproducing women's subordination are articulated. Similarly, differences arise over whether traditional culture and religion can and should be transformed and used as resources in feminist struggle or must be abandoned for a militant secularism.

Nevertheless, it should not be surprising that many feminists in the Two-Thirds World "seek the removal of all forms of inequality, domination and oppression through the creation of a just social and economic order in the home, nationally and internationally" (Bhasin and Khan 1986, 19). They refuse both antifeminist and non-integrative-feminist reductionisms in politics that both build and are built on integrative feminist principles.

WOMEN'S UNIVERSALITY, EQUALITY, AND SPECIFICITY

Many feminists from Asia, Africa, Latin America, the Caribbean, and the Pacific are articulating and further developing all the principles we have defined as characteristic of transformative feminisms. Their feminisms are not simply about women assimilating equally into existing social systems; they seek to transform those systems. An African feminist notes, for instance, that "If the major lesson from the anti-colonial struggle and the ongoing national libera-tion movements is that 'flag' independence is not a sufficient condition and hence should be accompanied by a much more profound social transforma-tion, feminism has also learnt that changing the position of women in society is a limited agenda that at best would benefit a few and that what is needed is transforming society as a whole" (Baffoun 1985, 3). A Sri Lankan feminist makes the point that, in any case, "changing the position of women in society" in any truly liberating way requires total social transformation:

> Today the word feminism includes but goes beyond reforms for achieving equal status. It is used to highlight women's struggles against all the various aspects of patriarchy—including male dominance in the home and family, the unequal man-woman relationship, women's double burden in production at work and reproduction of the species, male control of woman's sexuality, woman's unpaid domestic labour, and woman's subordinate status in the culture (including religions) of the country. The women's struggle is not only for emancipation, but for liberation from all the oppressive structures and institutions of patriarchal society. (Jayawardena n.d.)

So, as integrative Indian feminists say, feminism is about questioning everything, redefining everything. It is a perspective on the whole of society and not just women: "Today we no longer say—'Give us more jobs, more rights, consider us your "equals" or even allow us to compete with you better.' But rather: Let us re-examine the whole question, all questions. Let us take nothing for granted. 'Let us not only re-define ourselves, our role, our image—but also the kind of society we want to live in'" (Manushi 1979, 244–45).

Women's empowerment is at the very center of these politics. This allows them to bring specifically feminist perspectives to general social questions and avoid becoming subcategories of any other general politics. Far from being recuperated by nonfeminist politics, these feminisms repudiate the latter's claims to comprehensiveness and offer deeper, more inclusive analyses and visions. Two-Thirds World integrative feminists are absolutely clear that they are not abandoning but transforming, enriching, and broadening progressive struggle in general (AAWORD n.d., 5; Baffoun 1985, 6; Bhasin and Khan 1986, 21; Dakar 1982, 15; WAND/APCWD 1980, 27). The articulation of specific women's points of view and the development of new autonomous women-centered politics thus ground the claim that feminism is a politics of general significance. The dialectical process of naming both women's specificity and their universality allows feminists to argue that "women's struggle is not only crucial but central to the transformation of exploitative social structures and the creation of a more just society" (WAND/APCWD 1980, 27).

PERSONAL-POLITICAL AND MEANS-ENDS INTEGRATION

Enlarging the political agenda to include women is important because "true development, just development, cannot happen when the needs, talents, and potentialities of half of the world's population are seen as secondary and marginal" (Anand 1980, 11). It is equally true, however, that the "needs of half the world's population" cannot be integrated into politics as they exist. As Maria Teresa Blandon, coordinator of the National Feminist Committee of Nicaragua states, moving women from the political margins involves transforming politics: "One cannot speak of a democratic state if it does not take into account women's perspectives, interests and demands in a direct and permanent way. But democracy, from this perspective, goes even further, reaching into domestic life. You can't talk about democracy in homes filled with authoritarianism, violence, impositions, physical and psychological abuse, blackmail, and arbitrary, absolute hierarchies" (cited in Miranda and Alemán 1993, 21). Third World integrative feminists extend the notion of the political to include the personal, the private, the domestic, and the everyday; challenge the separations between the psychological, social, economic, and cultural; and bring personal change to the center of the process of social change. The recognition that real social change will require changing oneself and one's relationships brings the struggle home in ways that are both threatening and exhilarating. For the aim is not only to gain power but to transform it:

> If we continue . . . to use the same concept of power that exists, then we would have changed nothing: Power to use, to manipulate, to dominate, to control, to coerce, is the masculine understanding of power. . . . We women, coming as we do from the peripheries of power, may together with other oppressed people find through our powerlessness a redefinition of power, an alternative concept of power that encourages and enhances the potential of each one, and then perhaps collectively we may find new human strengths that will help us to find new possibilities. (D'Souza 1992, 49)

The progressive values of equality, democracy, freedom, peace, autonomy, respect, and dignity are sought in personal life as desirable ends in themselves and as necessary preconditions to their realization in the wider society. In the process their very definition is transformed: "We cannot talk of democracy outside the family yet allow male dictatorship inside it. In fact we believe that real democracies and egalitarian societies can only be established if we practice democracy, equality and mutual respect within the family. Real peace in society can only be established if we experience peace at home" (Bhasin and Khan 1986, 14).

Integrative feminists in the South are committed to constructing equal and cooperative relationships in their politics as well as their personal lives. They try to realize in their political practice the values they seek in the new society, "to create or transform women's organizations to be non-hierarchical non-competitive and truly reciprocal" (AAWORD 1985, 3). For they believe that the means of struggle must mirror its ends—that a free and caring society cannot be established by unfree and uncaring processes: "The experience of women who supported the revolution in Nicaragua is a lesson for women in El Salvador, and tells us: 'Be careful, don't fall into the trap of believing that first you must take power and then you can begin to develop egalitarian relationships.' The lesson of Nicaragua is that we must begin to build a new kind of power now, based on equal participation, on equality of decision-making, on consensus, and equality" (Ascencio 1992, 13).

Integrative feminists' commitment to create new women-defined and women-affirming understandings of the world and to build new nonoppressive ways of working politically means that consciousness raising is a key feature of these feminisms: "The fundamental aim of feminism is to lead women not only to a collective awareness of their oppression but above all to create within us a desire to radically change society" (Eteki 1990, 4). An essential part of this process is women coming to respect and value themselves and their work, and gaining the space, confidence, and knowledge to act individually and collectively. The affirmation of women involved is understood as deeply political: "Self-confidence is the beginning of all power. The recognition of self as valuable for being what it is can be a strong basis for solidarity among the oppressed whether black in a white society, female in a male dominated society, or Muslim in a Hindu society" (Jain 1978, 12–13). The resulting growth of pride, strength, consciousness, and solidarity among women is widely celebrated and often presented as the essence of integrative Third World feminisms. The Senegalese group Yewwu-Yewwi Pour la Libération des Femmes, for instance, emphasizes this in a poem on the masthead of its periodical, entitled *Fippu,* a Wolof word synonymous with rebellion:

Fippu is the acute consciousness of a necessary break with our present as women

Fippu is rebelling against the oppressive patriarchal order

Fippu is the recurrent quest of the need to change our everyday lives and prepare our future

Fippu is to build a feminist culture of proud women

Empowerment for Third World feminists depends on women-only spaces to support women's changing view of the world and of their relationship to themselves and others: "Adopting a feminist position means . . . creating the space and the conditions in which women, especially poor Third World women, can do their own gender analysis and—on the basis of this analysis—organize to define for themselves the long-term requirements for change. . . . In short, it means support for autonomous women's organizations" (Antrobus 1989, 203). In Third World contexts this may mean finding ways to support and rejuvenate or transform traditional women's organizations and culture as well as creating new organizations (Amadiume 1987; Gevins 1985; Leghorn and Parker 1981; Tauli-Corpuz 1992).

Autonomous political organization, whether built from tradition or its repudiation, provides a basis from which women can cooperate with other movements without sacrificing their commitment to women or their resistance to men's power.[9] As Rosa, Secretary for Women's Affairs of the Lima Shantytown Confederation, says:

> I am a feminist because there is no political party that values women's views, accepts women as leaders or deals with issues that specifically affect women. We must become feminists in order to raise the question of sexism, because that has been our experience as women. . . . The unions, the popular organizations and the political parties won't include women's demands in their platforms. . . . They don't take up the issues of family life, of women's situation, of what it means to be a wife. It is women's groups themselves that must deal with these issues because we are the one's being assaulted, raped and ignored. (cited in Rupert 1985/86, 47)

Feminist autonomy has to be consciously created and defended against attack and co-optation by other radicalisms: "The African feminist movement supports any struggle for a change in the social structure, however, it has to avoid falling into the trap of being recuperated by a number of (national or left-wing) parties which intend to make the struggle between sexes into a conflict which is secondary to a number of stakes they see as being major" (Anand 1980, 6).

WOMEN'S SPECIFICITY, COMMONALITY, AND DIVERSITY

For Third World integrative feminists, the articulation of feminist perspectives on society is the political achievement of diverse women. Far from assuming women's commonality, these feminists maintain the possibility of a shared women's struggle despite the overwhelmingly obvious divisions among women. Indian feminists have asked: "But is it possible to talk of women as an undifferentiated mass? Isn't life very different for a tribal woman, a Dalit woman in rural India, a factory worker, a clerk, a doctor, a university student, a middle-class or working-class housewife, an air hostess, a woman in purdah, or a common prostitute?" and have answered: "Yes, there are a lot of factors dividing women from each other—class, caste, religion, race, education (or the lack of it), one's field of work (in the house or out of it), and many other complex historical forces. Yet if we look at the nature and basis of women's oppression, we discover that our sex determines our common predicament in a very fundamental way" (*Manushi* 1979, 242). African feminists have answered the same question similarly:

> There are many factors dividing us. But if you look at the nature of our oppression, our sex does determine our situation in a very fundamental way. As women

we all carry a double burden. As women we all have to be concerned about reproductive rights. As women we face situations which men do not have to e.g. sexual harassment at work. As women our role as homemakers gets trivialised and unacknowledged, and our reproductive role is portrayed as our biggest liability. These are some of the issues we face as women. (Alloo 1988, 2)

Integrative feminists name the various systems of oppression that crosscut gender and actively point out differences among women,[10] yet they are also strongly committed to the challenge of building feminist struggle across those differences.[11]

Hope of building solidarity across women's differences lies in analyses of patriarchal oppressions as oppressions that women share despite their enormously diverse circumstances. As Aotearoa (New Zealand) feminists put it, "We women are—all of us—foreigners in our own land. Concepts of equality and liberty are not permitted us. Our work has no value. We are invisible except to each other" (Awekotuku and Waring 1984, 484). Nawal El Saadawi, an Egyptian feminist, makes the same point in an interview: "Women have always been viewed as second class citizens all over the North and the South. . . . Women's problems are everywhere, of course we might have to use different strategies to fight them, but eventually our goals are the same" (Kalemara 1988, 16).[12]

The recognition of shared oppression that these analyses represent requires that women identify as women; see themselves in each other; sympathize with and support, rather than distance and condemn, the "other woman"/other women. In a world in which women are so divided and despised, this deeply radical act requires that white, middle-class, and First World women renounce their dependent loyalties to men (and systems) whose race, class, and colonial power has privileged them.[13] It also requires that Black, working-class, and Two-Thirds World women break with mandated forms of uncritical loyalty to partial, male-defined resistances to this power.[14]

Only broader women-centered analyses and struggles based on alternative women- and life-affirming values can provide the necessary frame for this largely unprecedented development of women identification and solidarity. Yet in practice these alternative analyses and values can only emerge from a conscious women identification that must always involve a leap of faith. Identification with other women is therefore an always risky extension of self in the name of political possibilities; it both requires and is necessary for feminist revisioning and revaluing.

Identifying as a sex enables women to see and name the world as diverse women experience it rather than as it is interpreted by men. For women of all classes and communities all over the world, challenging patriarchal myths involves the frightening process of facing one's structural dependence and basic powerlessness. For integrative feminists, however, it also involves seeing and naming women's particular strengths and values and claiming power and voice for women on this basis:

> Many people (including women) interpret the call for equality for women as an assertion of women's right to be and be treated the same as men—to adopt their values, life style, behaviour, goals and aspirations ("integration" into the existing systems).
>
> And yet if women were simply pale carbon copies of men (or even stronger versions like some of our more famous female leaders), we would lose the essence of our claim to a share in decision-making. (Antrobus 1983, 13)

Insisting that women's equality with men need not, indeed should not, be claimed on the basis of sameness with men, these feminists reject the simple equality model of feminism. They claim women's specific skills, experience, and responsibility for the reproduction and preservation of life as important resources in the struggle to create a new world in which life, rather than profit, is the defining concern and the women-associated values of cooperation and nurturing are the defining values. "The women's movement too can have an ethic drawn from women's daily lives. At its deepest it is not an effort to play 'catch up' with the competitive, aggressive 'dog-eat-dog' spirit of the dominant system. It is, rather, an attempt to convert men and the system to the sense of responsibility, nurturance, openness, and rejection of hierarchy that are part of our vision" (Sen and Grown 1987, 72–73).

Far from narrowing and homogenizing the group "women," the integrative-feminist emphasis on diverse women's specificity provides the basis for perspectives whose values offer alternatives to all dominations and can unite women across many divisions. Thus integrative feminisms that emphasize women's shared values and strengths as well as their oppression and diversity are more inclusive than feminisms that, on varying grounds, deny or choose not to deal with women's specificity.

The strong integrative-feminist emphasis on women identification within and across different cultures and groups provides a framework for feminists to explore their particular identities and affinities with women inside and outside their own group. For many Third World women, growing pride and awareness as women go hand in hand with growing pride and awareness of their group's culture and history. Strong women identification enables them to claim more active and defining relationships to their own cultural traditions and/or national identity. The two are linked for women and often develop together.

This process involves criticizing the oppressive aspects of one's own culture (as well as others) while claiming one's place within it[15]—a task made particularly difficult and necessary for Third World women and women of color in the North by racist, colonialist, and capitalist attacks on their communities and by forces always ready to brand any feminist assertion as a betrayal of "community," and to dismiss feminist views as a product of colonized mentalities.

MULTICENTERED MOVEMENT

Transformative feminisms recognize and resist the differences within and between communities and among women that are grounded in power imbalances, while they welcome other differences as potential resources in broadening and deepening feminist analysis and movement. So for some integrative Third World feminists struggle involves a selective reclaiming of cultural traditions. Victoria Tauli-Corpuz, speaking of indigenous women's struggle in the Philippines, says, for instance:

> The culture of resistance and struggle lives among many of our Igorot sisters. The embers of this culture need to be fanned constantly. But while there is a need to introduce and reinforce the culture which is liberating and empowering for women, there is also a need to alter those aspects which are oppressive to women. One negative aspect is the minimal participation of women in formal indigenous decision-making structures such as in the "bodong" (peace pact) and the council of elders (male elders). Another is the practice of arranged marriages, dowry and bride price. (1992, 18).

Tauli-Corpuz is echoed by Egyptian feminist Nawal El Saadawi: "In the traditions and culture of the Arabs and Islam, there are positive aspects which must be sought for and emphasized. Negative aspects should be exposed and discarded without hesitation. Women at the time of the Prophet obtained rights of which today they are deprived in most Arab countries" (1981, 212).

This type of exploration and articulation of particular identities builds places from which to reach out and participate in wider multicentered movement—that is, movement in which there is no "typical" feminist, in which all women are equally central and any woman's experience can shed light on all women's condition. The women's movement is thus understood to be both particular and universal, international in scope and national/local in expression (Anonymous 1985, 7; Dakar 1982).

Mutual learning takes place in all directions among diverse feminisms and across the divisions among women. Yet particular attention is paid to ensuring that all women, including and especially the least powerful, find their voices and are heard. The mandate of the international Third World feminist group DAWN (Development Alternatives with Women for a New Era) is to develop Third World feminist voices, definitions of the world, and ideas about what is to be done. DAWN members emphasize the least powerful and most marginal among Third World women as particularly important in this project because their understanding of multiple oppressions will be greater and because alternative visions are best generated from the margins of any society by those responsible for the survival and nurturance of human beings. Maria Mies and Vandana Shiva (1993, 12–13,19–20) and others also see poor women's particular contribution stemming mainly from the fact that their work most directly concerns the necessities of life and most directly depends on keeping life-sustaining networks and processes alive.

The autonomy and specificity of particular feminisms grounded in particular realities thus enrich feminist politics generally. Diversity and commonality are essential aspects of dialectical practice. As a feminist from Bangladesh explained in a speech in Canada, global feminism is not uniform but stems from and encompasses enormous variety. In fact, it is variety that makes solidarity possible:

> We believe in the concept of spinning local threads, weaving global feminism. We may have different threads both in colors and texture from many local areas. But we are rich with experiences from various parts of the world, from Africa, Latin America, Asia and Pacific, Australia, Europe and America. We have experiences where women are fighting against poverty, against external domination, against the business corporate exploitation, against racism, against patriarchal social and cultural systems. The experiences are diverse and sometimes far from each other even in terms of understanding. We do not think that there can be only one design to be followed as an "answer." The diversity in design and color but woven in a single cloth will make us united and strong. (Das 1991, 17)

Two-Thirds World feminists are subject to both antifeminist charges of being foreign-dominated and to the actual limitations of some narrow Western feminisms. They experience the tensions between autonomy and solidarity constantly and immediately. At the same time, their more exploited position internationally means they understand both the difficulty and the necessity of working across the North-South divide more clearly and more urgently than many of us yet do in the North. For both these reasons Third World feminist commitment to the double project of building indigenous as well as international feminisms is explicit and articulate. Their understanding of the creative possibilities of the tension between the two is often more developed and their practice more conscious of that tension than is generally the case in North America. As we shall see in the next chapter, however, global awareness is growing among North American feminists.

7

NORTH AMERICAN GLOBAL AWARENESS

Clearly, global solidarity and movement are not about achieving centralized and uniform orthodoxy. Feminists committed to global visions call for the worldwide development of indigenous transformative feminisms with strong local practices both informed by and informing global perspectives and loyalties to women.

North American feminists most committed to global transformation tend to be those most aware both of exploitative and colonial international relationships and of women's activism around the world,[1] and therefore most resistant to dominant ethnocentric and racist myths. There are feminists in North America, however, who have not thought to question the cultural stereotypes of Two-Thirds World women as more passive, powerless, and oppressed than First World women or the patriarchal myth that industrialization and urbanization have invariably meant increased equality, respect, and liberty for women. They may also make unexamined and arrogant presumptions that liberation for Third World women will involve simply moving closer in condition to First World women and will be best attained by adopting methods of struggle learned from them.[2] These delusions are more often cause and consequence of unhealthy insularity than of destructive involvement. Western feminists' general lack of awareness of struggles abroad presents more of an obstacle to global feminist movement at the moment than does their domineering concern. But these two apparently opposed weaknesses are two sides of the same coin of ethnocentric ignorance.

Growing numbers of feminists in North America do, however, understand their efforts as part of a global struggle of women whose activism they respect and draw strength from.[3] Their women identification is not simply a projection of their own reality onto the world's women and is certainly not a denial of nongender dominations. As Adrienne Rich explains in a commencement address to elite Smith College graduates, it is the necessary political basis for radical commitment to diverse women around the world, including and especially the least advantaged:

> Because you are, within the limits of all women's ultimate outsiderhood, a privileged group of women, it is extremely important for your future sanity that you understand the way tokenism functions.... [In] losing her outsider's vision, [the token] loses the insight which both binds her to other women and affirms her in herself. Tokenism essentially demands that the token deny her identification with women as a group, especially with women less privileged than herself....
>
> [But] no woman is really an insider in the institutions fathered by masculine consciousness. When we allow ourselves to believe we are, we lose touch with parts of ourselves defined as unacceptable by that consciousness; with the vital toughness and visionary strength of the angry grandmothers, the shamanesses, the fierce marketwomen of the Ibo Women's War, the marriage-resisting women silkworkers of prerevolutionary China, the millions of widows, midwives, and women healers tortured and burned as witches for three centuries in Europe. (1979b, 7)

Educated, urban, middle-class women have found it especially difficult to consciously recognize women's strength and, on that basis, affirm their own identity and connections as women. For, whether Black or white, First or Two-Thirds World, they have been most colonized by patriarchal assimilation, are most divided from other women, and remain most susceptible to patriarchal myths that divide them from other women.[4] As Third World feminisms develop and the North American women's movement diversifies, women identification and global awareness have strengthened in North America. Afro-American women connect with and draw strength from African women and their writing[5] and are pursuing international links and building networks; native feminists identify with the anticolonial resistance of tribal cultures worldwide and affirm their values as resources in integrative change;[6] ecofeminists and feminist peace activists are inspired by the struggles of women around the world[7]; spiritual feminists expose the fact that "Western religion is not simply sexist but racist, imperialist, ethnocentric, and heterosexist as well" (Plaskow and Christ 1989, 2); immigrant women and the daughters of immigrants, often economic, political, and/or military refugees, bring knowledge of and commitment to women and struggles all over the world.[8]

The same events and policies that are displacing women in the Two-Thirds World directly affect the United States and Canada, generating an atmosphere increasingly receptive to the issues immigrant women are raising and stimulating organizations and activities with an international frame of reference. In responding to the North American Free Trade Agreement, the Gulf War, U.S. involvement in El Salvador and Nicaragua, the Arab-Israli conflict, war and destruction in the former Yugoslavia, and environmental crisis, feminists here become more gobally aware and concerned to build global links.

The group MADRE represents such an attempt. It was founded in 1983 as: "A woman-to-woman, people-to-people connection, [to link] the problems women and children face every day in [the United States] with challenges women and children in other parts of the world face as a result of U.S. policies. We are a multi-cultural, cross-class network firm in our commitment to human rights, peace and justice" (MADRE 1991, n.p.). In 1991, during the Gulf War, MADRE organized the Mother Courage Peace Tour. Women from Egypt, Iraq, Israel, Jordan, Kuwait, the Occupied Territories of Palestine, and the United States toured twelve U.S. and Canadian cities helping to generate "an international chorus of women's voices for peace" (ibid.). U.S. and Canadian women were also among the two hundred women and children in the Ship of Peace that sailed from Algiers in the fall of 1990 to take food and medicine to Iraq. Members of MADRE set out in a truck for Baghdad from Amman in Jordon in January 1992 with infant formula, vitamins, and antibiotics. In March and April 1993, MADRE sponsored Mother Courage II in response to the crisis in the former Yugoslavia. Women from Bosnia, Serbia, and Croatia joined women from Central America, the Middle East, Africa, the Caribbean, and Southeast Asia to "demonstrate the universality of the crime [of rape] and to demand immediate remedies at the U.N. and in each of our countries" (MADRE 1993, n.p.).

Feminist responses to international economic intitiatives have included the founding of Mujer a Mujer, a collective of Mexican, U.S., Canadian, and Caribbean women based in Mexico promoting communication, exchange and strategic connecting among activist women throughout the region. The group emphasizes sharing knowledge and developing common analyses of and resistance to the North American Free Trade Agreement and more general international structural adjustment programs. Its publication, *Correspondencia*, described on its masthead as "a bilingual [English and Spanish] forum for women active in labour, urban popular, lesbian, anti-violence, popular education and cultural movements in Mexico, Canada and the U.S.," is a fine source of information on activism within and among all three countries. The Woman to Woman Global Strategies Group, founded in Vancouver in 1991 to research the impact of global economic restructuring on women's lives, plans to link with women's groups internationally, nationally, and locally. The Women for Alternative Economics Network, made up of women from diverse regions and organizations in the United States searching for economic alternatives to systemic poverty, studies the global economy. The seminar entitled "Women and Economic Justice: North-South Perspectives" held in Toronto in May 1992 and the forum entitled "Women and the Earth: Connecting for Life" organized by Toronto Women for a Just and Healthy Planet in March 1993 are just two indications of increasing global and economic awareness and education among North American feminists.

Global feminism is not only, or even primarily, international activity so much as strong local activity with global awareness. The distinction between global movement and international practice is an important one, because the measure of feminism's development as a global and globally aware movement does not reside primarily in the amount of international networking and dialogue. In fact, without strong and reciprocally supportive grounding in local practice, regional and international activity may take resources away from and ultimately undermine feminist strength globally.

Nonetheless, one of the best ways to build global feminisms is undoubtedly through exchanges among women internationally. These can help feminists everywhere identify their cultural blindnesses and broaden their sense of feminism and its possibilities. Mutual learning like this works very effectively among women who share some circumstances and/or histories. For instance, Women Living under Muslim Laws, a worldwide feminist network described later, provides the opportunity for women with a shared Muslim heritage living in very different circumstances to compare and question varying patriarchal interpretations of Islam. South African women involved in the democratization process in their country turn for lessons and support to African sisters in nations that have achieved independence by revolutionary and other means over the last fifty years. Palestinian feminists can have some assurance that Algerian feminists will understand their context, and by the same token, El Salvadoran women may find discussions with Nicaraguan feminists particularly productive for they are also negotiating their relationship with revolutionary movements in the same region in fast-changing circumstances.

There are also benefits to be gained, however, from dialogue across wider diversity. Patriarchal ideological mystifications of any culture are likely to be more evident to women *less* familiar with them. African women's questions about "romance" and Western marriage, for instance, may reveal to First World women how mistaken we are if we presume that couples share economic status and interests. In such situations respectful questions in either direction can stimulate new analysis. They can reveal that patterns of relationships, behaviors, and customs so taken for granted as to be invisible to or seen as natural by those who live with them, are actually social constructions to be challenged and changed or honored and built upon.

This kind of exchange, of course, whether local, regional, or global, requires participants who are "willing to recognize and accept differences even as they collectively define commonalities" (AAWORD 1985, 2). Feminists must acknowledge the forces that divide women while they look for the interests that connect them and the possibilities of building on these. North American femi-nists in particular have to recognize the history of exploitative racist colonial and neocolonial economic and political relations that the North has imposed and continues to enforce on indigenous peoples and the South.

It is generally more difficult to see power relationships from the "top" side. Feminists in English Canada, for instance, remain largely and culpably unaware of Quebecois feminist perspectives on constitutional issues (Roberts 1988). The lives of lesbians, working-class women, women of color, and Third World women teach them things about heterosexual, class, race, and colonial power that heterosexual, middle- and upper-class, white, or North American women can only learn with difficulty. Yet global feminisms depend on "privileged" women learning these lessons and other women believing they can.

International exploitation is North American women's problem in the same way that racism is white women's problem. Good intentions and sentiments of sisterhood will not build global solidarity unless we oppose the policies that protect, expand, and intensify global exploitation and incorporate this opposi-tion in all our practice. Zimbabwean feminist Rudo Gaidzanwa explains how absolutely necessary this is to the continued development of feminism's trans-formative struggle:

> Western feminisms should address more explicitly the issues of racism and imperialism in the feminist movement and in western societies. It is the recogni-tion of these major forces and also of their capacity to divide us that will enable us to transcend them. Our division reflects our inabiliity to interact outside the confines imposed by racism and imperialism, and the measure of our success in transcending these divisions will be our ability to organize effectively against the exploitation of all women. (*Signs* 1986, 597)

All North American women, from the least to the most privileged, benefit from this exploitation. While we are not responsible for having established these relations, we *are* responsible for acknowledging and opposing them. Under-standing this responsibility is a necessary basis for participating honestly, or even at all, in global dialogue.

> In Latin America ... we make a distinction between the U.S. government and *gringos* and *gringas* who work against such policies and approaches. While there are prejudices and ignorances between feminists in different regions which we must work to overcome, we see the political possibility of alliances in which we work together for change as important.
>
> But in order for us to make such a distinction among *gringos* and create alliances with you, we must first see that you acknowledge and take responsibil-ity for the oppressive consequences of your nation's power in our lives. (Carillo 1990, 205)

The Association of African Women for Research and Development makes this general point strongly with reference to the particular case of clitoridectomy in its "Statement on Genital Mutilation":

> The fight against genital mutilation, although necessary, should not take on such proportions that the wood cannot be seen for the trees. . . . To fight against genital mutilation without placing it in the context of ignorance, obscurantism, exploitation, poverty, etc., without questioning the structures and social relations which perpetuate this situation, is like "refusing to see the sun in the middle of the day." This, however, is precisely the approach taken by many Westerners, and is highly suspect, especially since Westerners necessarily profit from the exploitation of the peoples and women of Africa, whether directly or indirectly. (AAWORD 1983, 219)

When we work with women from other countries, no matter how long our track record of opposing U.S. or Canadian government policies, and no matter what our race, class, or sexual orientation, we are nationals of these countries and must acknowledge this status. While a woman's citizenship may not be a large part of her conscious radical identity at home, it will loom large for women from countries that are subject to Western impositions. North American women can't expect to be allowed to disown or take honorary exemption from their nationality in foreign contexts and should not be hurt or surprised that we have to shoulder this identity actively and critically as a necessary part of our global awareness and practice.[9]

This means, among other things, working to be aware of power differences and unequal access to resources in situations in which First World feminists are advantaged. It requires fighting our First World tendency to see the North as the center of the world and Northern definitions of issues as universal definitions. Almost all First World feminists of all ethnicities are raised with these presumptions. Overcoming them is harder to do than might at first appear and requires consistent effort. Dialogue between First and Third World women can be painful for women of color from the North when they find their sisters from the South stressing colonial divisions in contexts in which they want and feel the need to stress shared oppressions and conditions or when issues (especially racism and colonialism) are defined and prioritized in unexpected and unfamiliar ways (Ahmed 1981; NiCharthaigh 1981; Reddock 1993).[10] Dialogue can also be exhilarating and empowering for women of color in the North, for Third World feminists' presumptions of centrality in their own movements, provide powerful support for minority feminists making similar claims and committed to multicentered movement in North America. The racism and Eurocentrism that sustain white-centered concepts of women's movement here become untenable in the forceful presence of women from all over the world, most of them from countries with no significant white population.

Dialogue with feminists from the South is one of the best and most demanding ways for North American feminists to increase their understanding of global issues.[11] It is in vain, however, if we let what we learn about our own ethnocentrism, internalized colonial mentalities, and privilege, and our nations' death-dealing history and policies, disable us with guilt. Dialogue is a two-way process; global solidarity and mutual support require every woman's active participation. Willingness to see the cultural limits of one's own viewpoint, to ask questions, to accept challenges, to listen, to learn, and to grow is essential to productive dialogue. But North American feminists must also be willing to share insights from their own experience and practice. While it is important to avoid the arrogance of presuming to know more about other women's situations than they do, it is equally important not to let the awareness that saves us from this mistake lead us to dismiss our own knowledge.

To build a just and heterogeneous world and women's movement feminists need to defend and celebrate diverse cultures while opposing any and all oppressions imposed in the names of those cultures. Feminists must be strong and independent enough in their own community and in the wider women's movement to decide for themselves what to affirm and what to reject in their own culture and to be able to offer and accept support from other feminists waging the same struggle. We need to challenge claims that associate community strength with the patriarchal power of men and to resist not only that power but the charge that in doing so we are betraying the community.

Accepting "outside" support for struggles against aspects of one's own culture requires enormous trust, especially when potential feminist supporters are from groups with a history of oppressing one's own people. Feminists must be confident that their feminist supporters will not impose ignorant external judgments and conditions and will not, even unwittingly, allow their support to be used to the benefit their own patriarchal community. This kind of trust is only possible among autonomous women prepared to challenge the patriarchal relationships and definitions of their own cultures; committed to ending power relations between classes, races, and nations as well as between men and women; and able to avoid the use of feminist issues to fuel attacks on already weak and threatened communities. Hindu and Muslim feminists have faced this challenge in their campaigns for legal reform in India,[12] as have Israeli, Jewish, and Palestinian feminists resisting Israeli occupation (Bergman et al. 1990), nonnative and native Canadian feminists around First Nations women's battles for their rights (LaChapelle 1982), and African and First World feminists in the struggles against clitoridectomy and polygamy (Koso-Thomas 1987).

One example of the dilemmas involved in solidarity across communities in relations of power is the case of First World feminist support for African feminists' struggles for democracy. It can be difficult to offer this support without feeding the U.S. and Canadian populations' general ignorance of the role played by the West in undermining indigenous forms of organization and supporting only the most compliant and often the most repressive regimes in the Two-Thirds World. Criticism of human rights violations elsewhere in the world can be used by our governments to lend credence to their hypocritical human rights campaigns and self-serving claims to represent the democratic hope of the world. But simply remaining silent is no solution. African feminists among others require our support and are asking for it directly: "For African women today, [feminism] means struggling against the totalitarianism established and maintained on the African continent by the 'liberal' West! and we launch an appeal to the feminists of Canada and the world to recognize the totalitarian nature of power in Africa, of African totalitarianism.... It is urgent that feminists on all continents ... create a world feminist domain from which African women could propose a democratic alternative to African totalitarianism" (Eteki 1990, 4). The urgency of this call was brought home forcefully in 1992 when Wangari Maathai, founder of the Green movement in Kenya, was arrested with other women while demanding democratic reform there.

The practical requirements of resisting colonial worldviews and imperialist practices in the North may conflict with some African feminists' needs for immediate support in resisting local dictatorship. North American feminists have to find ways to support our African sisters' struggle against the tyranny of ruling groups in Africa while acknowledging and educating North Americans about the role of Western governments and business in establishing and supporting African dictatorships.

The paradoxical fact that anticolonialism may have to be emphasized more by feminists in the West, where colonial and Eurocentric presumptions still largely structure people's perceptions, than in other parts of the world with widespread understanding of colonialism and long histories of resistance, is illustrated by Lata Mani (1990). In her doctoral research in the U.S. Mani explored the colonial impetus behind much of the British opposition to the practice of suttee (widow burning). When she returned to India she found that the main struggle for feminists there had to be against the practice itself, which was and is enjoying a resurgence. Raising issues central to her research that made important contributions in the North ran the risk in India of aiding and abetting the increasingly vocal and powerful supporters of suttee in their effort to discredit current feminist opposition as Western-inspired and orchestrated.

This case indicates the necessity *both* for feminist issues and strategy to be defined locally *and* for feminists in different parts of the world to develop our analyses together and learn from each other's different priorities and pressures. When differences of priority reflect differences of circumstance and not of political perspective, they can lead to increased understanding for us all. In contexts in which diverse feminists have equal voices (and this is, of course, the major challenge), disagreements can represent opportunities rather than stalemates.

Global consciousness is not just an additional insight but a frame for broader synthesis. For instance, when feminism's relevance to the whole of society encompasses the globe, it becomes possible to see that what have been defined as "development" issues in the South are called social issues in the North. The distinction is revealed as a false one that hides common struggles and masks potentially common activist self-definitions behind unequal donor and recipient relations. Global perspectives and global activism have opened the way for these institutionalized, asymmetrical, state-defined relationships to be challenged by establishing alternative autonomous political links within and between the North and the South.[13]

Many feminists in the North lack international awareness. Others without a grounding in feminist practice in their own country have focused their work on Third World nations and women. These researchers, professionals, and development workers, who have not tended to think in terms of linked social movements or mutually defined political relationships between South and North, need to respond to the new potential for equal North-South relationships. The objectives and principles of the Association of African Women for Research and Development (AAWORD 1981) and Third World feminist criticisms of the Wellesley Conference on Women in Development in June 1976 both uncompromisingly insist that Northern feminist academics and development workers make the shift to mutual and reciprocal relationships built on common political commitments in their own societies. In their critique of the Wellesley conference, feminists from Egypt, Morocco, and Thailand exposed the damaging impact of conferences that claim to be international but are actually exchanges among mostly Western women about Third World women: "The absence of papers on American women restored for us the hardly-healed colonial experience wherein the detached outsiders define your world for you. To feel like a fish in a glass bowl is very uncomfortable, especially if you are women coming from far away, expecting a rare chance to shed oppression and passivity and engage in a meaningful egalitarian dialogue" (Saadawi, Mernissi, and Vajarathon 1978, 103).

Feminisms that do not actively create new and equal political relationships and consciously oppose Western exploitation are in danger of carrying its myths and becoming its creature. What is asked of North American feminists is not withdrawal and silence, however, but active engagement on the basis of their *own* struggles and conditions—the only possible basis for equal relationships.

First World feminisms in the "belly of the beast" are particularly well placed to resist Western exploitation. We are in a position to put direct pressure on the patriarchal-capitalist classes, governments, businesses, and banks that are ruling the world. First and Third World feminists need to work together to resist what are today global systems of oppression as well as the power of men in each of their communities. Numerous North American feminists have made important contributions to the global networking necessary for this effort. It is therefore imperative that our awareness of the shortcomings of some noninte-grative feminisms not lead us to disown wholesale "Western feminism" or even "white Western feminism." Misleading homogenization of Western feminists plays into the hands of those who use negative stereotypes of elitist, individual-istic, man-mimicking, colonizing "Western feminism" to attack our sisters in the Two-Thirds World. Apart from performing a disservice to these feminists, any general rejection of "Western feminism" disables First World feminists who, in making it, totally deny the local practice that is the only basis for their partic-ipation in global solidarity.[15]

We have a creditable, though not faultless, history of diverse feminist strug-gle in North America that we can and should share. We need to deepen and enrich it, not deny it. Rather than distancing ourselves from "Western femi-nism," integrative feminists need to find and foster the many North American feminisms capable of participating in global dialogue. And we need to let Third World feminists know that these exist.

8

GLOBAL PRACTICE

INTERNATIONAL FEMINIST DIALOGUE AND ORGANIZING

The period since 1975 has seen amazing growth in feminisms around the world and in relationships among those feminisms. Numerous reports, descriptions, and analyses, as well as my own experience and interviews, indicate that the United Nations' International Women's Year (1975) and Decade for Women (1975–1985) were major factors in fostering feminist progress, stimulating local activity in both North and South as well as international links and dialogue (Stienstra 1994). The three international conferences held during the Decade provide a good measure of women's shifting understanding of each other and the world. Each official U.N. conference of government representatives was accompanied by an unofficial forum of women and women's groups. Attendance at the unofficial forums rose from six thousand in Mexico City in 1975 to seven thousand in Copenhagen in 1980 to fourteen thousand in Nairobi in 1985, figures indicative of women's growing interest in and capacity for global dialogue.[1]

In the 1970s mutual mistrust was widespread. Women concerned with issues of colonialism and economic development were not uncommonly suspected of being antifeminist dupes of male-dominated governments or movements. Women concerned with questions of women's equality were often seen as uncritical agents of exploitative Westernization and "modernization," privileged, individualistic man-haters and man-imitators. These caricatures, fostered by male-dominated media and political groups in both the First and Two-Thirds Worlds, fed suspicion of each other among active women at the first U.N. conference in Mexico in 1975.

But antifeminist efforts could not completely contain the exciting exchanges that went on in a forum widely reported in the mainstream media as demonstrating only women's inability to work together. The opportunity for active women to share experiences with others from very different circumstances helped women from both North and South to broaden their understanding of the complexities of and connections among divergent issues. Increasing numbers of First World women came to respect the strength, history, and concerns of women in other regions and to recognize the limits of their own ethnocentrism. Third World women came to see that despite their relative wealth, women in the First World were not free from poverty, violence, and sexual exploitation, that, even at its most liberal, feminism is a mass movement for social justice, not to ape men, but to free women from male power.

At the mid-Decade conference in Copenhagen integrative feminists presented their views of "feminism as a political perspective on all issues of concern to human life, ... a political process that reaches beyond patriarchal political divisions and national boundaries," and discussed the "difficulty of defining feminism across regional and cultural lines" (Bunch in *Signs* 1981, 790). The dismissal of feminism as elitist, individualist, and Western gave way among many to questioning and interest. Issues of women's role and power were not so widely read as displacements of other issues of domination and were raised with more awareness of other dominations. Issues of colonialism and capitalism were less often presumed to imply denial of questions of gender and were less often raised in that spirit.

The process that went on locally and internationally before and during the U.N. Decade, one that continues today, is a process in which activist women counter misunderstandings and misrepresentations and expand and develop their politics. Women are taking control of relationships with each other from those who would divide us and forging the inclusive and integrative politics that can unite us.

Feminists have over the years taken full advantage of the opportunities for networking provided by male-dominated international organizations such as the World Council of Churches and individual religious denominations and academic, professional, and trade-union as well as education, sport, film, and arts groups. International women's groups such as the YWCA, Associated Country Women of the World, and female religious orders have also provided important contexts for cooperation. However, autonomous feminist-defined and feminist-friendly international events and networks have played an increasingly important role since 1975. Internationally, feminists have concentrated on (1) fostering communication; (2) creating opportunities for dialogue, theory building, and organizational development; and (3) fashioning new decentralized political forms to support more sustained collective action and solidarity. All these activities are closely related, and the international newsletters, resource centers, conferences, workshops, and networks described below contribute to all three.

Publications and Resource Centers: Communication

ISIS, the Women's International Information and Communication Service founded as a collective in 1974, provides information about local, regional, national, and international women's struggles to feminists around the world. It seeks to:
- promote communication channels among women around the world;
- strengthen women's networks nationally, regionally, and internationally;
- provide information and models of action for women who are organizing and mobilizing against the oppression of women;
- build links of support and solidarity among women's groups and organizations worldwide;
- build women's capacity by providing technical assistance and training and tools in communication skills and information management.

To these ends, it maintains a network of over ten thousand contacts in 150 countries, coordinates the International Feminist Network founded in 1976, runs a resource center and database, and publishes the *ISIS International Women's Journal*, *Women in Action*, and *Women's World* as well as influential resource guides.[2]

The International Women's Tribune Center was founded in 1976 following the first U.N. Decade conference and incorporated in 1978 in order to "respond to the requests for information and assistance from many of the 6,000 women who attended that conference." It has since grown into a "communications and technical assistance support service for more than 16,000 women and women's groups in 160 countries" and publishes a quarterly newsletter, the *Tribune*, to document and provide a network of support for women's social-change activities around the world.[3]

Also founded in the mid-1970s, *WIN News* (Women's International Network News) reports on women's issues and struggles around the world. "All people concerned about women's development, women's status or women's rights are invited to send news and information of concern to women." By 1979 *WIN News* had reported from more than 130 countries (Hosken 1978/79).

Connexions, founded in 1981, states on the masthead of each issues that it "is the collective product of feminists of diverse nationalities and political perspectives committed to an international women's movement and . . . the growth of a worldwide network connecting women working on similar projects by researching, establishing contacts, and exchanging information with other women's organizations."

Conferences and Workshops: Dialogue, Theory Building, Solidarity

In June 1979 an international workshop entitled "Feminist Ideology and Structures in the First Half of the Decade for Women," gathering First and Two-Thirds World participants was held in Bangkok. A follow-up "International Feminist Workshop" was organized at Stony Point, New York, in April 1980 to produce tools to "stimulate further discussion—initially at the international events taking place in Copenhagen, July 1980—as well as into the future" (WAND/APCWD 1980, 4). Both workshops "consciously [used] a methodology which would help to create a climate in which the participants could explore the possibilities of formulating an international perspective on feminism while respecting differences of background and ideology" (ibid., 5).

It is clear from workshop reports and other descriptions that these sessions were models of creative dialogue that had a significant impact on the influential "theorists, activists, planners and program managers" (ibid., 4) who participated and who continue to develop and spread the integrative global feminist perspectives they forged there.

Peggy Antrobus, for instance, said in a speech to the Associated Country Women of the World in 1983: "The Workshop represented a turning point of my journey. . . . I left Bangkok determined to find a way of linking the issues of 'Women in Development' and those of feminist theory, determined that the programmes and strategies for the Integration of Women in Development should reflect feminist principles, and pledged to use the word feminism wherever possible and to give it a Third World interpretation" (1983, 3–4)

In June 1982, following an earlier "Conference on Alternative Development" that had left women out, the Association of African Women for Research and Development (AAWORD) and the Dag Hammarskjöld Foundation held an international seminar entitled "Another Development with Women" in Dakar, Senegal, with forty-six participants from twenty-seven countries in Latin America, Asia, the Middle East, North America and Europe as well as Africa.[4] The "Declaration" from the conference outlined the principles of Another Development, which could only be realized through the struggles of women all over the world:

> [this] vision . . . will only be possible if patriarchal relations and practices are eliminated. . . . Social progress means not only improving the situation of women but also changing it by opposing all ideologies that define women's role as subordinate, dependent or passive. Feminism provides the basis for this new consciousness and for cultural resistance to all forms of domination. Such resis-

tance by women to domination has been present in many countries, and has provided the women's movement with continuity in its active struggle for equality. (Dakar 1982, 14–15)

Countless other international working gatherings with significant invited representation of women from both North and South addressing areas such as peace, media, law, trade unionism, women's studies, housing, education, and health have contributed to the global development of feminist theory and practice.

Larger, open international conferences have also been important. Attendance at those held periodically increases over time, giving them a significant cumulative impact. Because they are open to anyone who has the resources to attend, they often have a preponderance of European and North American participants, especially when held in the North. Their failure to achieve balanced representation is a problem and has been the subject of criticism. Nonetheless, the situation has gradually, though insufficiently, improved.

The International Women and Health Network builds on dynamic local activity and regional Women's Health Networks to organize conferences every four years or so, increasingly in the Third World, and with growing global participation. Written reports of these conferences are inspiring in their descriptions of real and sustained international solidarity and learning around the range of linked economic, social, cultural, sexual, psychological, religious, military, and commercial issues that determine women's health (Philippine Organizing Committee 1992).

"The International Interdisciplinary Congress on Women" has been held every three years since its inception in Haifa, Israel, in 1981. The most recent conference, in San José, Costa Rica, in 1993, with eight hundred participants from eighty countries, saw significant participation by nonacademics from Costa Rica and elsewhere and found the travel funds to enable Third World feminists to attend and play a formative role.

"The International Feminist Book Fair," a trade fair and literary/political event, has been held every two years since 1984 with thousands in attendance. The most recent conference, with an estimated twenty thousand participants, was in Melbourne, Australia, in July 1994 around the theme "Indigenous, Asian, and Pacific Writing and Publishing."

New Political Forms: Networks and Associations

The last decades have also seen the development of more structured, though flexible and decentralized forms of regional and international organization that can support common action. DAWN (Development Alternatives with Women for a New Era) was launched in 1984 in Bangalore, India, building partly on the meetings in Bangkok in 1979 and Stony Point in 1980. It is an international organization of Third World feminist-activist researchers committed to producing theory and practice from a specifically Third World perspective. With experienced members in Asia, Africa, Latin America, the Pacific, and the Caribbean, this group has mobilized global support for integrative-feminist analysis and new feminist visions of "development." The book in which the group outlines these perspectives, *Development, Crises, and Alternative Visions: Third World Women's Perspectives* (Sen and Grown 1987), had a large impact at the U.N. conference in Nairobi. It remains influential in international, national, regional, and local events and organizations, where the group's perpectives continue to be used and developed.[5]

These and other international initiatives support and are supported by the increasing local, regional, and national organizing and activism among women that has built the potential for truly reciprocal international politics. For instance, AAWORD in Africa, WAND (Women and Development) in the Caribbean, and numerous Asian and Pacific regional networks[6] were involved in organizing many of the more representative international working conferences described above, including the important meetings in Bangkok, Stony Point, and Dakar.

The Association of African Women for Research and Development (AAWORD) was founded in 1977. AAWORD's objectives are:
- to undertake research which calls for the participation of women and emphasizes their presence in all cultural, social, economic and political processes of change;
- to create networks among African women researchers and those concerned with problems of development in Africa;
- to identify resources to facilitate research by its members;
- to encourage the formation of national research working groups in conjunction with national research centers.

The group plays an important role as a voice for African women in international contexts, having done so most notably at the U.N. conferences in Copenhagen and Nairobi. It has organized regional conferences and workshops on such topics as "Research on African Women: What Type of Methodology?" and "Women and Rural Development in Africa." It publishes proceedings of these gatherings in an occasional-paper series as well as newsletters, bibliographic series, and statements on such issues as clitoridectomy (AAWORD 1983) and such events as the Nairobi conference (AAWORD n.d.).[7]

The Caribbean Association for Research and Action (CAFRA) was founded in 1985 as an autonomous umbrella organization for active women in the region and Caribbean women living outside the region "committed to understanding the relationship between the oppression of women and other forms of exploitation in the society and to working actively for change" (CAFRA 1990, 60). The group defines feminist politics "as a matter of both consciousness and action" (ibid.). It undertakes research/action projects and puts out a quarterly newsletter, *CAFRA News*.[8]

The Commonwealth Women's Network, founded at a six-day meeting in Toronto in 1991, is another example of networking among women that crosses geographical, religious, and other boundaries to bring extremely diverse women together to build common politics and create new political definitions and possibilities (Commonwealth Women's Network 1991). Likewise, the European Network for African Women was established in October 1993 at the "Strengthening Our Links: African Women in Europe" conference, organized by the London-based nongovernmental women's group Akina Mama wa Afrika. Participants discussed, among other things, the strategic importance of having strong African women's groups in Europe with links to Africa (Mammandaran 1993, 46).

At an Asian regional workshop in Bangalore in January 1989 participants from Bangladesh, India, Pakistan, and Sri Lanka spent nine days discussing the nature of feminism and patriarchy and the relation of South Asian feminism to Western feminism, of Hindu to Muslim and Indian to Pakistani feminists, and of feminism to mass womens movements, to radical/leftist groups, and to traditional cultures and religions. After intensive discussion, also, of the state, identity politics, international capitalism, Western dualism, militarism, development, and the environment, participants issued the "South Asian Feminist Declaration" affirming alternative women-centered visions and values and their commitment to work together across the deep communal and national animosities in the region (South Asian Workshop on Women and Development 1989).

Latin American feminists began meeting regionally in 1981 and have met every two years since then in ever larger and more diverse *Encuentros* during which key strategic, organizational, and theoretical debates are engaged. The first Encuentro Feminista Latinamericano y del Caribe, in Bogotá Colombia, was announced by flyer at the U.N.'s mid-Decade conference in Copenhagen as a place for Latin American feminists "to exchange experiences and opinions, identify problems and evaluate different practices, as well as plan tasks and projects for the future." At the most recent *Encuentro,* held in 1993 in Costa del Sol, El Salvador, a thousand women braved threats from the Salvadoran right wing to meet for the first time in Central America. The presence of committed feminists from all over the region strengthened El Salvadoran women's voices in negotiations under way between guerilla forces and the government (Alemán et al. 1993; Match 1992).[9]

Indigenous women are also developing regional and international networks and solidarities and contributing to South-South and North-South learning. Shared indigenous identity provides a frame for dialogue among diverse women in both the First and Two-Thirds Worlds who are active in a myriad of ways, with different priorities and approaches. Many know both "modern" and "traditional" cultures and social arrangements as well as the immediate and acute experience of colonialism, economic exploitation, and environmental destruction. Organizations such as the Indigenous Women's Network, established in 1984; the International Indigenous Women's Caucus at the World Women's Congress for a Healthy Planet in Miami, in November 1991; and numerous conferences, such as the first International Indigenous Women's Conference in Adelaide, Australia, in July 1989; the Women of the Americas Conference in Mexico City in July 1992; and the First Asian Indigenous Women's Conference, in Baguio City, the Philippines, in January 1993, have supported and built on exchanges that are giving indigenous women in all their diversity a powerful presence and influential voice in developing feminisms regionally and globally (Hanlon 1992; Senogles 1992; Tauli-Corpuz 1993).

Local Learning from Global Exchange

Only a very small proportion of feminists are active globally. Increasingly widespread local feminist practice sustains the global feminist presence, however, and is enriched by it. The international newsletters, conferences, resource centers, and decentralized forms of organizing described here are making it possible for feminists everywhere to be informed about, to learn from, and to support each other's analyses and struggles.

There is ample evidence of the reciprocally transforming global process among women's movements around the world. Successful feminist political forms developed in one corner of the globe, for instance, are picked up by feminists in other countries and spread spontaneously. Consciousness-raising groups, International Women's Day celebrations, public testimonies/tribunals, transition houses, peace camps, Action Alerts, Take Back the Night Marches, Women in Black groups and demonstrations, international petitions, and community policing of violence against women are just a few creative forms of practice that have spread from their initial sites to all regions of the world.[10]

Feminists are also more deliberately creating opportunities for far-flung local activists to learn from each other and to develop analysis and strategy together, both bilaterally and multilaterally. South African women invited activists from Bombay to discuss what improvement if any, poor women could expect in their lives from the democracy that was imminent in their country (SPARC 1992). Southall Black Sisters Group in England got help from Women Living under Muslim Laws in its campaign to defend Rabia Janjua under threat of deportation from Britain to certain persecution in Pakistan (Patel 1991). Toronto feminists invited Sistren from Jamaica to teach them about the possibilities of popular theater. Canadian and Chilean feminists arranged an exchange among women from diverse communities active around issues of violence against women (Burke and Sfier 1992).

There are also longer term residential programs designed to foster knowledge and networking among feminist activists internationally. Many of these are organized by and as a result of the regional and international networks and conferences described earlier, all of which emphasize communication and theory building among their aims. ISIS, the Women's International Information and Communication Service, for instance, organizes the Women's International Cross-Cultural Exchange (WICCE), which involves activists from all over the world in residential workshops allowing them to learn from each other. The Institute for Women's Global Leadership holds summer workshops in the U.S. for feminist activists from around the world.

The fruits of this global process of diverse women's mobilization and empowerment were visible at the Nairobi Forum in 1985, at the end of the U.N.'s Decade for Women:

> In Nairobi the Third World women were clearly an overwhelming majority. Third World women were setting the pace, defining the issues, proposing solutions, taking initiatives. The polarization between "Developed" and "Developing," North and South, which had been evident in Mexico City was absent. The growing feminist movement has helped women from North and South to find a basis for solidarity which respects and celebrates cultural and ideological differences. The new assertiveness of Third World women living in the North has also helped to break down barriers and bridge the gap between the "developed" and "developing." . . .
>
> But more significant than the numbers was the fact that more women represented themselves. . . . [W]omen involved in the liberation movements from South Africa to Nicaragua; those fighting the degradation of federal housing in the USA and the slums of Calcutta; to those struggling for recognition in Palestinian camps or for food or water in Africa; the young, eldery, the handicapped *all spoke for themselves.* (Antrobus 1985, 20)

THE CASE OF VIOLENCE AGAINST WOMEN

All over the world women are beaten, raped, burned, sexually abused and harassed, mutilated, confined, forced into marriage and into pregnancy, sold into prostitution and pornography, aborted after amniocentesis, killed as infants and as adults, denied food and medical treatment and education, and forced to work without pay *because they are women*. The forms of this abuse vary across cultures, classes, and nations, but it is universal. A survey by the Canadian group Match International in 1988 found that violence against women was the most frequent concern raised by women's groups in the Two-Thirds World (Match International Centre 1990). At the time, this finding and the testimony of the women surveyed helped feminists in Canada to refuse growing antifeminist charges that issues of sexual violence are middle-class

Western concerns irrelevant to women faced with such *real* threats as hunger, displacement, and military attack.[11]

All over the world women are resisting male violence. What men define as private or cultural matters, they call crimes against women and put on the agendas of communities, cooperatives, trade unions, educational institutions, health departments, and the media as well as governments and political parties and groups (Schuler 1992). Women have established special women-only police units in Brazil to deal with cases of violence against women, started a program designed to encourage community whistle blowing against batterers in Peruvian barrios, waged campaigns against dowry deaths and police rape in India, established rape-crisis centers and transition houses from Trinidad to Toronto, campaigned for abortion rights in Ireland, educated against clitoridectomy in Somalia, organized to prevent sex tourism in the Philippines, raised issues of violence through popular theater in Jamaica, and resisted demeaning media images of women in Tanzania.

El Salvador, Namibia, Nicaragua, Palestine, and South Africa are all countries where active women have had to respond quickly to new opportunities to influence processes of rapid change. In all these cases, as women won political space they united across large differences to put violence against women on the public agenda.[12]

The urgency of support across national boundaries is immediately clear to women involved in local campaigns directed at these issues, many of which concern emergency situations of individual women subjected to cruel patriarchal impositions. New decentralized forms of organization are being created to express the truly multicentered movement that feminism is becoming and to enable collective analysis and resistance. These organizations are based on autonomous local processes of dialogue and mutual theory building; emphasize women's experience as the basis of analysis and, therefore, put priority on the inclusion of all women as experts on their own conditions and needs; address patriarchal oppression in the context of all systems of domination and address the whole of society; reflect the kind of shared commitment to resistance that makes it possible for women to offer and accept support across and within deeply divided communities; and are built on and honor complementary and transformative affirmations of women's equality, specificity, diversity, and commonality.

The International Tribunal of Crimes against Women held in Brussels in 1976, one of the earliest autonomous international feminist exchanges, was organized over a period of two years by independent feminists partly as an alternative to the government-sponsored events of International Women's Year. Two thousand feminists from forty countries testified to the atrocities committed against women in their homelands in the classic feminist belief that

> by sharing personal experiences and problems, we come to see that these problems are not merely personal, but that they are caused and exacerbated by the

way women are regarded and treated in general, and the situations and roles we commonly find ourselves in. We come to see that many of our problems are externally or socially induced, and hence, widely shared by other women. By talking honestly with each other, our isolation can be transformed into solidarity and our self-blame into anger, which motivates action much more powerfully than self-hatred. (Russell and Van de Ven 1976, 219–20).

Although financial constraints and still only embryonic networking meant that participants were disproportionately from Western Europe, Third World women's testimony had a significant impact, along with that of immigrant, Black, native, and poor women of the North. "All man-made forms of oppression" were under consideration in a context that defined crimes against women broadly and inclusively enough to reflect the experience of all women.

The information pooled at the well-publicized hearings helped increase general awareness of the extent of women's victimization and its many forms, stimulated organizing in local contexts, and contributed to feminist analyses. It also generated communication and action networks such as ISIS and the International Feminist Network, the latter intended to "facilitate the mobilization of the women's liberation movements on an international scale when needed" (ibid., 212). With this activity the Tribunal furthered its aims "to reach women everywhere, to reinforce solidarity between women and to discover ways to combat crimes against women" (ibid., 228).

Since then regional, interregional, and international links have developed in response to the urgent requirements of practice in numerous areas: Israeli and Palestinian women rally and march for a just peace; Japanese and Korean women publicize the fate of Korean "comfort women" abducted for the use of Japanese soldiers during the invasion of China and World War II; Thai and Dutch feminists resist the practice of mail-order brides while supporting the brides; European and Asian feminists campaign against sexual tourism; European feminists alert the world to the mass abduction and rape of women by Serb and other forces in ex-Yugoslavia and draw attention to the fact that rape is endemic in all wars and periods of civil unrest, including, today, those in Somalia, Peru, Liberia, and Cambodia; African women work together against clitoridectomy.

In December 1982 the women of the International Commission for the Abolition of Sexual Mutilations held a conference in Dakar, Senegal entitled "Women in Their Societies" and proposed, among other things, "to work in cooperation with women worldwide toward the abolition of every form of sexist discrimination, and of all forms of violence practiced on women; to work toward a change of consciousness which will eradicate every form of sexism; to work for the effective abolition of the practice of sexual mutilation; to be in solidarity with all struggles for the liberation of women throughout the world" (Barry, Bunch, and Castley 1984, 141).[13]

In Rotterdam in April 1983 thirty activists from twenty-four countries met at the workshop entitled "International Feminism: Networking against Female Sexual Slavery." The interaction was designed not only to raise consciousness generally and stimulate local organizing but to develop common strategies, policy statements and positions, and establish an international action network to support communication and cooperation among regional and local groups.

Sexual torture of political prisoners, mail-order brides, child marriage, prostitition ("chosen" or forced), sex tourism, rape, battery, military brothels, incest, sexual mutilation, pornography, and many other practices were examined by women from all parts of the world. The framework that enabled them to treat these issues together defines sexual oppression as lack of sexual self-determination; examines all the forms of control, prohibition, and exploitation of women's sexuality in the broadest legal, economic, political, cultural, and religious terms; and "addresses the situation of violence against women ... within the larger context of creating structural changes in society" (Barry, Bunch, and Castley 1984, 53).

Participants extablished the regionally based International Network against Female Sexual Slavery and Traffic in Women. Kathleen Barry, one of the founding members, expresses the importance of its organizational form:

> Rather than rely on a hierarchical organization which dictates policy and action to the local groups, this Network is based in each world region where women are engaged in the day to day work of combating the traffic, forming shelters and training programs for women escaping from prostitution and demanding prosecution of pimps and procurers who traffic women. The difference now is that these local groups work with international support and can bring global attention to their causes through the Network. (Barry 1984, xiii–xiv)

The "Women's International Tribunal and Meeting on Reproductive Rights" in July 1984 in Amsterdam, with four hundred women from sixty-seven countries, is another example of a successful international gathering of activist women (Women's Global Network on Reproductive Rights 1984). Participants testified to the ways that women and women's bodies are used and abused through sexist and racist population-control programs, drug dumping, forced sterilization, forced and prohibited abortion, eugenic policies, and dangerous, even life-threatening contraceptives and reproductive technologies. They spoke to the roles of ideology, religion, economic greed and need in sustaining these practices and affirmed both women's diversity and unity: "With women from so many countries present, not only the many things we have in common were discussed, but also the differences between us which threaten to separate us. Those differences included colour, religion, class, sexuality, degrees of disability, and many others. One of the many successes of the conference was that a strong sense of unity in the face of our differences came out throughout the week" (Keysers 1985, 31).

In fact, participants reached consensus on a broad range of analytical and policy positions opposing population-control measures whether they prohibit or mandate childbearing; supporting alternatives such as sharing economic resources within countries and between First and Third World countries along with the redirection of spending from wasteful and destructive uses to positive purposes such as health care and education; and calling for women's involvement in decison making around health care and in all areas of their lives. Dozens of requests were made and responded to for support for ongoing national struggles. Initial connections among Muslim women led to the founding of the important international network, Women Living under Muslim Laws.

International getherings continue to be held, and more regional and inter-regional links and practices have developed supported by, and in turn reinforcing, the strongly integrative perspectives brought to the diverse issues of violence in the global dialogue. Activism around reproductive and genetic intervention is one example of the new decentralized forms of global organizing and theory building that are emerging. The Feminist International Network of Resistance to Reproductive Technologies and Genetic Engineering (FINRRAGE), founded in 1984, aims to stimulate and link worldwide feminist research on, analysis of, and resistance to the use, abuse, and control of women in reproductive and genetic research and technologies. FINRRAGE relies on national contacts in many countries who collect information from their locality for an international archive. The international coordinator then assembles and distributes this information to all the national contacts, who make it available in their own countries. Member groups benefit from this exchange in their autonomous but collective development of analysis, policy positions, and strategies—a process supported by periodic conferences (Brodribb 1985).

The FINRRAGE perspective is women-centered and integrates an awareness of colonial, racial, class, and patriarchal power to enable its members to consider and speak from the extremely diverse realities as well as the common interests of women around the world. The group worked with the Bangladeshi Social Research Organization, UBINIG, to bring 145 women (only thirty from Western countries) to a July 1985 conference in Comilla Bangladesh. The resulting exchanges reinforced feminists' sense of worldwide patterns of destruction and control of women and nature. Renate Klein, a founding member of FINRRAGE, described the value of the conference dialogue in an interview:

> Also on the line is an enormous contempt and hatred for women. It was very good to see that shared rage about what is happening to women is certainly common among women whether we come from the West or Asian countries. We have to work together. There is no way we can afford to not listen to one another, to not work with one another. Having to integrate and have an inclusiveness is very useful. I would start with woman there at the centre. For instance, start with common experiences of oppression.... It is very frightening to put the two sides of the coin together.... The women, especially Indian

women were very articulate and very strong and courageous resisters to population control policies. They told us a lot about what is going on in the latest push to change the whole contraceptive focus from using the pill or condoms or diaphragms to using [untested and dangerous] really long-acting contraceptives . . . where you give a woman an injection and she stays infertile for three months or, even worse, hormonal implants. . . . Then we add the other side of the coin which is the test-tube baby technology happening in the Western part of the world, but now moving on to these countries, as well as genetic engineering, particularly embryo experimentation. . . .

That is why it is very important to have this dialogue and to learn from them and they learn from us. What I felt was that we were learning from one another but finding there was much more in common than there were differences.

The "Declaration of Comilla" issued by conference participants warned that: "Initial experiences with reproductive and genetic engineering all over the world show that these technologies are aggravating the deteriorating position of women in society and intensifying the existing differences among people in terms of race, class, caste, sex, and religion. These technologies also contribute to the further destabilizing of the already critical ecological situation" (FINRRAGE 1989, 84).

The FINRRAGE dialogue and the analysis built from it link the fate of the world's women, poor populations, and nature by considering specific experiences and studies of coercive population-control programs; harmful birth-control medication and technologies; prenatal sex determination and selection, diagnosis, and genetic screening; intrusive and experimental in-vitro fertilization programs; national and international traffic in women, eggs and embryos, human organs, body parts, cells, and DNA; and the patenting of life forms. All these practices ignore and/or hide the real causes of poverty, hunger, disease, and pollution by attributing them to "overpopulation." They reflect a logic of eugenics and are the product of ruling interests that use women and nature as experimental subjects in the name of materialist, consumerist, and individualist views of the world, human beings, and all of life.

The "Declaration of Comilla" opposes to this scientistic, exploitative, and destructive worldview the age-old compassionate and holistic skills and values that women have developed and passed on over centuries of bearing and raising children, caring for the sick and disabled, and providing for people's basic needs in humane and ecologically sustainable ways. At the same time, it demands full recognition of women in all spheres of life, "access for women to resources, income, employment, social security, and a safe environment at work and at home," in short, "living and working conditions that assure a life of human dignity for women worldwide" (FINRRAGE 1989, 84). Thus, while recognizing differences and commonalities among women, FINRRAGE explicitly affirms both women's specificity and their equality. When the fate of all the world's women is considered, the need is clear for women-centered feminist practice grounded in alternative connective, life-affirming values that can challenge dominant structures and ideology in all their forms and manifestations.[14]

The International Solidarity Network of Women Living under Muslim Laws[15] (WLUML) grew from initiatives by nine women from Algeria, Morocco, Sudan, Iran, Mauritius, Tanzania, Bangladesh, and Pakistan. They originally came together at the "Tribunal on Reproductive Rights" in Amsterdam in July 1984 to respond to issues requiring urgent action:

> The case of three feminists arrested and jailed without trial, kept incommunicado for seven months in Algeria for having discussed with other women the project of law known as "Family Code," which was highly unfavourable to women.
>
> The case of an Indian Sunni woman who filed a petition in the Supreme Court arguing that the Muslim minority law applied to her in her divorce denied her the rights otherwise guaranteed by the Constitution of India to all citizens, and called for support.
>
> The case of a woman in Abu Dhabi, charged with adultery and sentenced to be stoned to death after delivering and feeding her child for two months.
>
> The case of the "Mothers of Algiers" who fought for custody of their children after divorce.(Women Living Under Muslim Laws Dossier, n.d.)

The network maintains active links among women and women's groups in Muslim countries and communities "to increase women's knowledge about both their common and diverse situations in various contexts, and to strengthen their struggles and create the means to support them internationally from within the Muslim world and outside" (ibid.). To this end, it produces information kits, working papers, and a series of dossiers; facilitates contact, communication, and exchanges; builds links and initiates campaigns among women from different geographical regions; works with other feminist networks and organizations such as FINRRAGE, International Women's Tribune Centre, ISIS, AAWORD, and Women against Fundamentalism to develop global feminist theory, practice, and solidarity.

Women Living under Muslim Laws works from a women-centered perspective committed to challenging patriarchal definitions of Islam and community and to protecting and empowering women individually and collectively. The network welcomes participation by women with very different relationships to Muslim experience, identity, and faith. It seeks to support both the more and the less traditional and devout in the particular struggles they each face rather than to define what these struggles should be. The network addresses itself to "women living where Islam is the religion of the State, as well as to women who belong to Muslim communities ruled by minority religious laws; to women in secular states where Islam is rapidly expanding and where fundamentalists demand a minority religious law, as well as to women from immigrant Muslim communties in Europe and the Americas; and to non-Muslim women, either nationals or foreigners, living in Muslim countries and communities, where Muslim laws are applied to them and to their children" (ibid.). The wide variety of viewpoint, circumstance, and experience represented here means that the fact of living under Muslim laws implies not so much sameness as a useful frame for collaboration across difference.[16] It is a shared condition but not necessarily a shared identity. The identity that is shared is one of struggle and resistance that does not deny but rather affirms as it transforms specific cultural, traditional, and/or religious existences and contexts.[17]

This form of women-centered and women-positive but otherwise open organization enables diverse women to offer support to and accept it from each other in the knowledge that they are all contesting power in their own communities. It provides a space for women to develop alternative interpretations of the world and to act on these. And it provides a way for women of Muslim heritage and/or faith to be strongly present in global dialogue *as Muslim women* even while challenging their diverse Muslim cultures and conditions. The explicitly Muslim context of their struggles enables them to gain strength from the support of women who are not living under Muslim laws without risking a diminution or loss of their specifically Muslim identification and voice. This is truly the articulation of specificity in diversity, of strategic identities as a basis for struggle and a place to reach out from.

The group Women against Fundamentalism is a further example of new forms of feminist organizing in which the principles of diversity and commonality are jointly articulated. The network was founded in Britain in 1989 by a number of groups, including Southall Black Sisters, Brent Asian Women's Refuge, and the Iranian Women's Organization in Britain to fight fundamentalism in all religions (Patel 1991). It has since expanded to include Christian and Jewish as well as Hindu and Muslim women. In this group, the political commitment to resist fundamentalism enables extremely diverse women to recognize common oppression and build common struggle. In fact the members' diversity gives them all more power to challenge patriarchal religious control without denying their own cultures and identities: "Fundamentalism appears in many different forms in religions throughout the world, but at the heart of all fundamentalist agendas is the control of women's minds and bodies. All religious fundamentalists support the patriarchal family as a central agent of such control. They view women as embodying the morals and traditional values of the family and the whole community. We must resist the increasing control that fundamentalism imposes on all our lives" (Women against Fundamentalism 1990: 2).

The Salman Rushdie affair precipitated the founding of Women against Fundamentalism. Rushdie's 1988 book *The Satanic Verses* was found offensive by orthodox Muslim leaders and communities all over the world, which initiated campaigns against the book's author, publisher, and sellers. A *fatwa,* or death sentence, was pronounced on the author by the Ayatollah Khomeini. Members of Women against Fundamentalism, in defiance of Muslim authorities and much of the antiracist Left in Britain, courageously defend Rushdie's right to publish. The group's statement against all fundamentalisms allows Muslim women to accept the support of other feminists against the "leaders" of their own community, confident that they recognize and actively oppose parallel patterns in their own cultures; it sharply distinguishes their position from racist and anti-Arab, anti-Muslim prejudice; and it enables feminists with political experience around the postcolonial world, such as Indian anticommunalists, Iranian oppositionists, Israeli opponents of the occupation, and Irish anticlerics to strengthen international awareness in British feminism as their own feminism is strengthened.

Although Women against Fundamentalism originally emerged in one nation, the feminist antifundamentalist perspective is used increasingly as a frame for international networking and solidarity. For instance, in 1989 a conference entitled "Women against Fundamentalism" was held in India.

The ways in which this perspective links apparently diverse issues all over the world, gives equal voice to all women in defining feminism, and builds solidarity through attention to the parallels between different cultures and struggles was seen at a panel called "Women and Religious Fundamentalism" at the Annual Conference of the Canadian Research Institute for the Advancement of Women in Toronto in November 1992. The panel brought together Christian, Muslim, and Hindu women from Algeria, Nigeria, the United States, the United Kingdom, and India to talk about their organizing activities to counteract and challenge religious fundamentalism as it affects women. In this context, the religious right's campaigns to take over local governments in the United States and their referendum attacks on gay and lesbian rights take on new significance. The struggle around abortion can be seen as part of a worldwide resistance to fundamentalist control of women. The fight of First Nations women in Canada for an equal voice in constitutional reform, and their insistence that the protection of the Charter of Rights and Freedoms should not be summarily removed from native communities at the behest of male leaders, while *not* a struggle against fundamentalism, *is* a struggle to prevent the imposition of patriarchal interpretations of religion, tradition, and culture by male community "leaders" (McIvor 1992; Stacey-Moore 1993).

In keeping with an integrative approach, these feminists and others around the world not only assert women's individual rights but seek to transform human rights/native rights to include women's rights. This is part of the worldwide feminist project of redefinition initiated in the late 1960s. Women fleeing forced marriage, female genital mutilation, or wifebeating are named as political refugees. Specific forms of violence against women, such as rape, wife beating, denial of abortion, degrading treatment in the media, and enforced economic dependence, are named as attacks on women's human rights. Feminists all over the world have worked locally to defend individual women and have launched general campaigns in the name of expanded and redefined concepts of human rights. Human rights currently recognized internationally do not encompass harms to women, which tend to be at best understood as a lower order of significance.

The violence inflicted on women would be recognized as an attack of major proportions if it were suffered by any other group. The fact that it is not named and not outlawed by governments reflects and encourages a view of women as not fully human, a species by nature constrained and limited and so undiminished by this treatment. Local campaigns that place harms against women in the context of human rights have emerged all over the world as a means of redressing violations against women, because drawing parallels to harms that are widely and easily recognized is powerfully consciousness raising and can be an effective strategy with real outcomes for individual women.

In October 1990 Aminata Diop, a twenty-two-year-old woman from Mali, applied for political asylum in France to escape female circumcision. The French Commission for Appeals of Refugees made a historic decision when it recognized genital mutilation as a form of persecution under the terms of the Geneva Convention, partly in response to pressure from all over the world. It refused to grant her political-refugee status, however, on the grounds that she had not appealed to the authorities in Mali for help!

In 1991 Canadian feminists argued that a Trinidadian woman who left her husband when she was beaten and faced deportation should be recognized as a refugee. They have also made a case for political asylum for an Iranian woman who had been whipped and imprisoned for twenty-four hours because she wasn't wearing a veil at a party. The refugee board in Toronto rejected her claim for refugee status on the grounds that she was punished for committing a crime, not for her beliefs; that the punishment was not arbitrary; and that the relevant Iranian law did not abridge any essential and inalienable human right.

These cases, even when unsuccessful, are important challenges to the sexual double standards and moral inconsistencies in human rights definitions that address only government-inflicted and not also individually inflicted harms, entrenching narrow definitions of government harms that exclude laws that constrict, punish, contain, and control women all over the world. In Canada the steady stream of these well-publicized cases along with feminist pressure forced the question onto the political agenda. Widespread support was expressed for Nada, for instance, a woman from Saudi Arabia who actively resisted gender-based laws there. As part of the campaign, the National Action Committee on the Status of Women released and publicized the details of the cases of fourteen women facing deportations that would put them at risk as women. As a result, in March 1993 the Immigration and Refugee Board of Canada released ground-breaking guidelines that its then new chairperson, Nurjehan Mawani, reports "are making a difference.... We are now seeing women's situations ... in a holistic manner where their experiences (which are quite different from men's) are fully studied" (*Match* 1993a, 1).

Feminists in many different countries have drawn parallels between women's rights and human rights in more general campaigns (Barry 1992; Center for Women's Global Leadership 1991; Kerr 1993; Schuler 1992). During the struggle against the Pinochet dictatorship in Chile, feminists raised the slogan "democracia en el pais y en la casa" (democracy in the nation and the home). In the Philippines, the women's coalition Gabriela campaigned for the recognition that "Women's Rights Are Human Rights." When the National Resistance Movement government in Uganda set up a Human Rights Commission "to look into human rights violations by the agents of state during past years of misrule and terror," women called for an "expanded sense of human rights" (Kakwenzire 1991).

These campaigns use parallels with recognized human rights abuses to reveal the extreme and systemic nature of violence against women and to illuminate the political nature of such violence as product and enforcer of men's power. They bring to attention abuse that is so much a part of most cultures that it tends to go unnoticed or to be seen as natural and inevitable. Revealing this abuse as a series of social relationships that can and must be changed involves a truly revolutionary shift in thinking that contests the dominant male-defined view of reality.

These national campaigns create the climate for such international initiatives as the Convention on the Elimination of All Forms of Discrimination against Women, adopted by the U.N. General Assembly in 1979 and ratified by 101 countries to date; they support global monitoring of discrimination, for instance, by the International Women's Rights Action Watch, which was launched in February 1986 following the Nairobi Forum to support and coordinate campaigns to bring pressure on national and international bodies, including established human rights groups; and they provide the local foundations for international human rights lobbying by such organizations as the "Coalition against Trafficking in Women" and the "Women's Rights Are Human Rights Network."

The Coalition against Trafficking in Women "is a feminist human rights organization that is confronting the exploitation of women in prostitution as a form of sexual exploitation" (Coalition against Trafficking in Women 1993, 1). In 1991, with members and other groups active against prostitution in each world region, the Coalition launched a project with UNESCO to examine international human rights instruments in terms of their ability to confront the current crisis in the sexual exploitation of women. Finding the existing instruments wanting, the Coalition initiated a process of regional and international consultation to develop a proposed "Convention on the Elimination of All Forms of Sexual Exploitation of Women," which it took through regional preparatory conferences for refinement and NGO endorsement before introducing it at the Second U.N. World Conference on Human Rights in Vienna, held 14–25 June 1993.[18]

The Coalition affirms that "it is a fundamental human right to be free of sexual exploitation." It defines sexual exploitation as any "practice by which persons achieve sexual gratification or financial gain or advancement through abuse of a person's sexuality by abrogating that person's human right to dignity, equality, autonomy, and physical and mental well-being." And it defines all prostitution, whether apparently voluntary or not, as sexual exploitation that "violates the human rights of anyone subjected to it, female or male, adult or child, Western or Third World persons". It "rejects any of these distinctions as artificial and serving to legitimize some prostitution" as chosen and therefore nonexploitative.

Awareness of class, race, colonial, and patriarchal power, and activist experiences worldwide keep Coalition members sensitive to the extreme vulnerability of growing groups of women and children who are easy prey for sex industries and businesses (often government- and/or police-supported) because national and international economic, political, and military policies impoverish and disrupt whole communities, displace peoples, produce refugees, and promote migrant labor. At the same time, the Coalition's women-centered approach allows it to see the cost to the human dignity of *all women* when *any form* of prostitution or other sexual exploitation is countenanced: "Sexual exploitation of women through prostitution victimizes women both inside and outside of prostitution. When prostitution is accepted and normalized, what is legitimized is the sale of the body and sex of the individual prostitute and it is the sale of any woman. It reinforces the societal equation of women and sex which reduces women to less than human and contributes to sustaining women's second class status throughout the world" (From the proposed Convention).

The Network on Women's Rights Are Human Rights, founded in 1991, is a loose international association of women and women's groups espousing in their local work the view that women's rights are human rights (Bunch 1993). In preparation for the U.N. Conference on Human Rights the association collected stories of the abuse of women's human rights from around the world. It also launched a petition signed by over half a million women from 124 countries to urge the inclusion of women's human rights and gender violence as central concerns at this global forum. It reads in part:

> The Universal Declaration of Human Rights states that everyone has the right to life, liberty and security of person, and further no one shall be subject to torture,

or to cruel, inhuman or degrading treatment. Yet, everywhere women and girls are systematically subjected to violence, torture, coercion, sexual abuse, starvation, and economic deprivation because they are female. For example, in the United States, battery is the greatest single cause of injury to women each year; in the Punjab state of India girls aged 2–4 die at twice the rate of boys because of systematic malnutrition and neglect; an Inter-African Committee report estimates that half of Kenya's high maternal mortality rate is due to complications from female genital mutilation. Such violence is a pervasive form of human rights abuse cutting across social, ethnic, and national boundaries, and still, it is often excluded from the international human rights agenda.[19]

In this statement, the situations of diverse women document a common oppression. Emphasis on the specificity of women's experience combines with a claim for equal inclusion in human rights law in a way that has transformative implications for the concept and practice of human rights generally. Women as a diverse group are claiming a specific but equally defining place in human concerns and society and in so doing are changing the very nature of both.

At the Second International Conference on Human Rights in June 1993 thousands of women from around the world worked together, building on previous regional dialogue and cooperation, to develop and present women-centered recommendations to the official conference and to lobby the 160 governments in attendance, among other things for instance, for the adoption and ratification of the "Convention on the Elimination of All Forms of Sexual Exploitation of Women." They also organized a global tribunal at which thirty-three women from twenty-four countries presented powerful personal testimony to the harms suffered by women from political persecution, lack of economic and social rights, the violation of women's human rights in the family, and war crimes against women in ways that graphically demonstrated both the particular harms suffered by women in diverse situations and women's shared vulnerability to harms specific to women (see 1993).[20]

While not all their lobbying was successful, women's concerted action at this conference has ensured that the official declaration from the conference includes a section on women. The declaration recognizes that violence against women in both public and private is a human rights abuse; calls for the Human Rights Commission to appoint a Special Rapporteur on Violence against Women; calls for states to eradicate conflicts between the rights of women and the harmful effects of certain traditional or customary practices, cultural prejudices and religious extremism; and urges all U.N. agencies to specifically address the violation of women's human rights.

Feminists' local, national, and international resistance to violence against women is just one aspect of the developing theory and practice that are illuminating the links between issues in many crucial areas—violence against women, militarism, economic dependence, environmental degradation, and the exploitation of women, nature, and indigenous peoples—revealing them all as products of a hierarchical, dualistic world system oriented to the profit of the few and using all forms of life in its service. We shall see in Chapter 9 that dialogue and networking in all these areas are enriching feminist visions and building global consensus.

9

GLOBAL VISIONS

GLOBAL SISTERHOOD AGAINST GLOBALIZATION

Global economic, political, and military relationships connect us all through a series of ties that do not bind but rather alienate us from one another. Daily, we in the North deal with and depend on products of the global commodity and labor markets, most of us unaware of our own place or the role of others in these far-flung networks. We ourselves, as well as others, are rendered invisible in associations that are never named, that are, in fact, actively hidden:

> When we as local consumers in the North buy ... the bananas from Central America, tea from Assam, jeans from Sri Lanka, shampoo from Malaysia, a camera from the Philippines, we are not aware of the global dimension incorporated in these goods. We know nothing of the product-path of the T-shirt on our body, which may have cost only two dollars, we know nothing about the local effects which the production of the raw material may have caused for the environment in this case the cultivation of cotton for export. We do not know whether this cotton production destroyed the local food production, or how the chemicals used in cotton cultivation affected the soil and the water in that area. We also know nothing about the production conditions of those who have worked in the cotton fields, in the Free Trade Zones in Sri Lanka or in Mauritius—they are mostly women—where they have sewn the T-shirts together. We do not care to know of their incomes, their work and living conditions. All we are interested in is usually the price of the commodity in front of our eyes. (Mies 1992, 58)[1]

131

Feminists are criticizing this system from both "developed" and "developing" locations. First World feminists testify to the poverty, powerlessness, objectification, and vulnerability to violence of women in rich capitalist nations. Third World feminists document the ways the process of modernization is injuring women. In dialogue, and increasingly in collaboration, feminists are developing compatible critical analyses shaped by the integrative values and affirming integrative visions.[2]

The large and growing integrative feminist literature on the current global situation argues that the existing world system is in crisis on all levels in all parts of the world and that this crisis is reflected in ecological, economic, social, cultural, and ethical breakdown. The unequal, competitive, profit based, individualistic market relations at its core are essentially exploitative, violent, and destructive. The establishment and protection of these relationships in both the First and Two-Thirds worlds, called modernization or development, has historically depended on military conquest and control (of nature, women, workers, and traditional cultures and communities) and continues to do so today.

Feminists need not only to resist the worst consequences of the global market system and its spread but to work toward totally different, equal, cooperative, life-sustaining communal forms of social and economic organization. These new ways of living cannot be achieved without recognizing the worth of women's work[3] and of nature and the importance of women's and other traditional knowledges, all of which are currently denied, devalued, marginalized, and rendered invisible in the process of appropriation. Finding ways to include these things in existing measures of value, production, and growth can be a useful consciousness-raising exercise. However, changing accounting practices to include economic measures of the value of women's work and of nature may simply extend the logic of exchange relations and increase opportunities for profit; if it is done as an end in itself, it becomes a rationalization rather than a repudiation of the existing system.

The worth of these things needs to be seen in terms of an altogether different value system—one that is holistic (integrative) as opposed to dualistic (separative) and grounded in the value of life rather than profit. Measuring value in terms of what contributes to the sustenance of human and nonhuman life reveals the absurdity, even criminality, of measuring only production for the market and for profit. It makes it possible to see that what is called progress/ growth/modernization/development entails a process of relative or absolute deprivation for women, colonies, and marginal groups and communities. Expansion of the market and production for exchange at the expense of production for use (1) removes the means of subsistence from individuals and communities; (2) institutionalizes men's dependence on wages and women's dependence on men; and (3) fuels the concentration of wealth and power in fewer and fewer hands, ultimately in a few nonaccountable transnational corporations and financial institutions.

The alternative vision that undergirds an integrative understanding of the world involves redefining everything from mainstream and radical views of history to wealth, worth, work, progress, growth, and development. It also makes it possible to see the ways in which current separations between production and reproduction, investment and consumption, individual and community and society and nature (and between culture, economics, and politics) are both false ideological constructions that reflect and serve the competitive, individualistic system and, at the same time, actual products of this system. These separations need to be revealed as false even as we resist their actual impact.

Global feminisms hold the seeds of the world they want to create. Their response to alienated and exploitative globalization is not simple withdrawal, refusal, or reaction but the creation of autonomous, democratic, and empowering global relations in the struggle for alternative visions. The global understanding of women's oppression as the product of a long historical process of colonization and control of women, workers, nature, and indigenous and colonized peoples links all oppressions organically, not as add-ons or a litany of separate dominations; expands and integrates the field of struggle; underlines women's central role in resistance and reconstruction; enriches the integrative conception of women's equality, specificity, diversity, and commonality; and reinforces the conviction that what is needed is a paradigm shift of enormous proportions: "Women's voices have moved on from the modest ambition of being heard on public matters to the far more subversive endeavour of plotting a different path to civilization" (Oliviera 1992, 71).[4]

WOMEN'S SPECIFICITY AND AUTONOMY AND GENERAL SOCIAL CHANGE

The feminist struggle for transformation rather than assimilation is articulated explicitly by Third World and First World activists. Indian feminist Kamla Bhasin asks, for instance, "[Do] we want to be integrated into the present system and move only faster towards destruction? Or do we women want to challenge it?" And she answers: "I believe that we must challenge it and I know that we *can*. We must look for a new vision, new types of development so that we can transform knowledge and relationships with the poor, with the oppressed, with women, with nature" (1990, 24). The Boston Women's Health Collective, which wrote and published in 1971 the classic activist feminist health book *Our Bodies Ourselves,* and continues its work today, shares this commitment to core social change:

> We are among the women who want to let our long-time experience of being the ones *without* power shape a vision that challenges the existing power structures themselves. Instead of our own piece of the pie, in other words, we want to change the recipe. Running through our work on health and parenting issues is a wider vision of social change—a dream of eliminating the exploitation and suffering that result from racism, sexism, classism, and oppressive economic and political systems. We see, for instance, that the proliferation of nuclear power and violence against women in the media, street, and home are spawned by the same mindset and political systems that have denied women control over their bodies. (Norsigian and Sandford 1979, 18)

The problematic "mindset" identified here is one that reflects, legitimizes, and fuels the competitive production of commodities and profit, while it renders invisible and devalues life producing and sustaining activity. "The most important life activities have consistently been held by the powers that be to be unworthy of those who are fully human, most centrally because of their close connections with necessity and life: motherwork (the rearing of children), housework, and until the rise of capitalism in the West, any work necessary to subsistence. In addition, these activities in contemporary capitalism are all constructed in ways that systematically degrade and destroy the minds and bodies of those who perform them" (Hartsock 1983, 245). We have seen that integrative feminists see women's exclusion from all institutionalized power and their customary responsibility for individual and community survival as resources in the struggle to consciously develop alternatives. The analyses and visions of integrative feminists in both North and South selectively and critically incorporate aspects of women's traditional knowledge and concerns.[5] The appreciation of women's work and interests is generally harder won and more fragile in the North, however, than in the South, where women's subcultures and consciousness have not been so thoroughly disrupted. In fact, in North America the connection of feminist and traditional women's cultures in integrative practice is often experienced as a paradox even by feminists who realize its power: "What is emerging from this contradictory situation is a feminist peace movement *paradoxically* grounded both in traditional women's culture and contemporary feminism. . . . In the contemporary scene, women's political actions synthesize conventional women's imagery with militance. Women encircle Greenham base by weaving yarn to close the gates against missiles" (Harris and King 1989, 1–3). (Emphasis added).

The fact that when women speak they speak with recognizable women's voices is far less surprising to many Third World feminists and to those feminists in the North from working-class, rural, or minority communities in which vestiges of women's separate organization and identity remain (Christiansen-

Ruffman 1982; Miles 1991). These women also more often expect women to be organized and to continue to organize separately from men. Separation from men is not the highly theorized, consciously constructed, much contested, often marginal space that it tends to be in urban contexts in the North (Amadiume 1987; Gevins 1985; Goldberg 1991; Hanlon 1992; Leghorn and Parker 1981).[6]

In many communities in the South women's separate space is the norm for women's activities—activities that are subordinate to those of men but nevertheless central to the functioning of communities. Women, when they act and speak, presume to have a specific presence as women. And in communities where they are largely responsible for community life and survival, they presume that their interests, issues, and actions will have general relevance and impact. Accordingly, Third World feminists often more easily conceive of their struggle as women-centered community struggle and transformation rather than the sectional struggle of only one, albeit large, subordinate group. The simultaneous insistence on both women's necessarily separate voice and women's central role in general change that integrative feminists in the North have had to fight to articulate is more firmly understood and entrenched in many of the feminisms of the South.

In poor communities in both South and North where women are organized separately from men and men have few resources to buttress their power, women are more able not only to conceive of their concerns as general community concerns but to pursue them as such.[7] Once they win the autonomy to define their own interests, native women in North America and women in the barrios of Latin America, for instance, who are concerned with violence against women and children can hope to initiate community healing and change to eliminate the violence rather than just remove the victims for their own protection.

The articulation of general community concerns by women from women's points of view is not the abandonment of feminist vision but potentially its full realization—a process that requires that autonomous women's and general community struggles be brought together to become one. Mutually enriching interaction between women-focused and communitywide activism thrives in the North as well as in the South (Garland 1988). Nevertheless, it is true that many feminists in the Two-Thirds World are particularly well placed to conceive of this possibility and to understand its importance for developing global feminisms that go beyond pressure for women, to move the whole of society in women-defined directions.

Global feminist dialogue has thus supported integrative-feminist revaluing of the female, confirmed its radical political potential, and strengthened both feminist autonomy and the conceptualization of feminist struggle as women-defined general social change. It has deepened the mutually reinforcing articulation of women's particular interests and feminism's universal relevance and has sustained integrative feminism's dialectical refusal to see these as mutually exclusive possibilities.

WOMEN AND NATURE, FEMINISM AND ECOLOGY

The articulation of feminism's ecological politics has also been enhanced by global perspectives. Globally informed challenges to profit-centered rather than life-centered measures of productivity necessarily make visible the value of nature's as well as women's production. Global struggles for a society organized around the cooperative requirements of life rather than competition and profit have to name and resist the destructive dynamics that deny, control, and destroy women, workers, nature, and indigenous peoples: "Feminism as the affirmation of women and women's work allows a redefinition of growth and productivity as categories linked to the production, not destruction, of life. It is thus simultaneously an ecological and a feminist political project which legitimises the ways of knowing and being that create wealth by enhancing life and diversity, and which delegitimises the knowledge and practise of a culture of death as the basis for capital accumulation" (Shiva 1989a, 13).

Ecological awareness expands our notion of women's specificity and our understanding of the significance of diversity in the process of social change. Although the expression of feminism as simultaneously a women-centered and an ecological principle involves drawing parallels between women and nature as denied and devalued "resources" of "development," the main association of women and nature is "not in passivity but in creativity and the maintenance of life providing new categories of thought and new exploratory directions" (Shiva 1989b, 38). It is an extension of women's responsibility and concern for human life to the life of the planet.

This is neither a simple victim stance nor a reductionist biological argument.[8] Feminists claim women's association with nature as a part of the creative and conscious *political* process of reconstructing femininity, humanity, human society, nature, and their relationships:

> The Feminine is no longer the same nor the opposite of the Masculine. Neither is it an essence linked to an immobile Nature, but rather experience linked to a historical nature, a becoming. In this way, femininity is entering a region of freedom. . . . Femininity's freedom to define itself in due course will relate to nature, not as essence but as experience. It will not deny the body as its original point of departure for living in and thinking about the world, but will integrate this thinking into the world. . . . This plan to integrate the history of female Nature into the design for femininity's future is both feminist and ecological. (Oliviera 1992, 71–72)

The project articulated here aims to claim and create new forms of freedom in remaking history and society as well as the feminine in a conscious and deliberate process of grounding human/female reason in the body (physicality) and nature. It is a spiritual and emotional as well as political and rational project that claims a far broader, more complex, and inclusive field of action and (redefined) freedom than has ever been carved out before.

Third World feminists have played an integral role in supporting a broader, ecological conception of feminism. The destructive environmental and social impacts of "development" occur at a much faster rate there than in the West. Two-Thirds World peoples have experienced in a much more concentrated time span and with more devastating results the social dislocation and environmental destruction that Western Europe suffered over five hundred years of changes in land ownership and agricultural and industrial technologies. Where these changes directly threaten whole ways of life and communities, women's struggle has been a struggle in defense of community against this devastation.[9] The necessary connection between defending and affirming women, workers, nature, and community is more evident in these contexts than in North America, where environmental impacts, though extensive, are generally slower moving, less obvious, and less immediately dangerous to whole communities.

It is not, however, unknown in North America for environmental damage to threaten whole communities. Not surprisingly, the least powerful communities by virtue of race and class are most vulnerable: Love Canal to chemical waste, the Innu in the North of Labrador to military overflying, the Western Shoshone to nuclear testing, and fishing villages to the depletion of fish stocks, to name only a few examples. Women from these communities in the North are, like women from the South, raising environmental issues as economic- and social-justice issues. For instance, the "Statement by Women of Color of North America" to the World Women's Congress for a Healthy Planet in Miami in November 1991 reminded participants that:

> [growth] has left a trail of horrors in communities of color which includes the following:
> - These communities have experienced the most severe deindustrialization as well as the greatest contamination from industrialization;
> - Three out of five of the largest commercial hazardous waste landfills in the U.S. are located in predominantly Black or Hispanic communities. . . .
> - Three out of every five Black and Hispanic Americans live in communities with uncontrolled toxic waste sites. (World Women's Congress for a Healthy Planet 1992, 35)

A number of Third World feminists have adopted and are independently defining the term "ecofeminist" which originated in the North (Mies and Shiva 1993; Oliviera 1992; Perpiñan 1993). At the same time, integrative ecofeminists in the First World are being drawn to a more organic conceptualization of their politics (Diamond and Orenstein 1990; Plant 1989). What many used to describe as combining environmental and women's-movement concerns is now more frequently conceived as articulating the ecological aspects inherent in feminism itself[10] Certainly, global economic analyses,[11] analyses of war, militarism, and violence against women,[12] and indigenous feminist analyses[13] all share and reciprocally support a concern for nature and ecology as essential aspects of women-centered and women-defined social transformation.

DIVERSITY AND UNIVERSALITY

An awareness of the ecological vision inherent in feminism also enriches our appreciation of diversity as both the means and the end of feminist struggle. Integrative feminists welcome diverse political positions as building blocks of politics that they expect will always be in process: "It is precisely the diversity of thought and action that makes this new politics so promising as a catalyst for change in these troubled times" (Diamond and Orenstein 1990, xii). Sectarian thinking is explicitly rejected (D'Souza 1992, 46) in such a large project, which requires radical departures into uncharted waters and bold new questions rather than closed systems of thought: "Feminism is a developing world-view evolving through practice rather than dogma, and as such our attempt at definitions should be seen as part of an ongoing process. Charges . . . of being a 'partial world-view' and of offering no real alternatives, must be seen against this process" (Gandhi and Kannabiran 1989, 13).

Sectarian practice is also discouraged in a context in which feminists have little power and are under constant external attack. The hope is that debate can thrive in ways that do not lend aid and comfort and ammunition to feminism's enemies. Integrative feminists believe that we must learn to engage fully, to value debate, and to take it and our differences of condition and viewpoint seriously while we honor, appreciate, and support each other. The ability to both criticize and support each other, to explore differences while we build solidarity, involves nothing less than an ethics of interaction that is an emotional and spiritual as well as political commitment—an essential synthesis in the urgent efforts of feminists around the world to build new and inclusive politics and political forms (Apthekar 1989, 20; Ashrawi 1992, 17; Telling It Collective 1990, 128).

In Bihar, India, a conference is "organized to bring together diverse kinds of women's organizations and individuals" (Omvedt, Gala, and Kelkar 1988, 1). The theme of the the First Asian Indigenous Women's Conference in Baguio City, the Philippines, is "Sharing Commonalities and Diversities: Forging Unity towards Indigenous Women's Empowerment." In 1993 Israeli feminists organize a national conference, "Together beyond Our Differences." Nicaraguan feminists entitle their first national conference "Seeking Unity in Diversity." In South Africa in April 1992, sixty-seven national organizations participate in launching a National Women's Coalition to bring women together across the political spectrum, from political parties, women's organizations, churches, and other interest groups. The main objective of the coalition is to draw up a Women's Charter listing the demands of the majority of South African women. Mavivi Manzini, a participant in the process, explains in her keynote address to the 1992 "Women and Power" conference in Johannesburg that "the process of drawing up this document will serve as an educational campaign and will ... bring together South African women, who over the years have been divided on the basis of race, class and political affiliation. In mobilising and building unity, it is necessary to guard against creating false sisterhood. Differences existing among women must be taken into consideration and used to build bridges, and unity must be built on what is common for all women" (World University Service Women's Development Programme 1992, 7–8).

For integrative feminists diversity is an essential characteristic not only of political dialogue and organization but of the society to be achieved. June Jordan, U.S. Black feminist writer, expresses this aspect of integrative feminism in a recent interview in which it is clear that diversity within as well as among communities is valued. Respect for diverse and self-reliant communities is not a call for exclusive, isolated, or homogeneous communities. Diversity in community, unity in diversity are sought, not division: "Human life, and the life of the planet altogether, all of the creatures, the earth, depends upon diversity, the preservation of diversity and the protection of diversity, it really does. . . . [T]hat's like a naturalist kind of wisdom which most of us I think embrace now—and in knowing that, it's my business, I feel, as a human being here, to try to really make all the peoples of the world a family to which I can belong and be useful in. And to make the entire planet a home for my spirit and my dreams" (Christakos 1992, 38).

When the global and ecological aspects of feminism become explicit, the revaluation of women's skills and concerns as resources in developing alternatives to existing social organizations and values becomes part of a more general recognition and defense of knowledges and practices devalued and displaced by the spread of industrial patriarchy. Not only diverse women but diverse communities and cultures become potential resources in social movement toward a new society. The value placed on diversity in ecological thinking adds weight to the identification of female and tribal cultures as important sources of alternative knowledges and values not yet entirely eclipsed by monolithic Western constructs: "Mother Earth, women and colonized cultures. It is from these fringes that we are beginning to discern the economic, political and cultural mechanisms that have allowed a parochial science to dominate and how mechanisms of power and violence can be eliminated for a degendered, humanly inclusive knowledge" (Shiva 1989a, 21).

For integrative feminists, however, the significance of female and tribal cultures lies not only in their distance from the "diseased mainstream" (46) of society but also and primarily in the holistic principles they share. The global and ecological awareness that reveals the common colonization of women, workers, nature, and indigenous peoples also reveals remarkable parallels between indigenous worldviews and the women-associated values that inform integrative feminisms—parallels that are widely and increasingly recognized in both the First and Two-Thirds Worlds. Irene Diamond and Gloria Orenstein, for instance, call ecofeminism "a new term for an ancient wisdom" (1990, xv). Maori feminist Ngahuia Te Awekotuku suggests that "for the future, despite the depletion and abuse of natural resources, we must find hope in the wisdom of the past. . . . This knowledge, if emulated and perpetuated, will serve as our strength and foundation for the times that lie ahead" (1982, 139–40). U.S. Black feminist Patricia Hill Collins notes that "the search for the distinguishing features of an alternative epistemology used by African-American women reveals that values and ideas Africanist scholars identify as characteristically 'Black' often bear remarkable resemblance to similar ideas claimed by feminist scholars as characteristically 'female'" (1990, 206–7). And Native American writer Paula Gunn Allen sees parallels between integrative-feminist principles and basic concepts in many traditional American Indian systems: "Traditional American Indian systems depended on basic concepts that are at present being reformulated and to some extent practiced by western feminists, including cooperation (but by that traditional Indians generally meant something other than noncompetitiveness or passivity), harmony (again, this did not necessarily mean absence of conflict), balance, kinship, and respect" (1986, 206).

So global understanding broadens integrative feminists' concept of valued diversity from diverse women to diverse communities and opens the possibility of organic solidarity between feminist and indigenous struggles. It enriches the dialectical redefinition of autonomy and community, unity and diversity, specificity and universality that is at the heart of integrative-feminist politics—politics that welcome differences even as they heal divisions: "[Feminism recognizes] that there is not only one way towards progress, but that there are various logic systems, numerous languages, many different concepts of time and space. . . . At the same time feminism seeks to break down the barriers that separate one discipline from another; between one job and another; between the personal and the political; between the emotional and the rational; between the mental and the physical; between them and us; and between you and me" (Bhasin 1990, 25).

Feminists are moving toward new conceptions and practices of solidarity and internationalism that both depend on and contribute to the creation of "political practice that is humanly more inclusive; . . . challenging the patriarchy's ideological claim to universalism not with another universalising tendency, but with diversity; and . . . challenging the dominant concept of power as violence with the alternative concept of nonviolence as power" (Shiva 1989b,

38). In this political practice, paradoxically, the recognition of diversity (including women's differences from men) is part of a general and inclusive human struggle that is universal but not universalizing—a vision of what Corinne Kumar D'Souza calls a "new universalism":

> not a universalism that denies the many and affirms the one, not a eurocentric universalism; not a patriarchal universalism. A universalism that will not deny the accumulated experience and knowledge of all the past generations . . . that . . . will not accept the imposition of any monolithic, "universal" structures under which it is presumed all other peoples must be subsumed. . . . A new universalism that will challenge the universal mode, the logic of our development, science, technology, militarization, the nuclear option. A new universalism that will respect the plurality of different societies—of their philosophy, of their ideology, their traditions and cultures, one that will be rooted in the particular, one which will develop in the context of the dialectics of different civilizations, birthing a new cosmology. (1992, 44)

Integrative feminists are envisioning wholly new forms of free yet connected ways of living in harmony, not harking back to or glorifying any golden ages. As we have seen, feminists can be among the fiercest critics of tradition. Holistic knowledge and practice and many of the values that have been hidden, pushed aside, and destroyed by capitalist and patriarchal enforcement of monolithic separative Western science and the Western worldview are prized in this project. But we are not retreating into parochial and patriarchal worlds. We are using the particular to create new universal and shared possibilities. Selected aspects of traditional alternatives are affirmed in the face of their erasure as part of the struggle against the current intensification and globalization of commodification and control: "Hope for the future . . . requires that women create new models, allowing for diversity and drawing from the best of the past, but refusing to accept any form of domination in the name of either tradition or modernization" (Bunch 1987, 304).

EMERGING GLOBAL CONSENSUS

Feminists in all regions of the world are committed to developing new models. They are consciously and explicitly engaged in defense and reform, not to save the old world, but to build a new one. They are convinced that even major reform of existing structures will not save the world or women. They hold no hope for anything short of fundamental change. Integrative feminists in international networks on health, housing, education, law reform, population, human rights, labor, reproductive and genetic engineering, female sexual slavery and trafficking in women, violence against women, spirituality, peace and militarism, external debt, fundamentalism, environment, development, media, alternative technology, film, art and literature, publishing, and women's studies are forging alternative forms of global relations. Without exception they are generating and working with new paradigms unashamedly informed by utopian goals. The Indian feminist Kamla Bhasin expresses this, using concepts she learned from Japanese activists: "Feminism is showing us the possibility of finding new kinds of space, of searching for new rhythms and of discovering new roots, dreaming new dreams. It seeks to integrate a radically new conception of progress and development in all aspects of our lives. We must all of us work harder to definite [*sic*] our vision of a more human life, more human development, of 'Janakashaba' (this is the word in Minimata dialect for an alternative world, as we learnt during our stay in Japan)" (Bhasin 1990, 24).

The fact that consensus is emerging globally around transformative perspectives among feminists active in all areas of practice was evident at the World Women's Congress for a Healthy Planet in Miami in November 1991.[14] The congress's broad mandate brought together fifteen hundred activists, researchers, and policymakers from eighty-four countries involved in diverse networks in all regions of the world to "develop policy goals and actions, for use in this decade and into the next century" and to guide women's intervention in preparations for and deliberations at The U.N. Conference on Environment and Development (the Earth Summit) in Brazil in June 1993.

Participants heard from women resisting dictatorship, militarism, violence against women, nuclear energy and weapons testing, forced migration and homelessness, the appropriation of tribal lands, poverty, starvation, external debt, biotechnology and biogenetics, toxic dumping, abusive and controlling population programs, and exploitative sexual policies and practices. Because women brought to this exchange prior experience of global dialogue in diverse preexisting networks, shared life-centered values, and women-centered perspectives that recognize class and colonial power, mutual learning was swift and discussion quickly led to unanimity around integrative positions.

Resolutions were passed acknowledging the links between issues and situating them all within the large feminist project of transforming the world—a project in which the Conference Report claimed a central and defining role for women: We come together to pledge our commitment to the empowerment of women, the central and powerful force in the search for equity among peoples of the Earth and for a balance between them and the life-support systems that sustain us all" (World Women's Congress for a Healthy Planet 1992, 16).

Regional caucus statements from Africa, Europe, International Indigenous Women, Latin America and the Caribbean, the Middle East, North America, Pacific, Women of the South, and Women of Color of North America articulate remarkably similar concerns, priorities, and principles, reflecting the influence of intensive exchanges in plenary meetings, hallways, workshops, and drafting sessions on already well-established shared perspectives. They express strong commitment to continued dialogue and solidarity and leave no doubt that Women's Action Agenda 21, the collectively written Conference Report, reflects a genuine and developing consensus of indigenous and nonindigenous participants from all regions of the world.

The "Statement from the Women of the South Caucus" reads in part:

> We, the women of the South, affirm that equity and justice must be the guiding principle between men and women, among communities and among nations, for a healthy people and a healthy planet.
> We believe that people have the right to sustainable livelihoods which encompass every aspect of human well being: material, spiritual, cultural, ecological and political. . . .
> We condemn the alienation of people from land, especially the indigenous peoples, the poor and women. (World Women's Congress for a Healthy Planet 1992, 34)

The women of the South demand an end to overconsumption "which underpins the lifestyles of the North and the elite of the South [and] is a central element of the Western development model" (ibid., 34). They condemn poverty, unequal trade relations, structural adjustment programs, coercive population-control strategies, militarism and nuclear testing, and the dumping of hazardous wastes. And they declare that:

> Traditional knowledge and technology, of which women and indigenous people have been the major creators and caretakers, must inform all national and international strategies to promote environmentally sound development.
> We urge greater South-South dialogue and cooperation, particularly among the women of our countries, in the search for common solutions to common human and environmental problems.
> Long live solidarity of Women of the World! (ibid., 34).

Both the European and North American Caucuses take clear stands against inequality in their own regions and declare their solidarity with their sisters of the South against Northern waste and exploitation as a basis for their participation in global dialogue and the development of a new future. They recognize the value of traditional knowledges and the need to end the hegemony of Western patriarchal science and the Western worldview as well as Western exploitation and domination. The report of the North American Caucus reads in part:

> We North American women are living in nations in which overconsumption by some co-exists with poverty and social deprivation for many and ecological degradation for all; and in which women and children everywhere are threatened

physically as well as economically. As a means of deepening our understanding and developing our alternative visions and values we welcome both the North-South dialogue and the dialogue among social movements.... We join with our sisters in the South in rejecting the world market economic and social order which is promoted, protected and sustained by both military might and military production. We support reforms that ... challenge the dualistic and destructive logic of this system. We particularly support changes which contribute to:

1) An equalizing redefinition and redistribution of power and resources within and between nations and regions;
2) A shift in the exploitative and hierarchical relations among and between people and the planet;
3) A basic redefinition of such concepts as power, human rights, wealth, work and progress, in terms which recognize and reaffirm the value of women, nature, and indigenous peoples;
4) The demilitarization of our economies and our cultures in order to free our creative genious for a more humane and renewable planet.

We see all these as necessary parts of a process in which the knowledge, values, wisdom and vision of women around the world can shape the priorities and ways of being in the world. (ibid., 32)

The emerging global consensus reflected in the regional caucus statements and the Conference Report as a whole testifies to the fact that the alternative values at the core of integrative feminisms challenge existing social relations at a level deep and radical enough to provide a frame for global solidarity.

CONCLUSION

Integrative feminists in North America, like those all over the world, recognize that the oppositions at the core of dominant Western culture are destructive and false, and they are committed to creating a world that fosters and celebrates, rather than masks and interrupts, connections. Their visions are of cooperative, egalitarian, life-centered social arrangements wherein the currently devalued, marginalized, and trivialized women-associated responsibilities and values of love and nurturing are the organizing principles of society; wherein differences do not mean inequality and can be celebrated as constitutive of commonality; wherein freedom is found in and won through community; and wherein humanity's embeddedness in nature is not only recognized but welcomed.

As we have seen, many of the diverse North American feminists who seek to transform their own communities and society in these integrative terms have a strong global awareness and presence. Not all integrative feminists in North America understand the global context of their visions, however. Not all yet see that the industrial patriarchy whose destructive logic they criticize in the North

is both product and producer of colonizing global processes of "modernization" and "development" that must be resisted worldwide.

As our global links and learning grow, reinforced by the increasing activism
and influence of women of color, and indigenous, immigrant, and working-
class women in the North, global knowledge is increasing in North America. It
is strengthening the transformative potential of our politics and our ability to
participate fully in the worldwide development of feminism. Like feminists
everywhere, we need global solidarity/support for our local struggles.

All over the world, integrative feminists are globally as well as locally realizing their connections in resistance and actively, creatively, and empathically
redefining the meaning and potential of these connections. They are building
equal, multicentered, mutually initiated and mutually beneficial relationships
with shared integrative goals defined and explored together, across and through
diversity. They are trying to change a political game women have never yet even
been "allowed" to play, levering from the outside and realizing that this is in
some ways the best, perhaps the only place from which to do so.

In the process they have to maintain a delicate balance between their local
autonomy and priorities and the demands of regional and international cooperation; they have to play a central role in the struggle to change the whole
world without losing themselves as women; and they have to create new possibilities from these dialectical tensions.

It is important to recognize the enormity of what feminists have achieved as
well as of what they need to do. Feminists have not yet built the power to halt
criminal economic, social, and environmental practices of increasing conservatism, fundamentalism, and militarism. But they have, with very few resources,
built the local and global connections and practice to conceptualize alternatives,
to keep these visions alive and developing, and to bring integrative values to bear
in political struggle and debate on issues ranging from local welfare policy
to U.N. population policy; from local bylaws on pornography to the U.N.
Human Rights Declaration; from local self-help groups to international alternative technology exchange.

In order to maximize our strength locally and play our full role globally, integrative feminists in North America need to recognize and make visible the often
unacknowledged integrative commitments we have found to be shared by
numerous feminisms; we need to consciously and strategically foster debates
and challenges within and among these feminisms that will broaden and
deepen all their politics. We need to resist disabling guilt; to recognize potential
allies; to be the center of our own practice while reaching out to others; to question everything while we build alternatives. This book has tried to show that
many and varied feminisms in North America and around the world are
engaged in this essential and dynamic process, and that their practice holds the
promise of a new world.

NOTES

Introduction

1. Although Mexico is officially considered part of North America, I use the term to refer to Quebec, English-speaking Canada, and the United States.
2. There has been much recent criticism of the too easy use of the terms "our" and "we" in the women's movement and the tendency of some feminists to appropriate the right to speak for other women. However, since I am writing about groups to which I belong, both women and feminists, the simple use of third-person pronouns throughout is not entirely accurate. It is also contrary to the spirit I intend in this work. Nevertheless, in the main body of the book I have used third-person pronouns with an occasional reversion to the first person. If the occasional switch from third to first person is jarring, this may serve to alert the reader to shifting identities, groupings, alliances, and their political significance and fragility, and to the fact that this is an engaged study.
3. When referring to self-consciously feminist-defined activism, I use the term "the women's movement" or "the women's liberation movement." Following bell hooks's suggestion, however, I use the term "women's movement" when I am referring to autonomous women's activism generally and want to communicate the breadth, diversity, informality and unknowableness of the ways in which women today are moving. By no means does all of this movement define itself as feminist or explicitly claim to be part of "*the* women's (liberation) movement." Therefore, using this term when referring to all women-centered and pro-women activity would tend to obscure the vitality and variety of women's personal and political practice today. It might also be read to claim for feminists an unintended and untenable proprietary relationship to this activism. Women's movement is the context within which feminism and the women's (liberation) movement grow and develop; they are not coterminous.

147

4. Here there are no really satisfactory solutions to the question of terminology. I have chosen to use the term "Third World" to refer collectively to those nations that share a history of colonization and exploitation by and resistance to the capitalist nations of the West. There is a danger that this collective term may seem to imply a homogeneity of history and condition among and within these countries that is very far from being the case and that I certainly do not wish to imply. The term "Third World" has also been read by some as uncritically reflecting the very colonial categories to which it is a response. Certainly, even those who use it have reservations. I have chosen to do so because most "Third World" feminists I have spoken to or read prefer this terminology as the best of a bad lot, and also because this term names historical power relations, of domination and resisted domination, that other terms, such as "North" and "South," do not. I do, however, use the latter terms on occasion for the sake of brevity and/or variety. It will be clear from the analysis that follows why such terms as "developed" and "underdeveloped" or "developing" are particularly inappropriate. I have heard the term "'Two-Thirds World" used recently and use it myself periodically because of the timely reminder it provides the North American reader of the South's predominance in both population and land mass.

5. This book focuses on feminist radicalisms in general and integrative feminisms in particular and mentions reform feminisms only in passing. This latter realm of feminist practice forms the context within which feminist radicals operate but receives no attention here. Generalizations about feminist weaknesses and strengths refer only to the feminisms under study.

Chapter 1

1. I am aware that the terms "domination," "exploitation," "oppression," and "subordination" have distinct meanings. However, in this book I use them interchangeably and loosely to refer to the whole complex of women's disadvantaged and relatively powerless position, which includes economic and sexual use and abuse as well as cultural devaluation and marginalization.

2. For information on early feminist radicalism, see Brodeur et al. 1982; The Clio Collective 1987; Freeman 1975; Hole and Levine 1971; Lamoureaux 1986; O'Leary and Toupin 1981, 1982; Ware 1970. For studies that do justice to the often overlooked continuities between sixties women's rights agitation and women's struggles in earlier decades, see Backhouse and Flaherty 1992; Clio Collective 1987; Dumont 1992; Evans 1989.

3. The influence of all these revolutionary movements on feminist radicalisms of the period is evident throughout the literature, including indebtedness: for aspects of analyis (Dworkin 1974); for inspiration, especially from anticolonial struggles (Asian Delegates from Berkeley 1971; O'Leary and Taupin 1982; Redstockings 1975); and for the acquisition of skills (Beal 1969; Chow 1987; Dumont 1992; Evans 1979; Garcia 1990; Giddings 1984 Chapter 17; Lopez 1977; Stephenson 1975).

4. The breadth of these visions exploded the normal categories of political thought: "That so profound a change cannot be easily fit into traditional categories of thought e.g. 'political' is not because these categories do not apply but because they are not big enough: radical feminism bursts through them. If there were a word more all-embracing than *revolution* we would use it" (Firestone 1970, 1).

5. Criticism of the New Left's failed commitment to the liberation of *all* is widespread in the Quebecois and English Canadian feminist literature of the early '70s. See, for example, Bernstein et al. 1972, 37–38; Front de Libération des Femmes 1971, 119.

Disappointment in male-defined radicalisms is also a major theme in early Black, Chicana, and white U.S. feminist writing about the student movement (Morgan 1977, 60); the Black movement (Cade 1970, 103); the Chicano movement (Lopez 1977, 24; Garcia 1990). These tensions between male-defined resistances and feminisms that reject them as partial continue into the nineties in all communities.

6. The broad liberatory commitment of early feminist radicals (and my description of it here) should not be read to displace a commitment to or devalue the significance of women's liberation for its own sake and in its own right. The fact that women's liberation is an essential aspect of the struggles against class, race, and colonial oppression is recognized by integrative feminist radicals and influences their politics, but it is not needed or presented as justification for their struggles as women.

7. Celestine Ware's important book, unfortunately, is out of print and not well known. Written by a Black radical feminist activist and participant in the political developments and debates she describes, it was an important resource when it was published and remains so today.

   For radical group statements that the personal is political, see Brossard 1976b; New York Radical Feminists 1970; Redstockings 1969.

8. Consciousness-raising groups have been compared to the "speak bitterness" meetings of the Chinese Communist Party and to the process of "conscientization" advocated by Paulo Freire. Despite the significant similarities, consciousness-raising groups are unique in being self-initiated and self-sustaining formations.

9. The necessity/possibility of integrating personal experience, feelings, and activity with intellectual and theoretical analysis and collective practice is a well-developed theme in the feminist literature on consciousness raising. See, among others, Allen 1971; Bunch 1970; Redstockings 1969; Susan 1970.

10. Later chapters examine in more detail the ways in which women identification complements and completes rather than supplants other identities such as class and race and the ways in which integrative feminisms have developed to more fully and successfully articulate women's commonality and diversity in their transformative politics.

11. I have not designated Black or Third World feminisms here because there are no particular forms of Black feminist reductionism in this period. Although women of color were active in each of the categories named, sometimes in identity-based groups, Black and Third World feminisms were not publicly proclaimed as separate politics by autonomous feminists until close to the end of this early period. The Combahee River Collective Statement, April 1977, is one of the earliest and most influential statements outlining the principles of autonomous Black feminism. This statement emphasizes the absolute indivisibility of the struggles against race, class, and gender power as the hallmark of Black feminisms and a valuable contribution to all feminisms. It is very different in spirit from many earlier claims that Black feminism is a separate feminism. These often stressed not so much the need for all feminists to fight racism as for Black feminists to prioritize the struggle against racism.

12. For a more developed argument of this point, see the first section of Chapter 2.

13. For Furies publications see Bunch and Myron 1974; Myron and Bunch 1975.

14. The Redstockings are a U.S. group. For a collection of members' writing see Redstockings 1975.

15. Wages for Housework is a tightly organized international grouping. Its units in the 1970s included the "Power of Women Group" in London, England, and "The Toronto Wages for Housework Committee" as well as groups in Quebec, the United States, and Italy.

   The central control of these units was so strong and direct that it is possible to refer to them collectively in this period as "The Wages for Housework Group" and to treat their publications as a single literature. Early sources include Dalla Costa and James 1972, 1973.

Chapter 2

1. Claiming their connection with other women is especially difficult for middle-class urban women who in industrial society live in isolation from each other and in close proximity to individuals in the group that has power over them and has monopolized the power of defining reality and society. The fact that this is less true of rural, working-class, and Third World women, many of whom still live in communities with more intact women's spaces and connections, has significance for integrative feminisms' potential, as we shall see in later chapters.
2. The essential political connection between the affirmation of a woman's gender and culture and race is examined more fully in Chapter 3.
3. For interesting interview material testifying to the extent of personal change and the importance of group participation for feminists in radical groups in Montreal, Vancouver, and Chicago respectively, see Saint-Jean 1980; Stephenson 1975; Strobel 1994.
4. For examples of this Black-feminist literature, see Bell-Scott et al. eds. 1991; Davis 1971; Hamilton and Prieto 1989; Moraga and Anzaldúa 1983; Morrison 1971; Murray 1970; Reagan 1982; Sage 1984; Walker 1974.
5. In her analysis of the English Canadian women's movement, Lynn Teather (1976) recognized the importance of women's desire to remain true to feminism's original ideas in the founding of alternative institutions: "When the politicos/feminist split occurred many of these women entered service groups and formed women's centres and consciousness-raising cells in order to pursue their ideals" (329).
6. For valuable accounts of diverse feminist organizations and projects, see Bunch and Pollack 1983; Ferree and Martin 1994; Wine and Ristock 1991.
7. In an interview in 1984, for example, Barbara Smith is asked, "How does it feel to be in the vanguard of Black feminist thought and struggle?" and replies, "Vanguard is a word I never use. That's not what it's about; let's not get into that or seeing Black Lesbian feminists as a vanguard. I mean, who wants to be in that position anyway?" (Parkerson 1984, 26)
8. The commitment to openness is stated clearly in the editorial of the first issue of *La vie en rose* in March 1980: "Nous ne prétendons pas cerner la réalité ou lui faire suivre une ligne; nous nous contenterons de regarder et de commenter le monde qui nous entoure sans chercher refuge derrière les paravents sacrés de l'objectivité et de la représentativité. Nous ne chercherons pas à véhiculer des certitudes; simplement nous indiquerons les pistes qui se présentent à nous."

   ["We (in the magazine) don't pretend to encompass reality or to follow any set line; we are content to look at and comment on the world around us without hiding behind claims of objectivity and representativeness. We don't seek to communicate certainties; simply to point out paths that present themselves to us."]

Chapter 3

1. See, for instance, Bersianik 1976; Boulding 1976; Brossard 1977; Bunch 1976; Chicago 1975; Clark 1976; Combahee River Collective 1977; Deming 1977; Dinnerstein 1977; Dworkin 1976; Gagnon 1977; Janeway 1974, 1976; Jordan 1977;

Kingston 1977; Lorde 1978; Miller 1976; Morgan 1977; O'Brien 1976; Peters and Samuels 1976; Rich 1976; Les têtes de pioche 1977; Walker 1974, 1976.

2. For early collections that illustrate this shift to transformative perspectives in a wide variety of areas of scholarship, see Cohen 1981; Harding and Hintikka 1983; Miles and Finn 1989 (1982); Moraga and Anzaldúa 1983.

3. "Physicality" is an awkward expression, but the word "body" does not accurately communicate the concerns of feminists committed to breaking down patriarchally imposed and enforced divisions between the body and the mind, reason and emotion, motherhood and sexuality and to encompass all this and more in an exploration of all women's embodied capacities and desires in an integrated journey of personal and political transformation. Nicole Brossard, in dialogue with Adrienne Rich, explained that the word "skin" (*peau*) often expressed her inclusive vision more accurately than the word "body" (*corps*), with all its patriarchal overtones/ baggage (Brossard and Rich 1981). This word will clearly not serve the purpose here, however.

4. Feminist analytical speculation on male-female differences was not unknown before the late seventies. Nevertheless, it was not until the second half of the seventies that the question of male-female differences emerged as a central theoretical and strategic project in politics that integrate material and psychological, social and individual analyses.

5. While feminists committed to equality with men had come over time to name and value women's difference from men, traditional female subcultures have always tended to discount men and male preoccupations while affirming women and women's concerns. This development in feminism has brought it in touch with important female truths that had been lost to urban, assimilated women but that remain very much alive around the world and in rural and working-class women's communities.

6. Self-defined socialist feminists I interviewed expressed this clearly: "The reason why I call myself a socialist feminist is that I think it's really important to try to figure out some way to pull together, into one sort of unified politics ... the ways we've learned to look at the world through the women's movement, with certain socialist traditions.... There are good and bad things in those socialist traditions and there are good things and bad things in the women's movement too. And what we have to figure out is how to use the best of those things and build on them to create something different" (Lorraine).

   But the concern with class and gender was not restricted to those who defined themselves as socialist-feminist: "I think unless we can really come to grips with the differences between women and somehow incorporate that in a fairly cohesive analysis of what women's liberation and the women's movement is all about, we won't be able to get very much further. I think we have differences between women, different levels of oppression, and that essentially means ... class. How it relates between women as well as how women relate to class as a Marxist concept is crucial" (Elizabeth).

7. "Motherhood" here refers to the whole process of child care and child rearing, not just the giving of birth, whose necessary biological association with women can, of course, not be denied. Feminist radicalism's emerging integrative analysis of motherhood/reproduction is evidenced in a wide variety of literature that is clearly a product of a mutually influential dialogue in the mid-1970s. See, for instance, Brossard 1977; Deming 1977; Jean and Théoret 1976; Lazarre 1976; Lecavalier, Laprade, and Pelletier 1978; Morgan 1977; O'Brien 1976; Rich 1976; Walker 1974.

8. The parallels of tone and content between the poem "Natural Resources" by Adrienne Rich (1978b) and the article/poem "My Black Mothers and Sisters; or, On Beginning a Cultural Autobiography" by Berenice Johnson Reagan (1982) are an interesting illustration of the extent to which the radical rediscovery, renaming, and revaluing of women and women's work, against traditions that have left them invisible and unvalued, are tasks shared by diverse feminists. The work of redefining the world both requires and enables the participation of all women. It could never be the project of any single group of women.

9. Identity-based groups were, however, far from rare. The first national conference for and by Chicanas, La Conferencia de Mujeres Por la Raza, sometimes referred to as the National Chicana Conference, was held in 1971 in Houston, Texas. Early groups in the U.S. and Canada include the Ad Hoc Committee on Indian Rights for Indian Women; the Alliance for Displaced Homemakers; Appalachian Women for a Coal Employment Project; Black Women Concerned, Baltimore; Black Women Organized for Action, San Francisco; Hijas de Cuauhtemoc (Long Beach State University); the Coalition of Labour Union Women; the Congress of Black Women; the Gray Panthers; Las Chicanas (San Diego State University); Les Femmes Acadiennes de Moncton (Les FAM); the League of Black Women, Chicago; the Mexican American Women's National Association (MANA); the National Alliance of Black Feminists; the National Black Feminist Organization; the National Congress of Neighbourhood Women; the Native Women's Association of Canada; the New York Black Women's Group, Mt. Vernon, New York; 9 to 5 (office workers); Pan Asian American Women; Sisters Getting Ourselves Together (Black women), Davis, California; the Third World Women's Alliance, California; the Welfare Rights Movement; Women of All Red Nations; and Women against Repression, Los Angeles.

10 See, for instance, early movement anthologies: Babcox and Belkin 1971; Cade 1970; Canadian Women's Educational Press 1972; Cooke and Bunch-Weeks 1971; Jenness 1972; Koedt, Levine, and Rapone 1973; Morgan 1970; Tanner 1971; Thompson 1970.

11. The title of the important anthology *All the Women Are White and All the Men Are Black, but Some of Us Are Brave,* edited by Gloria T. Hull, Patricia Bell Scott, and Barbara Smith (1982), testifies eloquently to this refusal to choose between race and gender identity.

12. This is a paraphrase of the title of Michelle Cliff's book *Claiming an Identity They Taught Me to Despise* 1980.

13. Autonomous women identification is not a denial of women's ethnic, class, or other allegiances (traditional or revolutionary) but a challenge to the ways in which women have been constructed by them, as well as by mainstream culture. See Alarcon 1983; Allen 1986, 30; Beal 1969, 92; Cheng 1984; Collins 1990, 67; H. 1989; hooks 1990, 16 Vidal 1972, 53.

14. "When women (manage to) come together in a shared project and desire (what I call the beautiful energy of women for and with women) we have a movement, a movement capable of achieving radical changes that make us vibrate with all our body, our sweat, our tenderness, our muscle and our strength toward other women. This is called a rising of consciousness. It stirs the patriarchal shit around us, makes it visible and unlivable. So out of our daily life a movement arises which, in a metaphoric sense, 'brings us to life.'"

15. "To whose camp, then, should the lesbian of color retreat? Her very presence violates the ranking and abstraction of oppressions" (Moraga 1983a, 29). "I am Latina, Jewish and an immigrant (all at once)" (Moschkovich 1983, 79). For other statements about crosscutting identities, see Allen 1986; Beck 1982; Cole 1986, 3–4;

hooks 1990, 20; Moraga and Anzaldúa 1983, 91, 123,1 26; Peters and Samuels 1976, 12; Smith 1983.

16. See Chapter 4 for a more extended discussion of the political articulation of identity that has emerged in recent years.

17. The lesbian feminist group the Furies was among the first to try to deal systematically in practice and in theory with differences of class among them (Bunch and Myron 1974). Smith, Stein, and Golding (1981) report on attempts at dialogue among diverse lesbian feminists. The Necessary Bread Affinity Group (1982) is an example of a self-consciously diverse lesbian-feminist group.

18. The DAWN address is Ste 120, 180 Dundas St. West, Toronto, Ontario M5G1Z8, Canada; tel. 416-598-2438. For an account of the network's founding and development, see Doucette 1991.

19. Charlotte Bunch's article "Self-Definition and Political Struggle" (1975b) is, if possible, more relevant on this point today than when it was written.

20. Melanie Kaye/Kantrowitz 1992, Minnie Bruce Pratt 1988, and Adrienne Rich 1978a all discuss the political dangers of liberal guilt. Rich, for instance, stresses the importance of white feminists being able to work actively against their own and society's racism rather than being overcome by "impotent guilt reflexes, which have little or no long-term, continuing momentum or political usefulness" (1978a, 24). She explains at greater length in the same article: "It . . . seems to me that guilt feelings—so easily provoked in women that they have become almost a form of social control—can also be a form of solipsism, a preoccupation with our own feelings which prevents us from ever connecting with the experience of others. Guilt feelings paralyze, but paralysis can become a convenient means of remaining passive and instrumental. If I cannot even approach you because I feel so much guilt toward you, I need never listen to what you actually have to say; I need never risk making common cause with you as two women with choices as to how we might exist and act" (1978a, 24).

21. The point that passive defensiveness is not an adequate response to issues of racism is made urgently by, among others, Gayatri Spivak, when she notes that what is required is "not only [being] able to listen to that other constituency, but [learning] to speak in such a way that one will be taken seriously by [it] (1990, 42, also 62–63), and Trinh Minh-ha, when she warns that "the danger of speaking for the other [should not] serve as an excuse for . . . complacent ignorance and . . . reluctance to involve [oneself] (1989, 80). Bell hooks urges an active and political stance on white feminists when she says, "we [Black feminists] inhabit marginal space that is not a place of domination but a place of resistance" and invites white feminists to "enter that space" (1990, 151). Himani Bannerji reminds us, however, that the margins are not automatically sites of struggle, that making them so must be all women's aim: "The point is to shift the centre itself from the mainstream to the margin. By understanding 'representation' to mean re-presentation of our realities from a foundationally critical/revolutionary perspective, there can emerge the possibility of making our very marginality itself the epicentre for change. This has always been the principle of any fundamentally revolutionary or critical perspective" (1993, xvi). This is very much my own argument, with the exception that I would pluralize margin in a concept in which multiple margins become multiple centers of diverse social movement.

22. The title of bell hooks's book *Black Feminist Theory: From Margin to Center* (1984) clearly states this essential political project. Other feminists who stress the importance of claiming the center, write of "developing a feminist movement based on the realities and priorities of third world wimmen" (davenport 1983, 89); framing "our social action around our own agenda for change"(Radford-Hill 1986, 162);

recognizing that the "differential consciousness [of Third World feminism] is vital to a next 'third wave' women's movement" (Sandoval 1991, 4).

Although these feminists differ in their views of the short-term desirability/ effectiveness of trying to work with white/heterosexual/middle-class feminists, the autonomy they advocate is not separatism. In the long term they are all committed to building their own autonomy/identity as part of the general development of a broad-based, inclusive feminist movement that is "international in scope and universal in application" (davenport 1983, 90): "The political viability of feminism as an agency of change depends in the final analysis both on its ability to foster women's solidarity and on its ability to build a movement that is inclusive rather than exclusive, one that can mobilize against sexist oppression from a broad base of support" (Radford-Hill 1986, 169).

23. On this important point see Christian 1985; Russell 1976; Sandoval 1991; Simms 1992.

24. Deconstuctionist theoretical positions, by contrast, discussed in Chapter 5, read the fact of diversity in opposition to universal values and struggle and posit a decentered rather than multicentered women's movement.

Chapter 4

1. "Active and political women, whether independist, marxist or syndicalist, currently work in a context constructed and defined by men for the benefit of generations of men to come."

2. Kathleen Lahey (1989) has called this "equality with a vengeance." For feminist discussion of difference in law, see Baron 1987 regarding the United States and Boyle et al. 1985 regarding Canadian criminal law.

3. What is called pay equity in Canada and comparable worth in the United States allows (at least in theory) for women's paid work in traditional areas to be revalued and their wages in these large areas of employment to be raised because it does not require women to do the same work as men to receive equivalent wages. Despite the advantages of its departure from a simple equality frame, relations of power limit its achievements in practice (Evans and Nelson 1989).

4. Activist groups include prostitutes, poor women, trade-union women (office workers, air hostesses, nurses), immigrant women, native women, and professional women as well as women struggling in their communities around such issues as the environment, housing, safety, violence, poverty, and health.

5. Following are a few examples of the vast number of identity-based feminist collections that have appeared in large and growing numbers since the mid-80s: Anzaldúa 1990; Asian Women United of California 1989; Baxter 1988; Beck 1982; Brant 1988; Driedger and Gray 1992; Dubois and Ruiz 1990; Hull, Bell-Scott, and Smith 1982; Kaye/Kantrowitz and Lipfisz 1986; Moraga and Anzaldúa 1983; Mukherjie 1993; Rooney and Israel 1985; Smith 1983; Trujillo 1991; White 1990; Women's Book Collective, Chinese Canadian National Council 1992. Numerous identity-based journals and magazines also began to appear in the 1980s, for instance, to name just two: *Sage: A Scholarly Journal on Black Women* and *Shifra: A Jewish Feminist Magazine* both began publishing in 1984.

6. The Welfare Warriors' publication *Welfare Mothers' Voice,* a national bilingual publication, is available from 4504 North 47th, Milwaukee, WI, 5318.

7. I first heard the phrase "women living poverty" used in preference to the term "poor women" by Carolyn Lehmann, a founding member of Casa Sofia, a women's center in the barrios of Santiago, Chile.

8. Poor mothers' lives and fears reflect in heightened form the vulnerability of all mothers. "Like all women, poor moms must live in fear of rape and battery (more frequent for us since we often live with angry men, take buses, and walk in war zones.) ... All mothers in patriarchy lose our children, in some degree, to the Fathers. But impoverished mothers suffer wrenching, heartbreaking violent, literal losses of our children—disappeared in El Salvador, gunned down in Milwaukee, legally snatched *whenever, wherever they will bring in a profit for the Fathers.*" (Welfare Warriors 1991, 20).

9. Information on the National Black Women's Health Project comes from Avery 1990a, 1990b, the project's newspaper, *Vital Signs,* talks and workshops I have heard given by Byllye Avery, and reports in the feminist press. Contact the National Black Women's Health Project, 1237 Ralph Abernathy Blvd. S.W., Atlanta, Ga 30310; tel. 404-758-9590.

10. Contact the National Women's Health Network, 1325 G St. N.W., Washington D.C. 20005; tel. 202-347-1140; the National Latina Health Organization, P.O. Box 7667, Oakland, CA 94601; tel. 510-534-1362; and the Native American Women's Health Education Resource Center, P.O. Box 572, Lake Andes, S.D. 57356; tel. 605-487-7072.

11. Information provided on WHISPER is from the group's newsletter, *WHISPER,* and its educational pamphlets. The group's address is Lake Street Station, Box 8719, Minneapolis, MN 55408; tel. 612-644-6301. For more information on the development of the group, see a long interview with founder-member Evelina Giobbe (Mayne and Wingfield 1993).

12. WHISPER has carried reports, to name just a few, on the Nairobi Conference; UNESCO Conferences and resolutions on prostitution; prostitution laws in Moscow; trafficking in Asian women; and sex tourism between Norway and Thailand, and between Japan and the Philippines, as well as articles on Peru, China, and Kenya; a large overview of global trafficking in women; and information about the antiprostitution struggles of Gabriela in the Philippines and the Rainbow Project in Thailand.

13. The following are just a few examples of the thousands of local and national Conferences held recently on themes of racism and diversity among women: "Telling It: Women and Language Across Cultures," Vancouver, November 1988; "Parallels and Intersections: Racism and Other Forms of Oppression," Iowa City, April 1989; "I Am Your Sister: Forging Global Connections Across Differences," Boston, October 1990; "An African American and Asian American Feminist Dialogue: Forging Alliances Across the Color Line" with Merle Woo and Barbara Smith, San Francisco, November 1990; "Making Links: Anti-Racism and Feminism," Canadian Research Institute for the Advancement of Women Conference, Toronto, March 1992.

14. Pamela Harris's photo exhibition and her book *Faces of Feminism* (1992), for instance, capture the wealth of feminist diversity in Quebec and English-speaking Canada.

15. Part of Brand's speech appears in the videotape of the "Making the Links" conference entitled *Wings of the Same Bird,* by Marjorie Beaucage (1993).

16. Information on the Latinamerican Coalition is from the Coalition Report (Latinamerican Community 1992), and from conversations with a founding member, Carolyn Lehmann, as well as her unpublished paper "Protecting and Caring for Children in the Community Through Group Work Connections" (1993). The Coalition's address is: P.O. Box 36, Station C, Toronto, Ontario, M6J 3M7, Canada.

17. See, for instance, the collections listed in note 5 and Albrecht and Brewer 1990; Apthekar 1989; Bannerji 1993; Bunch 1987; Cardinal 1992; Dill 1983; Doucette 1986, 1991; hooks 1990; Reagan 1983; Rich 1986.

Chapter 5

1. The ethnocentrism of reductionist refusals of women's specificity is also evident in the analysis that leads Alice Echols (1989) to conclude that "true" radical feminism only existed for a few early years in a few young, mainly white feminist groups, in a few Eastern U.S. cities. She reads the history of increasingly broad, diverse, and integrative feminisms since those years as a continuous decline from this early high point largely because she sees all recognition of women's specificities as an essentialist undermining of feminism.

2. As Barbara Smith has stated, "There was a concerted effort in the early seventies to turn the Black community off to feminism. You can look at publications, particularly Black publications making pronouncements about what the feminist movement was and who it reached that would trivialize it, that would say no Black women were involved, that did everything possible to prevent those coalitons between Black and white women from happening because there was a great deal of fear. Black men did not want to lose Black women as allies. And the white power structure did not want to see all women bond across racial lines because they knew that would be an unbeatable, unstoppable combination. They did a very good job" (Smith and Smith 1983, 125).

3. But feminist reductionism is not rare. Both integrative and nonintegrative feminisms are often falsely accused of essentialism. The blanket use of this pejorative results from the mislabeling of both dialectical politics and politics that are reductionist without being essentialist.

   For a well-balanced discussion of the limitations that essentialism, accurately defined, places on the possibilities for feminist practice against violence against women, see Liz Kelly 1991. Kelly defines essentialism narrowly and accurately as "the belief that aggression is inherent in men" (15). Andrea Dworkin (1977) has also usefully critiqued feminist tendencies to biological determinism and essentialism, in this case the mirror belief that women are inherently superior. Carol Anne Douglas's book *Love and Politics: Radical Feminist and Lesbian Theories* does a very good job of recognizing and describing the varied radical and lesbian feminist "perspectives on biological differences." She also makes and illustrates the important point that these differences do not provide "in themselves adequate information to predict a given feminist's other political ideas or actions" (1990, 3). This kind of nuanced analysis, with attention to actual theory and practice, is all too rare in a literature dominated by broad, unsupported, undocumented general criticism of "essentialism."

4. The address of the Revolutionary Feminist Organizing Committee is: 109 Ellerbee St., Durham, North Carolina 27704.

5. For materialist, radical, and socialist defenses of a simple equality frame for feminist politics, see, respectively, Delphy 1992; Echols 1989; Segal 1987. Historical treatments of earlier "maternal" or "social" forms of feminism also often mistakenly view any recognition of women's specificity as a betrayal of the feminist claim for equality. For a more detailed development of this point see Miles 1985.

6. Alice Echols recognizes Dworkin's and MacKinnon's deep social constructionism but retains the right to criticize these authors as essentialist: "Both Andrea Dworkin and Catharine MacKinnon have repudiated essentialism. . . . However, their view of male dominance as eternal and unchanging makes social constructionism, in their hands, virtually indistinguishable from essentialism. Gender might be socially constructed rather than biologically determined, but if the social structure is as imper-

vious to change as they suggest, it might as well be biologically fixed" (1989, 363).

The distorting effect of the hegemony of antiessentialist orothodoxy in academic feminist circles is nowhere more evident. Instead of a rigorous argument against the claims that sexuality is deeply constructed socially, we have a magical and dismissive invocation of "essentialism." Instead of a serious debate about just what it will take to change these biological, psychological, legal, and social structures and how we should proceed strategically, there is an amazing assertion that two feminists who are devoting most of their energy to changing these structures might as well believe them to be immutable.

Even looser and more encompassing definitions of essentialism without Echols's acknowledgment that the usage is idiosyncratic are not uncommonly employed to dismiss the most basic tenets of feminism and with them the majority of feminist movement. For instance, we find in a review of Catharine MacKinnon's, *Toward a Feminist Theory of the State* (Menkel-Meadows 1991), "MacKinnon holds tenaciously to an essentialist position that women are united by their sexual oppression." If this position is essentialist, then feminism is, by definition, essentialist.

7. Numerous problems of terminology are evident here, not for the first time. Black feminists and Quebecois feminists, for instance, are self-identified as radical, socialist, eco-, materialist, and many other types of feminist. A different difficulty is found in the fact that Alison Jaggar (1983) cites Elizabeth Fee, Jane Flax, Sandra Harding, Nancy Hartsock, Evelyn Fox Keller, and Dorothy Smith as socialist feminists, though not all are self-defined as socialist feminists. They are, however, all integrative feminists with a concern for class oppression and a knowledge of Marxist theory. The common presumption that integrative feminist principles and vision are unique to one's own brand of integrative feminism contributes to the difficulty of seeing their extent and diversity.

8. The refusal to discuss sexuality in value terms has been most developed in defense of sadomasochism but extends for some to a general refusal of any reflection on sexuality that implies collective values and visions.

9. For sources on the sexuality debates within feminism, see Lederer 1980; Leidholdt and Raymond 1990; Snitow, Stansell, and Thompson 1983.

10. Di Stefano posits a third "postrationalist" feminism roughly corresponding to the reductionist postmodern feminist positions I discuss later. Her argument that both "rationalist" and "antirationalist" feminisms are inadequate does not recognize the existence of integrative feminisms that incorporate and transform these two. Ultimately, she defends the need to retain a notion of women's specificity against rationalist and postmodern refusals, but it is an apologetic defense (Di Stefano 1988, 20).

11. Here Snitow is referring to a need to speak beyond the specific category "woman" to the general category "human," not arguing for a need to "deconstruct" the general category "woman." This political issue, which I deal with in the next section, is not her concern in this article.

12. Actually, in a footnote Snitow acknowledges the existence of "'third course' thinking." However, she sees it as an extreme minority position. She does not recognize the extent of the diverse feminisms that pursue this integrative "third course" in practice.

13. There is a growing but scattered feminist literature critical of feminist postmodernism/poststructuralism. See, for instance, Barry 1990; Benhabib and Cornell 1987; Brodribb 1992; Busia 1989/90; Carby 1990; Christian 1987; Di Stefano 1988; Gordon 1990; Hawksworth 1989; Jackson 1992; Juteau 1990; Lauretis 1989; Lazreg

1988; E. MacDonald 1991; I. MacDonald 1991; MacKinnon 1991; Modleski 1991; Newman 1991; Spretnak 1991; Thiele 1989.

14. Kathleen Barry (1990) and Danielle Juteau (1990) point out the untenable conflation of women as a social class and women as a biological category in their respectively radical and materialist critiques of feminist poststructuralism.

15. Donna Haraway argues that although Marxist/socialist feminism does not "naturalize unity [but sees it as] a possible achievement based on a possible standpoint rooted in social relations, ... the essentializing move is in the ontological structure of labour or of its analogue, women's activity" (1990, 200).

    Linda Nicholson and Nancy Fraser (1990, 28–32) criticize Shulamith Firestone, Michelle Zimbalist Rosaldo, Nancy Chodorow, Ann Ferguson, Nancy Folbre, Nancy Hartsock, Catharine MacKinnon, and Carol Gilligan as essentialist.

16. Haraway, for instance, charges both socialist and radical feminists with homogenizing differences: "If my complaint about socialist/Marxist standpoints is their unintended erasure of polyvocal, unassimilable, radical difference made visible in anti-colonial discourse and practice, [radical feminist] MacKinnon's intentional erasure of all difference through the device of the 'essential' non-existence of women is not reassuring" (Haraway 1990, 201). Here Haraway dismisses as essentialist even MacKinnon's argument that women do not exist for themselves—the ultimate nonesssentialist social-constructionist argument.

17. The misunderstanding and dismissal of dialectics as a misguided belief in easy, simple, and unmediated resolutions or reconciliations of contradictions is widespread. Transformative struggles informed by visions of a society in which these dualisms (though not all of them) are overcome (though not for all time) and by active commitments to honour this ideal in daily political practice are left invisible. Feminist poststucturalists, for whom this vision is simplistic, are left trying to resist these dualisms while theorizing the impossibility of so doing and refusing the articulation of alternatives. Hence the unnecessarily complex, almost inaccessible suggestions of deconstructionist approaches that focus on feminist "discourse" without attention to feminist values or to the actual practice of feminist movement.

18. For an exciting film celebrating the visionary power of Quebec feminist writers see Hénaut 1986.

19. Smith's straightforward approach leaves Nancy Miller, by contrast, unable "to imagine a relation between the [deconstructionist] logic and ethics of deferral and the (regrettable) assumption of immediacy and transparence that [she thinks] animates ... Barbara Smith" (1986, 108).

20. Among the feminists claimed for poststructuralism are Barbara Smith, Cherríe Moraga, bell hooks, Toni Cade Bambara, Gloria Hull, Patricia Bell-Scott, Audre Lorde, Berenice Reagan.

21. Chris Weedon is only one among many deconstructionists who outrageously misrepresent feminists' collective political analysis of women's experience as a simplistic assumption "that women's experience, unmediated by further theory is the source of true knowledge" (1987, 8).

22. Drucilla Cornell's (1991) detailed reading of Toni Morrison's *Beloved* is another example of a tortuous deconstructionist analysis that "saves" the author from far-fetched charges of essentialism invented by deconstructionists in the first place.

23. This has moved many of them, ironically, to comment on the limits, even dangers, of simple or fundamentalist "antiessentialist" positions. See, for instance, Fuss 1989; Lauretis 1989, 4; Martin and Mohanty 1986, 208; Spivak 1989, 129, 143.

24. Diana Fuss puts the issue thus: "The problem of identity has long been a problem for feminist poststructuralists seeking to base a politics on something other than

'essence.' Is it possible to generate a theory of feminism's specificity that is not essentialist? How do we reconcile the poststructural project to displace identity with the feminist project to reclaim it?" (1989, 69–70).

25. See, for instance, Fuss 1989, 71, 118; Scott 1988, 43–44; Spivak 1990, 134; Trinh 1989, 39–40, 113.

26. The poststructuralist embrace of disorder/incoherence and concentration on individual sensation rather than communication are captured in the following quotation where the celebration of many meanings becomes the invention of no meaning: "My dream of counter theory takes place in a huge pharmacy with a moving soda counter packed with people sipping and gulping with liquid straws on swiveling chairs. This is speech. A horizontal tower of babel where everyone has walkmans whose dials translate different straw dialects. You're always behind the conversation, waiting for deeper, thirstier ears. But you don't worry anxiously about all you're missing because what you do tune into is absolutely, fantastically, instructive and transporting. Often, soda spills. The soda drinkers invent readings of the meanings and patterns of these spills: these readings are the stuff of counter-theory" (Phelan 1990, 5).

Chapter 6

1. In speaking generally of "Third World feminisms," I risk being read as homogenizing extremely diverse phenomena. I have decided to take this risk because I am concerned to point out principles that are shared across diversity by feminisms in a great number of countries and continents. My focus is primarily on integrative feminisms in both the First and Two-Thirds worlds. There are, of course, noninte-grative Third World feminists, just as there are nonintegrative feminists of all classes and ethnicities in the West.

2. I have heard the term "Two-Thirds World" used recently and use it here periodically as a substitute for Third World because of the timely reminder it provides the North American reader of the South's predominance in both population and land mass.

3. See Maathai 1988.

4. See Shiva 1989a Chapter 4.

5. See Bhatt and Patel 1986.

6. See Zabaleta 1983.

7. For general descriptions and analyses of the marked development of feminism and other autonomous women's activism in different regions, see AAWORD 1985; Hélie-Lucas 1993; Shadmi 1993a; South Asian Workshop on Women and Development 1989; Sternbach et al. 1992. For information on specific Third World-feminist-defined or explicitly feminist-friendly groups and activities, see Davies 1983, 1987; Kerr 1993; Kishwar and Vanita 1984; Mbilinyi and Meena 1991; Morgan 1984; Schuler 1986, 1990, 1992; Yudelman 1987.

8. Feminists of color in the North are subjected to analogous charges. The arguments presented in the pamphlet *Some Questions about Feminism and Its Relevance to South Asia* (Bhasin and Khan 1986) and in Barbara Smith's introduction to *Home Girls: A Black Feminist Anthology* (1983) are interesting parallel defences of feminism by Asian and Black U.S. feminists. See also statements of the National Black Feminist Organization in the United States (1974); Women in Nigeria (Kihoro 1992); and Chicana feminists in the United States (Lopez 1977).

9. For accounts of parallel but particular feminist debates among Muslim women around the world and in Asia and Latin Americ, respectively, on autonomy and

feminism's relationship to other radical forces see Hélie-Lucas 1993; Omvedt, Gala, and Kelkar 1988; and Sternbach et al. 1992.

10. However, feminists from the North who are well aware of diversity within the North may overlook diversity in the South. The best corrective for any tendency to homogenize is the learning that comes from active dialogue, networking, and practice. This is a point that Cynthia Enloe (1989) makes eloquently. Her detailed case studies show very clearly that women and feminists in the South are as diverse as in the North and that there is a First World in the Third World and a Third World in the First World.

11. "Contrary to assertions both within and outside the movement, feminism is not a homogeneous movement. It is this vast terrain of struggle and the heterogeneity of its form that makes feminism one of the most dynamic and powerful challenges to the status quo. It is also these same complexities that block the way to quick and lasting victories. . . .

    To accept the existence of class, race, ethnicity and generational differences among women and to devise multiple fronts of struggle in order to eliminate domination in any of its forms is what gives feminism its vitality." (AAWORD 1985, 1–3)

12. For additional statements about diverse women's shared oppression as women, see, for instance, Afshar 1993, 5; Antrobus 1983, 6; D'Souza 1992, 40; Jain 1978, 15.

13. The kind of awareness of interests shared with other women that leads to and sustains feminists' "disloyalty to civilization" and its structures of domination, even among relatively privileged women associated with men of ruling races and classes, is grounded in close feminist examination of women's own lives and experience. For it is particularly difficult for urban middle-class educated women, whose women identification has been blocked and whose access to female subcultures has been broken, to recognize the fragility of their own privilege, power, and status and face the fact that in a male-dominated society all these are conditional upon, derived from, and dependent on men. Adrienne Rich (1978a), Marilyn Frye (1983), and Minnie Bruce Pratt (1988) are three white lesbian radical feminists who have explored the ways in which women identification/feminist solidarity and a full understanding of their own interests enable as well as require racial disloyalty of white women. The U.S. Black feminists Pauli Murray (1970), Barbara Smith (1980), Michelle Russell (1981), and doris davenport (1983) are among the many feminists of color who challenge white feminists to recognize the interests they have in common with women of color.

14. "Women are caught in between two legitimacies: belonging to their people and loyalty to their female oppressed group. We are made to feel that protesting in the name of women's interests and rights is not to be done now. (It is never, has never been the right moment: not during the liberation struggle against colonialism, because all forces should be mobilised against the principal enemy: French colonialism; not after Independence, because all forces should be mobilised to build up the devastated country; not now that racist imperialist Western governments are attacking Islam and the Third World, etc.) Defending women's rights 'now' (this 'now being ANY historical moment) is always betrayal—of the people, of the nation, of the revolution, of Islam, of national identity, of cultural roots, of the Third World . . . according to the terminologies in use *hic et nunc*" (Hélie-Lucas 1987, 13).

15. Criticisms of traditional culture and/or current patriarchal interpretations of tradition abound in Third World feminist literature. See, for instance, Eteki 1990; Mernissi 1987; Omvedt, Gala and Kelkar 1988; Saadawi 1981; Savane 1985.

Chapter 7

1. See Bernard 1987; Leghorn and Parker 1981; Morgan 1984.
2. One letter to the editor of *Off Our Backs* (March 1991), for instance, seems to equate global feminism with the spread of NOW. Canadian feminists are only too aware that it is hard for U.S. feminists to escape the mainstream illusion that the United States is the center of the world. We have suffered from their tendency to conceptualize global/international feminism as simply the spread of U.S. feminism.

   Another form of ethnocentrism that Canadian women are as prone to as U.S. women is a misplaced belief in the propaganda that women in each of our nations are the most "liberated" women against whom other women's condition should be measured.
3. For examples of North American feminist literature reflecting global awareness see Anzaldúa 1990; Apthekar 1989; Bunch 1987; Cole 1986; Enloe 1989; hooks 1990; Jordan 1992; Kaye/Kantrowitz 1992; King 1989; Moraga 1993; Rich 1986; Walker 1983.
4. Third World feminists often comment on the more intact bonds among women in their own less "developed" parts of the world: "The feminist struggle in the West is to get women together, to get the bonding, and already in Africa we have the bonding, we have the structures, all we need to do is direct the power of these structures" (Stella Effua Graham from Ghana in Gevins 1985, 47).
5. See Christian 1985; Collins 1990; Lorde 1988; Walker 1983.
6. See Allen 1986; Chai and Cambra 1989; Green 1990; Hanlon 1992; Sanchez 1989; Trask 1984.
7. See Caldecott and Leland 1983; Diamond and Orenstein 1990; Harris and King 1989, Plant 1989.
8. See Anzaldúa 1987; Kaye/Kantrowitz and Lepfisz 1986; Morales and Morales 1986.
9. Some U.S. feminists with little international experience, for instance, were surprised and hurt to be challenged on U.S. government policies at the U.N. End of the Decade Conference in Nairobi in 1985. Other U.S. feminists at the Second International Interdisciplinary Congress on Women, in Groningen, Holland, in 1984 met unexpected challenges to their presumptions to be central. At the World Women's Congress for a Healthy Planet in November 1991 in Miami, as well, some U.S. women who had spent most of their adult lives struggling against U.S. government policies were surprised that their experience did not entitle them to leadership roles in workshops. They were personally offended when women from other countries resisted their playing these roles.
10. A certain amount of pain and confusion was experienced, for example, by African American women (many of them not feminists) at the Conference on Women in Africa and the African Diaspora in Nsukka, Nigeria, in July 1992. Third World-First World tensions among women of color are sometimes commented on by First World minority feminists in accounts of International gatherings. See, for instance, reports of the First Latin American Feminist Lesbian *Encuentro* (popp 1988) and the Asian Lesbian Network Conference (Rahim, Renay, and Matsuyama 1992).

    One crucial organizational challenge for the development of global feminisms is to find ways to build on the potential for solidarity among feminists of color across colonial divisions and at the same time protect the autonomy and equality of Third World voices and definitions in these relationships. This challenge is being faced in an immediate and ongoing way by groups such as DAWN (Development Alternatives with Women for a New Era), which is generating a lot of interest and a large following in the North, and CAFRA (Caribbean Association for Feminist Research and Action), which has a large and proportionately significant membership in the diaspora, as well as in such gatherings as the Latin American Feminist *Encuentros,* where Latin American women resident in South and North come together. Two exciting plenary sessions at the Fifth International Interdisciplinary Congress on Women in San José, Costa Rica, in February 1993 with diverse Black feminists from around the world provided an opportunity for dialogue around these and many other issues in public forums and intense discussions held in workshops, caucuses, and hallways.

11. One case in point was a poetry reading at the University of Toronto, where the Ghanaian feminist poet Ama Ata Aidoo challenged the self-definition of some Canadian feminists as "Third World feminists." This was the first time that many of us there had actually been in dialogue with a feminist from the Two-Thirds World. What we saw was an important political term that had been adopted by North American women of color to express their commitment to solidarity across their diversity being challenged as even broader dialogue and solidarities became possible.

    Aidoo also rejected being designated on the poster for the event as a "Third World" rather than African poet. She objected to the obliteration of her African identity and commitment in a general term that defined hugely diverse regions of the world only in their relation to the West (a point she has also made in a published interview [James 1990, 15]). The discussion of these points with a sister who, in turn, appreciated learning about the political context in North America and respected the particular imperatives of practice here was inspiring for the participants.

12. In an interview during a visit to Halifax, Nova Scotia, a few years ago Madhu Kishwar, founder of the Indian feminist journal *Manushi,* spoke about how difficult it is for feminists in India to find ways of supporting the struggle to reform Muslim law when so much communal hatred is directed by the dominant Hindu group against minority Muslims and much of the criticism of the law is fueled by anti-Muslim sentiment. The urgency of this challenge has increased since that time with the escalation of communal violence.

13. The political links between the North and the South in question here should be distinguished from "women and development" and "gender and development" initiatives, which tend to be contained within, rather than transcend, the "development" field and definitions.

    For an interesting description of one Canadian organization's shift toward more equal and more political relations with Third World women's groups, made possible by global feminist understandings, see Woroniuk and Lafrenière 1989.

14. Yifat Susskind states this clearly when she points out that solidarity with Women in Black is expressed more effectively through supporters' activism against the same forces in their own contexts than by standing with them in their vigils (1992/93, 9).

Chapter 8

1. For reports and comments on the U.N. Decade for Women and its conferences, see feminists from around the world in *Signs* 1981, 1986; AAWORD n.d.; Antrobus 1983, 1985; Bunch 1987; "Connexions" 1985; Pelletier 1985; Yudelman 1987.

2. My information about ISIS comes from ISIS publications and Davies 1987.

3. The quotations are from the International Women's Tribune Center's list of publications, published in October 1992. Contact the International Women's Tribune Center, 777 United Nations Plaza, New York, NY 10017. See also Dankelman and Davidson 1988.

4. "The Dakar Declaration on Another Development with Women" was published with a list of participants and a number of their presentations in *Development Dialogue* 1–2 (1982).

5. Information provided on DAWN comes from discussions and interviews with DAWN members and from DAWN publications. See also Davies 1987; Dankelman and Davidson 1988. DAWN has regional representatives in a number of locations around the world. The address of *DAWN Informs,* the network's newsletter is c/o Women and Development Unit, School of Continuing Studies, University of the West Indies, Pinelands, St. Michael, Barbados; tel. 809-426-9288/436-6312; fax. 809-426-3006.

6. Asian and Pacific feminist networks include Asia Pacific Forum on Women Law and Development Secretariat (APWLD), 9th Floor, AFDC Building, Persiaran Duta, P.O. Box 12224, Kuala Lumpur, Malaysia; Asian and Pacific Centre for Women and Development, Persiaran Duta, P.O. Box 12224, Kuala Lumpur, 50770, Malaysia; Asian and Pacific Women's Research and Action Network, P.O. Box 208, Davao City, 9501 Philippines; Research Centre for Asian Women Sook Myng Women's University, 53-12, 2-KA Shungpa-Dong, Yongsan-ku, Seoul, South Korea; Pacific and Asian Women's Forum (PAWF) 623/27 Rajagiriya Gardens, Rajagiriya, Sri Lanka; Committee for Asian Women (CAW), CCA-URM, 57 Peking Road, 5/F, Kowloon, Hong Kong.

7. For an account of the founding and development of AAWORD, see AAWORD 1981.

8. The CAFRA address is P.O. Box 442, Tunapuna Post Office, Tunapuna, Trinidad and Tobago; tel 809-662-1231/663-8670; fax 809-663-6482, attn. CAFRA.

9. For political analyses of all the *Encuentros* from 1981 to 1990, see Carillo 1990; Sternbach et al. 1992.

10. Israeli *Women in Black National Newsletters,* for instance, include letters from, and mention of, Women in Black groups in the United States, Canada, Italy, Yugoslavia, Holland, and Germany. Some of these groups have formed in support of peace in the Middle East; others are adopting the same symbolic form in their own struggles against the rise of fundamentalism in Germany, the war in ex-Yugoslavia, or communal violence in India.

11. Third World feminist support for attention to violence against women is just one of the many very real and immediate ways that growing feminist activism around the world is supporting our struggle in the North at a time when some of the most important early feminist insights about the oppression of all women *as women* and the interests women therefore potentially share across our deep divisions are being challenged.

12. Nicaraguan feminists I interviewed in 1991 described the space that had been opened up for autonomous feminist organizing since the Sandinista electoral defeat in February 1990 and the speed with which issues of violence had emerged. In speeches they gave in Toronto in 1992 about women's role in the process of reconciliation in El Salvador, Yanira Argueta, president of AMS (the El Salvadoran Women's Association), and Ana Lucia Martinez of ADEMUSA (the Association of El Salvadoran Women) named violence against women as one of the key issues women are raising. South African and Namibian feminists I met at the International Conference on Women in Africa and the African Diaspora in Nsukka, Nigeria, in July 1992 mentioned in conversation that intracommunal violence against women became an issue in mass women's organizations in both places as possibilities for political movement appeared.

13. Networking and organizing continues, in June 1988, for instance, the Somali Women's Democratic Organization (SWDO) hosted an international seminar in

Mogadishu, "Female Circumcision: Strategies to Bring About Change," with participants from Egypt, Nigeria, Sudan, The Gambia, Indonesia, Italy, Britain, and the United States (*Off Our Backs* 1988). See A'Haleem 1992; Koso-Thomas 1987.

14. Maria Mies (1989) illustrates the limits of a simple individual equality frame for feminist practice in some detail, with reference to the experience of North-South dialogue in FINRRAGE.

15. Addresses for the International Solidarity Network of Women Living under Muslim Laws are Central Coordination and Dossier Editorial Committee, Boite Postale 23, 34790 Grabels, France; Coordination for Asia, 18a, Mian Mir Road, Po Moghlapura, Lahore 15, Pakistan.

16. In providing a frame for connections among diverse women, WLUMLS is like the integrative North American groups the Welfare Warriors, the National Black Women's Health Project, and WHISPER. The shared identity/conditions of their members, too, is a basis for inclusive and broad outreach to otherwise extremely diverse women. Another even more marked and exciting development of this nature is the global and regional networking among indigenous women mentioned earlier in the chapter.

17. As Marie-Aimée Hélie-Lucas, a founding member of Women Living under Muslim Laws, explains, "Building up information and support networks within the Muslim world allows women at last to cut through . . . religion, traditions and the political use of both of them, together with the subsequent prohibition to question any aspect of the enforced lifestyle, without betraying country, community, religion and so on. It allows women at last to defend their rights without questioning their identity and their belonging to their community" (1993, 221).

18. A draft of the proposed "Convention on the Elimination of All Forms of Sexual Exploitation of Women" may be obtained from the Coalition against Trafficking in Women, P.O. Box 10077, Calder Square, State College, PA 16805. The Coalition's newsletter, *Coalition Report,* has accounts of the development of a preliminary draft of the "Convention" in meetings at the U.N. in October 1992 and of the discussion, amendment, and/or endorsement of the document at "La Conférence de Bruxelles —Commerce du sexe et droits humains" and the U.N.-sponsored Latin America and Caribbean, and at the Asia/Pacific Regional Preparatory Meetings for the Second U.N. Conference on Human Rights (fall 1992, spring 1993, and summer 1992).

19. The contact address for the petition is the Center for Women's Global Leadership, 27 Clifton College, New Brunswick, NJ 08903. It is sponsored by many church, business, and professional groups as well as feminist groups mentioned elsewhere in this book, such as ISIS, the International Women's Tribune Center; the Match International Centre; the Asia Pacific Forum on Women, Law, and Development; the Association of African Women for Research and Development; DAWN; Gabriela, the Philippines; the Arab Women's Solidarity Association, Egypt; and the Tanzanian Media Women's Association.

20. For two feminist films on the Global Tribunal on Violations of Women's Human Rights, see Anand 1994; Rogers 1994,

Chapter 9

1. Sweet Honey in the Rock, a U.S. Black feminist a cappella group, brings these hidden links to view in their song "Are My Hands Clean?" written by Berenice Johnson Reagan. (Songtalk Publishing Co., copyright 1985).

2. See Agarwal 1992; Allen 1986; Anand 1980; Antrobus 1985; Bandarage 1991; Bhasin 1990; Boulding 1980; Bunch and Carillo 1990; Dakar 1982; D'Souza 1992;

Franklin 1990; ISIS 1983; Leghorn and Parker 1981; Mies 1986; Mies and Shiva 1993; Mitter 1986; Moraga 1993; Oliviera and Corral 1992; Perpiñan 1993; Pietilä 1993; Sen and Grown 1987; Shiva 1989a, 1989b; Waring 1988.

3. I am using the term 'women's work' to refer to the enormous amount of diverse and changing subsistence work associated with women and done, with or without (low) pay, in dependent circumstances in hugely varied societies.

4. Early in this phase of feminism in North America, feminists drew powerful parallels between colonialism and women's oppression that served an important function in helping women see patriarchal oppression that was so pervasive and "naturalized" as to be almost invisible: for instance, men's ownership, control, and use of women's bodies and labor. They also used these parallels to counter the prevailing (even monolithic) opinion of the time that women's oppression was trivial and of an entirely different order from serious race, class, and colonial oppression.

   Not surprisingly, the exploration of the parallels and tensions between feminism and nationalism and patriarchy and colonialism was particularly rich in Quebec (Jean 1977, 5). However, the early arguments paralleling patriarchy and colonialism differ from those presented here, because they did not generally extend to an analysis of the common underlying historical dynamics of domination that actually reveals these oppressions and their causes and consequences to be linked aspects of the same process of "development."

5. The fact that the incorporation of women's knowledge and concerns into integrative feminist analysis is selective is very important. For integrative feminisms are not simply glorifying women's traditional knowledge and concerns but are using these as a basis from which to do the hard and challenging political work of constructing conscious feminist values and visions to inform and shape both resistance to dominant patriarchal forms and the struggle to establish new ones (Apthekar 1989, 183; Bhasin 1990, 25).

6. In the North, where women have been so effectively separated from each other and have lost most traditional women-defined spaces, the contribution of lesbian feminism to articulating women-to-women connections and bonding as well as carving out alternatives to cultural, social, sexual, and economic dependence on men has been formative. Paula Gunn Allen, Bettina Aptheker, and Cherríe Moraga are three authors who develop this theme extensively in their exploration of women-centered politics and perspectives

   The important positive political role of lesbian-feminist community and culture in North America continues to be denied by some nonintegrative feminists who see in it an abandonment of politics. See Taylor and Rupp 1993 for a detailed participant study of the Columbus, Ohio "women's community" that makes an effective counter to this criticism.

7. In conversation, Prema Gopalan of SPARC in Bombay made the point that among pavement dwellers who have nothing, women commonly play defining and leadership roles in their communities' struggles. Among squatters with only a few more resources, however, men have disproportionate power based on these resources, established political groupings are active, and women are marginalized. For an interesting description of the pavement dwellers' struggles and SPARC's relationship to them, see Bapat and Patel 1992.

8. For explicit repudiations of biological essentialism by feminists who call on women's specificity as a resource in transformative global struggle, see Agarwal 1992, 149–50; Bhasin 1990, 25; Mies and Shiva 1993, passim; Oliviera 1992, 71–73; Seager 1993, 269–70; Shiva 1989b, 38–39; Tauli-Corpuz 1992, 17–18.

9. For descriptions of women's struggles for community survival in the Two-Thirds

and First worlds, see Agarwal 1992; Anand 1980; Dankelman and Davidson 1988; Garland 1988; Mies and Shiva 1993; Shiva 1989a.

10. The following quotation from Judith Plant is typical in its implication that ecological concerns are unique to explicitly ecofeminist-defined politics and are, in a sense, an import to feminism from environmentalism: "Historically, women had no real power in the outside world, no place in decision-making and intellectual life. Today, however ecology speaks for the Earth, for the 'other' in human/environmental relationships; and feminism speaks for the 'other' in female/male relations. And ecofeminism, by speaking for *both* the original others, seeks to understand the interconnected roots of all domination as well as ways to resist and change. The ecofeminist's task is one of developing the ability to take the place of the other when considering the consequences of possible actions, and ensuring that we do not forget that we are all part of one another" (1989, 156).

Anne Cameron refuses to call her politics "ecofeminist" on the ground that "the term 'ecofeminism' suggests that the old 'feminism' was not at all concerned with ecology, could not have cared less about the environment, had no analysis of industrial exploitation, and ignored the need for peace" (1989, 63). The view that ecological concerns are integral to feminism is closer to most Third World, indigenous, and Black integrative-feminist views—and one that ecofeminists are increasingly coming to share.

11. See the sources listed in note 2.

12. See especially Enloe 1989; FINRRAGE 1989; Harris and King 1989; Kishwar and Vanita 1984; Morgan 1990; Schuler 1992; Women against Fundametalism 1990; Women Living under Muslim Laws n.d.

13. See, for instance, Allen 1986; Awekotuku 1982; Chai and Cambra 1989; Green 1990; Hanlon 1992; Sanchez 1989; Tauli-Corpuz 1992, 1993; Trask 1984.

14. The best single source of information about the World Women's Congress is the Official Report (World Women's Congress for a Healthy Planet 1992), from which all the quotations here are taken. It is available from World Women's Congress Report, c/o WEDO (Women's Environment and Development Organization), 845 Third Avenue, 15th floor, New York, NY 10022. Despite the almost deafening silence of mainstream media in North America about this important event, information can be found in the feminist press around the world.

BIBLIOGRAPHY

AAWORD. 1981. "The Experience of the Association of African Women for Research and Development (AAWORD): A Workshop Report Prepared for the High-Level Meeting on the Review of Technical Cooperation among Developing Countries," *Development Dialogue* 1, no. 2:101–13.

———. 1983. "A Statement on Genital Mutilation," in Davies 1983. 217–20. Originally issued in 1980.

———. n.d. *AAWORD in Nairobi '85*. Occasional Paper Series no. 3.

———. 1985. "Feminism in Africa," *ECHOE, AAWORD Newsletter* 2/3: 1–11.

Afshar, Haleh, ed. 1993. *Women in the Middle East: Perceptions, Realities and Struggles for Liberation*. London: Macmillan.

Agarwal, Bina. 1992. "The Gender and Environment Debate: Lessons from India," *Feminist Studies* 18, no. 1 (spring): 119–58.

A'Haleem, Asma Mohammed. 1992. "Claiming Our Bodies and Our Rights: Exploring Female Circumcision as an Act of Violence in Africa." In Schuler 1992. 141–56.

Ahmed, Leila. 1981. "What about 'The Rest of Us'?" *Women's Studies Quarterly* 9, no. 3 (fall): 16–17.

Alarcon, Norma. 1983. "Chicana's Feminist Literature: A Re-Visioning through malintzin/or Malintzin: Putting Flesh Back on the Object." In Moraga and Anzaldúa 1983. 182–90.

Albrecht, Lisa, and Rose M. Brewer, eds. 1990. *Bridges of Power: Women's Multicultural Alliances*. Philadelphia: New Society.

Alcoff, Linda. 1988. "Cultural Feminism versus Post-Structuralism: The Identity Crisis in Feminist Theory." *Signs* 13, no. 3 (spring):405–36.

Alemán, Verónica, Carla Miranda, and Tania Montenegro. 1993. "Women = Subjects = Power = Feminist Movement." *Barricada Internacional*, November/December, 17–24.

Al-Hibri, Azizah. 1981. "Capitalism is an Advanced Stage of Patriarchy: But Marxism Is Not Feminism." In Sargent 1981. 165–93.

Allen, Pamela. 1971. "Free Space." In Koedt, Levine, and Rapone 1973. 271–79.

Allen, Paula Gunn. 1986. *The Sacred Hoop*. Boston: Beacon Press.

Alloo, Fatma. 1988. "The Need for a Women's Magazine." *Sauti Ya Siti* no. 1 (March): 2, 23.

Amadiume, Ifi. 1987. *Male Daughters, Female Husbands: Gender and Sex in an African Society*. London: Zed.

Anand, Anita. 1980. "Rethinking Women and Development." In ISIS 1983. 5–11.

———. 1994. *Breaking the Silence*, a film about the Global Tribunal on Violations of Women's Human Rights, Women's Feature News Service, 49 Golf Links, New Delhi 110 003, India tel/fax 462-9886 fax 462-6699.

Angeles, Leonora Calderon. 1989. "Feminism and Nationalism. The Discourse on the Woman Question and Politics of the Women's Movement in the Philippines." Master's thesis, University of the Philippines.

Anonymous. 1985. "Wherefore African Feminism." *ECHOE, AAWORD Newsletter* 2/3: 7–8.

Antrobus, Peggy. 1983. "Equality, Development, and Peace: A Second Look at the Goals of the UN Decade for Women." Address to the Associated Country Women of the World, Vancouver, British Columbia, 18–29 June.

———. 1985. "Changes in the Status and Position of Women in the Last Decade: Pointers for the Future." *Women and Development: Beyond the Decade, Proceedings*. Conference Report, Guelph University, Ontario: 19–27.

———. 1989. "The Empowerment of Women." In *The Women and International Development Annual*, vol. I, ed. Rita S. Gallin, Marylyn Aronoff, and Ann Ferguson. Boulder, Colo.: Westview Press.

Anzaldúa, Gloria. 1983. "La Prieta." In Moraga and Anzaldúa 1983. 189–209.

———. 1987. *Borderlands/La Frontera: The New Mestiza*. San Francisco: Spinsters/Aunt Lute.

———, ed. 1990. *Making Face, Making Soul; Haciendo Caras: Creative and Critical Perspectives by Women of Color*, San Francisco: Aunt Lute.

Aptheker, Bettina. 1989. *Tapestries of Life: Women's Work, Women's Consciousness, and the Meaning of Daily Experience*. Amherst: University of Massachusetts Press.

Ascencio, Isabel. 1992. "Women: Challenging the Revolution in Latin America." *Challenge: Faith and Action in Central America* 3, no. 1 (spring): 1, 13.

Ashrawi, Hanan. 1992. "The Feminist behind the Spokeswoman—A Candid Talk with Hanan Ashrawi." *Ms.*, April, 14–17.

Asian Delegates from Berkeley. 1971. "Indochinese Women's Conference." *Asian Women* 1, no. 1. 77–80.

Asian Women. 1971. "Politics of the Interior." *Asian Women* 1, no. 1. 77–80.

Asian Women United of California, ed. 1989. *Making Waves: An Anthology of Writings by and about Asian-American Women*. Boston: Beacon Press.

Austin, Regina. 1989. "Sapphire Bound!" *Wisconsin Law Review* 3:539–78.

Avery, Byllye. 1990a. "Breathing Life into Ourselves: The Evolution of the National Black Women's Health Project." In White 1990.

———. 1990b. "Reproductive Rights and Coalition-Building." In Fried 1990. 307–8.

Awekotuku, Ngahuia Te. 1982. "He Wahine, He Whenua: Maori Women and the Environment." In Caldecott and Leland 1982. 136–40.

Awekotuku, Ngahuia Te, and Marilyn Waring. 1984. "New Zealand: Foreigners in Our Own Land." In Morgan 1984. 480–84.

Babcox, Deborah, and Madeline Belkin, eds. 1971. *Liberation Now*. New York: Dell.

Backhouse, Constance, and David H. Flaherty, eds. 1992. *Challenging Times: The Women's Movement in Canada and the United States.* Montreal: McGill-Queen's University Press.

Baffoun, Alya. 1985. "Future of Feminism in Africa." *ECHOE, AAWORD Newsletter* 2/3: 4–6.

Bandarage, Asoka. 1983. "Toward International Feminism." *Brandeis Review* 3. Cited in Bernard 1987. 34.

———. 1991. "In Search of a New World Order." *Women's Studies International Forum* 14, no. 4:345–55.

Bannerji, Himani, ed. 1993. *Returning the Gaze: Essays on Racism, Feminism, and Politics.* Toronto: Sister Vision Press.

Bapat, Meera, and Sheela Patel. 1992. "Beating a Path: Towards Defining Women's Participation." Unpublished paper, available from SPARC, P.O. Box 9389, Bhulabhai Dewai Road, Bombay, India.

Baron, Ava. 1987. "Feminist Legal Strategies: The Powers of Difference." In *Analyzing Gender: A Handbook of Social Science Research,* ed. Beth B. Hess and Myra Marx Ferrel. Newbury Park, Calif.: Sage. 474–503.

Barry, Kathleen. 1984. Introduction. *Female Sexual Slavery.* 2d ed. New York: New York University Press. xi–xiv.

———. 1990. "The New Historical Synthesis: Women's Biography." *Journal of Women's History* 1, no. 3 (winter): 75–105.

———. 1992. "Sexual Exploitation Violates Human Rights." *Coalition Report,* fall, 1–2.

Barry, Kathleen, Charlotte Bunch, and Shirley Castley, eds. 1984. *International Feminism: Networking against Female Sexual Slavery: Report of the Global Feminist Workshop to Organize against Traffic in Women, Rotterdam, the Netherlands, April 6–15, 1983.* New York: International Women's Tribune Center.

Bartlett, Elizabeth Ann. 1986. "Liberty, Equality, Sorority: Contradiction and Integrative Feminist Thought and Practice." *Women's Studies International Forum* 9, no. 5: 521–29.

Baxter, Sheila. 1988. *No Way to Live: Poor Women Speak.* Vancouver: New Star Books.

Beal, Frances M. 1969. "Double Jeopardy: To Be Black and Female." In Cooke and Bunch-Weeks 1971: 63–76; Cade 1970: 90–100; Morgan 1970: 340–53; Babcox and Belkin 1971: 185–97.

———. 1981. "Slave of a Slave No More: Black Women in Struggle." *Black Scholar,* December,16–24. Originally published in *Black Scholar* vol. 12, no. 6 (March 1975).

Beaucage, Marjorie. 1993. *Wings of the Same Bird.* Film available from CRIAW (Canadian Research Institute for the Advancement of Women), 152 Slater St., Ste. 408, Ottawa, Ontoario, K1P 5H3.

Beauvoir, Simone de. [1953] 1974. *The Second Sex.* New York: Alfred A. Knopf.

Beck, Evelyn Torton, ed. 1982. *Nice Jewish Girls: A Lesbian Anthology.* Trumansberg, N.Y.: Crossing Press.

Before You Turn Another Trick. . . . n.d. Pamphlet published by WHISPER.

Bell-Scott, Patricia, Beverly Guy-Sheftall, Jacqueline Jones Royster, Janet Sims-Wood, Miriam De Costa Willis, and Lucie Fultz, eds. 1991. *Double Stitch: Black Women Write about Mothers and Daughters.* Boston: Beacon Press.

Benhabib, Seyla, and Drucilla Cornell, eds. 1987. *Feminism as Critique: Essays on the Politics of Gender in Late Capitalist Societies.* Cambridge: Polity Press.

Benston, Margaret. 1969. "The Political Economy of Women's Liberation." *Monthly Review* 21, no. 4 (September): 13–27.

Bergman, Miranda, Susan Greene, Dina Redman, and Marlene Tobias. 1990. "Painting for Peace: Break the Silence Mural Project." *Bridges* 1, no. 2:39–57.

Bernard, Jessie. 1987. *The Female World from a Global Perspective*. Bloomington: Indiana University Press.

Bernstein, J., P. Morton, L. Seese, and M. Wood. 1972. "Sisters, Brothers, Lovers … Listen …" In Canadian Women's Educational Press 1972. 31–39.

Bersianik, Louky. 1976. *L'Euguélionne*. Montreal: La Presse.

Bhasin, Kamla. 1990. "Asian Women against Mal-development" (keynote address to the Third International Interdisciplinary Congress on Women, Dublin, Ireland, 1987). *Fenix* no. 00:22–26.

Bhasin, Kamla, and Nighat Said Khan. 1986. *Some Questions about Feminism and Its Relevance in South Asia*. New Delhi: Kali for Women Press.

Bhatt, Ela, and Veena Patel. 1986. "India: Self-Employed Women Workers." In Schuler 1986. 358–63.

Bhavnani, Kum-Kum. 1989. "Complexity, Activism, Optimism: An Interview with Angela Y. Davis." *Feminist Review* 31 (spring): 67–81.

Black Women's Collective. 1988. "Building a Global Movement: Black Women's Collective Statement, February 26, 1988." *Our Lives,* summer/fall, 10.

Black Women's Liberation Group, Mount Vernon, New York. 1970. "Statement on Birth Control." In Morgan 1970. 360–61.

Boulding, Elise. 1976. *The Underside of History: A View of Women through Time*. Boulder, Colo.: Westview Press.

———. 1980. "Integration into What? Reflections on Development Planning for Women." *Convergence* 13, nos. 1–2: 50–59.

Boyle, Christine L. M., Marie-Andrée Bertrand, Céline Lacert-Lamontagne, and Rebecca Shamai. 1985. *A Feminist Review of Criminal Law in Canada/Un examen féministe du droit criminel au Canada*. Status of Women Canada. Ottawa: Ministry of Supplies and Services.

Brant, Beth (Degonwadonti), ed. 1988. *A Gathering of Spirit: A Collection by North American Indian Women*. 3d ed. Toronto: Women's Press. Originally published in 1984 by Sinister Wisdom Books.

Brodeur, Violette, Suzanne G. Chartrand, Louise Corriveau, and Béatrice Valay. 1982. *Le mouvement des Femmes au Québec: Étude des groupes Montréalais et nationaux*. Montreal: Centrede formation populaire.

Brodribb, Somer. 1985. "Conference Report: Feminist International Network of Resistance to Reproductive and Genetic Engineering, Sweden, July 1985." *Resources for Feminist Research* 14, no. 3 (November): 54–55.

———. 1992. *Nothing Matters: A Feminist Critique of Postmodernism*. North Melbourne, Victoria: Spinifex Press. (PhD thesis University of Toronto 1988).

Brooke. 1975. "The Retreat to Cultural Feminism." In Redstockings 1975. 65–68.

Brossard, Nicole. 1976a. "Un mouvement de femmes?" *Les têtes de pioche* 1, no. 5 (September): 2.

———. 1976b. "La vie privée est politique." *Les têtes de pioche* 1, no. 1 (April): 1, 2.

———. 1977. *L'amèr ou Le chapitre effrité*. Montreal: Éditions Quinze. Trans. Barbara Godard. *These Our Mothers; or, The Disintegrating Chapter*. Toronto: Coach House Press, 1983.

———. 1978. "Libération de la femme/Mouvement des femmes." *Les têtes de pioche* 2, no. 9 (February); 3, no. 2 (March):2.

Brossard, Nicole, and Adrienne Rich. 1981. "Conscience lesbienne et littérature." *La vie en rose,* Octobre, 50–51.

Brown, Carol. 1981. "Mothers, Fathers, and Children: From Private to Public Patriarchy." In Sargent 1981. 239–68.

Brown, Rosemary. 1989. *Being Brown*. New York: Random House.

Bunch, Charlotte. 1970. "A Broom of One's Own." In Cooke and Bunch-Weeks 1971. 164–68.

———. 1975a. "Not for Lesbians Only." *Quest: A Feminist Quarterly* 2, no. 2: 50–56.

———. 1975b. "Self-Definition and Political Struggle." *Quest: A Feminist Quarterly* 1, no. 3 (winter): 2–15.

———. 1976. "Beyond Either/Or: Nonaligned Feminism." *Quest: A Feminist Quarterly* 3, no. 1 (summer): 3–15.

———. 1987. *Passionate Politics, Feminist Theory in Action: Essays, 1968–1986*. New York: St. Martin's Press.

———. 1993. "Organizing for Women's Human Rights Globally." In Kerr 1993. 141–94.

Bunch, Charlotte, and Roxanna Carrillo. 1990. "Feminist Perspectives on Women in Development." In *Persistent Inequalities*, ed. Irene Tinker. New York: Oxford University Press. 70–82.

Bunch, Charlotte, and Nancy Myron, eds. 1974. *Class and Feminism: A Collection of Essays from the Furies*. Baltimore, Md.: Diana Press.

Bunch, Charlotte, and Sandra Pollack, eds. 1983. *Learning Our Way: Essays in Feminist Education*. Trumansberg, N.Y.: Crossing Press.

Burke, Bev, and Marsha Sfeir, with Carolyn Lehmann. 1992. *As Women Together, Based on an Exchange among Women Working on the Issue of Violence against Women, 1987–1991*. Produced by Chile-Canadian Women Working Together to End Violence against Women. Available from Education Wife Assault, 427 Bloor St. West, Toronto, Ontario, Canada M5S 1X7.

Burris, Barbara. 1971. "The Fourth World Manifesto." In Koedt, Levine, and Rapone 1973. 322–57.

Busia, Abena P. A. 1989/90. "Silencing Sycorax: On African Colonial Discourse and the Unvoiced Female." *Cultural Critique* 14 (winter): 81–104.

Butler, Judith. 1990. "Gender Trouble: Feminist Theory and Psychoanalytic Discourse." In Nicholson 1990. 324–40.

Cade (Bambara), Toni, ed. 1970. *The Black Woman: An Anthology*. New York: New American Library.

CAFRA. 1990. "Caribbean Region." *Voices Rising*, October/November, 60.

Caldecott, Léonie, and Stephanie Leland, eds. 1983. *Reclaim the Earth: Women Speak Out for Life on Earth*. London: Women's Press.

Cameron, Anne. 1989. "First Mother and the Rainbow Children." In Plant 1989. 54–66.

Canaan, Andrea. 1983. "Browness." In Moraga and Anzaldúa 1983. 232–37.

Canadian Women's Educational Press, ed. 1972. *Women Unite!* Toronto: Canadian Women's Educational Press.

Carby, Hazel V. 1990. "The Politics of Difference." *Ms.*, September/October, 84–85.

Cardinal, Linda. 1992. "La recherche sur les femmes francophones vivant en milieu minoritaire: Un questionnement sur le féminisme." *Recherches féministes* 5, no. 1:5–29.

Carillo, Roxanna. 1990. "Feminist Alliances: A View from Peru." In Albrecht and Brewer 1990. 199–206.

Center for Women's Global Leadership 1991. *Gender Violence: A Development and Human Rights Issue*. New Brunswick, N.J.: Center for Women's Global Leadership.

Chai, Alice Yun, and Ho'oipo De Cambra. 1989. "Evolution of Global Feminism through Hawaiian Feminist Politics: The Case of Wai'anae Women's Support Group." *Women's Studies International Forum* 12, no. 1:59–64.

Cheng, Lucie. 1984. "Asian American Women and Feminism." *Sojourner* 10, no. 2 (October): 11–12.

Chicago, Judy. 1975. *Through the Flower: My Struggle as a Woman Artist.* New York: Doubleday.

Chisholm, Shirley. 1969. "Racism and Anti-feminism." *Black Scholar* 1 no. 1 (January/ February): 40–45.

Choderow, Nancy. 1978. *The Reproduction of Mothering: Psychoanalysis and the Sociology of Gender.* Berkeley: University of California Press.

Chow, Esther Ngan-Ling. 1987. "The Development of Feminist Consciousness among Asian American Women." *Gender and Society* 1, no. 3 (September): 284–99.

Christakos, Margaret. 1992. "The Craft that the Politics Requires: An Interview with June Jordan." *Fireweed* 36 (summer): 26–39.

Christian, Barbara. 1985. *Black Feminist Criticism: Perspectives on Black Women Writers.* New York: Pergamon Press. In Anzaldúa 1990. 335–345.

———. 1987. "The Race for Theory." *Cultural Critique* 6:51–53.

Christiansen-Ruffman, Linda. 1982. "Women's Political Culture and Feminist Political Culture." Paper given at the Tenth World Congress of Sociology, Mexico City (August 16–21).

Clark, Lorenne. 1976. "Politics and Law: The Theory and Practice of the Ideology of Male Supremacy." In Shea and King-Farlow 1976. 49–65.

Clarke, Cheryl. 1983a. "The Failure to Transform: Homophobia in the Black Community." In Smith 1983. 197–208.

———. 1983b. "Lesbianism: An Act of Resistance." In Moraga and Anzaldúa 1983. 128–137.

Cliff, Michelle. 1980. *Claiming an Identity They Taught Me to Despise.* Watertown, Mass.: Persephone Press.

Clio Collective (Micheline Dumont, Michelle Jean, Marie Lavigne, and Jennifer Stoddart). 1987. *Quebec Women: A History.* Toronto: Women's Press.

Coalition against Trafficking in Women. 1992. "Elements of a New U.N. Convention to Eliminate all Forms of Sexual Exploitation," *Coalition Report* (fall): 3.

———. 1993. "Convention on the Elimination of All Forms of Sexual Exploitation of Women: A Proposal for a New Convention."

Cohen, Leah and Constance Backhouse. 1980. "Putting Rape in Its (Legal) Place." *Macleans*, 30 June, 6.

Cohen, Yolande, ed. 1981. *Femmes et politique.* Montreal: Le Jour.

Cole, Johnneta B., ed. 1986. *All American Women: Lines That Divide, Ties That Bind*, New York: Free Press.

Collins, Patricia Hill. 1990. *Black Feminist Thought: Knowledge, Consciousness, and the Politics of Empowerment.* Boston: Unwin Hyman.

Combahee River Collective. 1977. "A Black Feminist Statement." In Eisenstein 1979. 259–91.

Commonwealth Women's Network. 1991. *Background Research Studies.* Toronto: Commonwealth Women's Network.

Confederation of National Trade Unions. 1972. *Quebec Labour.* Montreal: Black Rose Books.

Connexions. 1985. "Forum '85, Nairobi, Kenya." Special issue of *Connexions* 17–18 (summer/fall).

Cooke, Joanne, and Charlotte Bunch-Weeks, eds. 1971. *The New Woman: A Motive Anthology on Women's Liberation.* Indianapolis: Bobbs-Merrill.

Cornell, Drucilla. 1991. *Beyond Accommodation: Ethical Feminism, Deconstruction, and the Law.* New York: Routledge.

Dakar. 1982. "The Dakar Declaration on Another Development with Women." *Development Dialogue* 1, no. 2:11–16.

Dalla Costa, Maria Rosa, and Selma James. 1972. *The Power of Women and the Subversion of the Community*. Bristol, England: Falling Wall Press.

———. 1973. "Rencontre avec deux féministes marxistes." *Québecoises deboutte* 1, no. 6 (June): 26–39.

Dankelman, Irene, and Joan Davidson. 1988. *Women and Environment in the Third World: Alliance for the Future*. London: Earthscan Publications.

Das, Shima. 1991. "Women with Diverse Designs: Feminism from the Perspective of Real Experiences of Women in Bangladesh." *CRIAW Newsletter* 12, no. 1 (winter): 15–17.

davenport, doris. 1983. "The Pathology of Racism: A Conversation with Third World Wimmen." In Moraga and Anzaldúa 1983. 85–99.

Davies, Miranda, ed. 1983. *Third World, Second Sex: Women's Struggles and National Liberation*, vol. 1. London: Zed.

———. 1987. *Third World, Second Sex: Women's Struggles and National Liberation*, vol. 2. London: Zed.

Davis, Angela. 1971 "Reflections on the Black Woman's Role in the Community of Slaves." *Black Scholar* 3, no. 4 (December): 2–15.

Davis, Angela Y. 1990. "Sick and Tired of Being Sick and Tired: The Politics of Black Women's Health." In White 1990. 18–26.

Davis, Elizabeth Gould. 1972. *The First Sex*. Harmondsworth, England: Penguin.

Delphy, Christine. 1992. "Mothers' Union?" *Trouble and Strife* 24 (summer): 12–19.

Deming, Barbara. 1977. "Remembering Who We Are." *Quest: A Feminist Quarterly* 4, no. 1 (summer): 52–74.

Densmore, Dana. 1971. "On Celibacy." In Tanner 1971. 264–68.

Diamond, Irene, and Gloria Feman Orenstein, eds. 1990. *Reweaving the World: The Emergence of Ecofeminism*. San Francisco: Sierra Club Books.

Dill, Bonnie Thornton. 1983. "Race, Class, and Gender: Prospects of an All-Inclusive Sisterhood." *Feminist Studies* 9, no. 1 (spring): 131–50.

Dinnerstein, Dorothy. 1977. *The Mermaid and the Minotaur: Sexual Arrangements and Human Malaise*. New York: Harper and Row.

Di Stefano, Christine. 1988. "Dilemmas of Difference: Feminism, Modernity, and Postmodernism." *Women and Politics* 8, no. 3:1–24.

Dixon, Marlene. 1971. "Restless Eagles: Women's Liberation in 1969." In Cooke and Bunch-Weeks 1971. 32–42.

———. 1975. "Women's Liberation: Opening Chapter Two." *Canadian Dimension* 10, no. 8:56–68.

Doucette, Joanne. 1986. "An Open Letter from the DisAbled Women's Network, D.A.W.N. Toronto to the Women's Movement." D.A.W.N. Toronto, Ste 210, 180 Dundes St. West, Toronto, Ontario M5G 1Z8, Canada; tel. 416-598-2438.

———. 1991. "The Disabled Women's Network: A Fragile Success." In Wine and Ristock 1991. 221–35.

Douglas, Carol Anne. 1990. *Love and Politics: Radical Feminist and Lesbian Theories*. San Francisco: ism press.

Driedger, Diane, and Susan Gray, eds. 1992. *Imprinting Our Image: An International Anthology by Women with Disabilities*. Charlottetown, P.E.I.: Gynergy Books.

D'Souza, Corinne Kumar. 1992. "The South Wind." In Oliviera and Corral 1992. 24–53.

DuBois, Ellen Carol, and Vicki L. Ruiz, eds. 1990. *Unequal Sisters: A Multicultural Reader in U.S. Women's History*. New York: Routledge.

Dulude, Louise. 1984. *Love, Marriage, and Money: An Analysis of the Financial Relationships between the Spouses*. Ottawa: Canadian Advisory Council on the Status of Women.

Dumais, Monique. 1983. *La mère dans la société québecoise. Étude éthique d'un modèle à partir de deux journaux féministes: La bonne parole (1913–58) et Les têtes de pioche (1976–79)*. The CRIAW Papers/Les documents de l'ICRAF, No. 5. Ottawa: Canadian Research Institute for the Advancement of Women.

Dumont, Micheline. 1992. "The Origins of the Women's Movement in Quebec." In Backhouse and Flaherty 1992. 72–89.

Dworkin, Andrea. 1974. *Woman Hating*. New York: Dutton.

———. 1976. *Our Blood: Prophecies and Discourses on Sexual Politics*. New York: Wideview/Perigree Books.

———. 1977. "Biological Superiority: The World's Most Dangerous and Deadly Idea." In Dworkin 1989. 110–16.

———. 1989. *Letters from the War Zone: Writing, 1976–1989*. New York: Dutton.

Echols, Alice. 1983. "The New Feminism of Yin and Yang." In Snitow, Stansell, and Thompson1983. 439–59.

———. 1989. *Daring to Be Bad: A History of the Radical Feminist Movement in America, 1967–1975*. Minneapolis: University of Minnesota Press.

Ehrenreich, Barbara, and Deirdre English. 1973. *Witches, Midwives, and Nurses: A History of Women Healers*. Green Mountain Pamphlet no. 1. Old Westbury, N.Y.: The Feminist Press.

———. 1979. *For Her Own Good: 150 Years of the Experts' Advice to Women*. New York: Anchor Press/Doubleday.

Eisenstein, Hester. 1983. *Contemporary Feminist Thought*, Boston: Hall.

Eisenstein, Hester and Alice Jardine, eds. 1980. *The Future of Difference*. New Brunswick, N.J.: Rutgers University Press.

Eisenstein, Zillah R, ed. 1979. *Capitalist Patriarchy and the Case for Socialist Feminism*. New York: Monthly Review Press.

Elshtain, Jean Bethke. 1979. "Feminists against the Family." *Nation* 17 November, 1979, 496–500.

Enloe, Cynthia H. 1989. *Bananas, Beaches, and Bases: Making Feminist Sense of International Politics*. London: Pandora.

Eteki, Marie Louise. 1990. "Feminism and Democracy in Africa." *Match News* 14, no. 1 (fall): 1, 3, 4.

Evans, Sara M. 1979. *Personal Politics: The Roots of Women's Liberation in the Civil Rights Movement and the New Left*. New York: Vintage.

———. 1989. *Born for Liberty: A History of Women in America*. New York: Free Press.

Evans, Sara M., and Barbara Nelson. 1989. *Wage Justice: Comparable Worth and the Paradox of Technocratic Reform*. Chicago: University of Chicago Press.

Fallis, Guadelupe Valdés. 1974. "The Liberated Chicana—A Struggle against Tradition." *Women: A Journal of Liberation* 3, no. 4:20–21.

Federici, Sylvia. 1975. *Wages against Housework*. Bristol, England: Falling Wall Press.

Ferguson, Ann, and Nancy Folbre. 1981. "The Unhappy Marriage of Patriarchy and Capitalism." In Sargent 1981. 313–38.

Ferree, Myra Marx, and Patricia Yancy Martin, eds. 1994. *Feminist Organizations: Harvest of the New Women's Movement*. Philadelphia: Temple University Press.

Finley, Lucinda M. 1986. "Transcending Equality Theory: A Way Out of the Maternity and the Workplace Debate." *Columbia Law Review* 86, no. 6 (October): 1118–83.

FINRRAGE. 1989. "Declaration of Comilla." *Resources for Feminist Research* 18, no. 3 (September): 84–86.

Firestone, Shulamith. 1970. *The Dialectic of Sex*. New York: Morrow.

Fisher, Elizabeth. 1979. *Women's Creation*. Garden City, N.Y.: Anchor Doubleday.

Flax, Jane. 1990. "Postmodernism and Gender Relations in Feminist Theory." In Nicholson 1990. 39–62.

Ford-Smith, Honor. 1986. "Sistren: Exploring Women's Problems through Drama." *Jamaica Journal* 19, no. 1 (February–April): 2–12.

Franklin, Ursula. 1990. *The Real World of Technology*. Toronto: CBC Enterprises.

Freeman, Jo. 1975. *The Politics of Women's Liberation: A Case Study of an Emerging Social Movement and Its Relation to the Policy Process*. New York: David McKay.

Fried, Marlene Gerber, ed. 1990. *From Abortion to Reproductive Freedom: Transforming a Movement*. Boston, Mass.: South End Press.

Friedan, Betty. 1963. *The Feminine Mystique*. New York: Norton.

———. 1981. *The Second Stage*. London: Michael Joseph.

Front de Libération des Femmes. 1971. "Bulletin de Liaison No. 2, Août 1971." In O'Leary and Toupin 1981. 107–21.

Frye, Marilyn. 1983. "On Being White: Toward a Feminist Understanding of Race and Race Supremacy." In *The Politics of Reality: Essays in Feminist Theory*. Trumansberg, N.Y.: Crossing Press: 110–27.

Fuss, Diana. 1989. *Essentially Speaking: Feminism, Nature, and Difference*. New York: Routledge.

Gagnon, Madeleine. 1977. "Mon corps dans l'écriture." In *La venue à l'écriture*, Paris: Editions 10/18. Excerpts are translated in Miles and Finn 1989: 269–282.

Gandhi, Nandita, and Vasantha Kannabiran. 1989. "Feminism." In South Asian Workshop on Women and Development 1989. 12–15.

Garcia, Alma M. 1990. "The Development of Chicana Feminist Discourse, 1970–1980." In DuBois and Ruiz 1990. 418–431.

Garland, Anne Witte. 1988. *Women Activists Challenging the Abuse of Power*. New York: Feminist Press.

Gevins, Adi. 1985. "Tackling Tradition: Interview with Assitan Diallo (Mali) and Stella Efua Graham (Ghana)." *Connexions* 17/18 (summer/fall). 45–47.

Giddings, Paula. 1984. *When and Where I Enter: The Impact of Black Women on Race and Sex in America*. New York: Morrow.

Gilligan, Carol. 1982. *In a Different Voice: Psychological Theory and Women's Development*. Cambridge, Mass.: Harvard University Press.

Goldberg, Sharon. 1991. "Let Women Speak Their Diversity! An Interview with Charlotte Bunch." *Women's Education des femmes* 8, nos. 3–4 (winter): 22–26.

Gomes, Teresa Santa Clara. 1992. "A Feminine Utopia." In Oliviera and Corral 1992. 84–91.

Gordon, Linda. 1986. "What's New in Women's History?" In Lauretis 1986. 20–30.

———. 1990. Review of *Gender and the Politics of History* by Joan Wallach Scott. *Signs* 15, no. 4 (summer): 853–60.

Gowens, Pat. 1993. "Welfare Warriors." *Equal Means* 7, no. 4 (winter): 33.

Green, Rayna. 1990. "American Indian Women: Diverse Leadership for Social Change." In Albrecht and Brewer 1990. 52–64.

Griffin, Susan. 1978. *Woman and Nature: The Roaring Inside Her*. New York: Harper and Row.

Un groupe de femmes de Montréal. 1971. *Manifeste des femmes québecoises*. Montreal: La Maison Réédition-Québec.

Gupta, Nila, and Makeda Silvera, eds. 1989. *The Issue is 'Ism: Women of Colour Speak Out*. Toronto: Sister Vision (Black and Women of Colour Press).

H., Pamela. 1989. "Asian-American Lesbians: An Emerging Voice in the AsianAmerican Community." *Asian Women United of California* 1989. 282–90.

Hamilton, Sylvia, and Claire Prieto. 1989. "Black Mother, Black Daughter." Film by the National Film Board of Canada, Ottawa.

Hanlon, Gail. 1992. "Supporting Our Front-Line Struggles: An Interview with Winona LaDuke about *Indigenous Woman* Magazine." *Woman of Power* 21 (fall): 75–77.

Haraway, Donna J. 1990. "A Manifesto for Cyborgs: Science, Technology, and Socialist Feminism in the 1980s." In Nicholson 1990. 190–233.

Harding, Sandra. 1981. "What Is the Real Material Base of Patriarchy and Capital?" In Sargent 1981. 135–164.

Harding, Sandra, and Merrill B. Hintikka. 1983. *Discovering Reality: Feminist Perspectives on Epistemology, Metaphysics, Methodology, and Philosophy of Science.* Dordrecht: D. Reidel.

Harris, Adrienne and Ynestra King, eds. 1989. *Rocking the Ship of State: Toward a Feminist Peace Politics.* Boulder, Colo.: Westview Press.

Harris, Pamela. 1992. *Faces of Feminism.* Toronto: Second Story Press.

Hartsock, Nancy. 1983. *Money, Sex, and Power: Toward a Feminist Historical Materialism.* New York: Longman.

Hawksworth, Mary E. 1989. "Knowers, Knowing, Known: Feminist Theory and Claims of Truth." *Signs* 14, no. 3 (spring): 533–57.

Hélie-Lucas, Marie-Aimée. 1987. "Bound and Gagged by the Family Code." In Davies 1987. 3–15.

———. 1993. "Women's Struggles and Strategies in the Rise of Fundamentalism in the Muslim World: From Entryism to Internationalism." In Afshar 1993. 206–42.

Hénaut, Dorothy Todd. 1986. *Fireworks.* Film made for Studio D of the National Film Board of Canada, Ottawa.

Heyward, Carter. 1989. *Touching Our Strength: The Erotic as Power and the Love of God.* San Francisco: Harper and Row.

hinden, roanne. 1991. "Forging Alliances across the Color Line." *Off Our Backs: A Women's Newsjournal* 12, no. 1:21.

Ho, Chi-Kwan A. 1990. "Opportunities and Challenges: The Role of Feminists for Social Change in Hong Kong." In Albrecht and Brewer 1990. 182–98.

Hole, Judith, and Edith Levine. 1971. *The Rebirth of Feminism.* New York: Quadrangle Books.

hooks, bell. 1984. *Feminist Theory from Margin to Center.* Boston: South End Press.

———. 1990. *Yearning: Race, Gender, and Cultural Politics,.* Toronto: Between the Lines.

———. 1993. "Seduced by Violence No More: By Shaping Our Eroticism, We Oppose Rape Culture." *Z Magazine,* November, 20–21.

Hosken, Fran. 1978/79. "WIN—Women's International Network News." *ISIS International Bulletin* 10 (winter): 38.

Hull, Gloria, Patricia Bell-Scott, and Barbara Smith, eds. 1982. *All the Women Are White, All the Blacks are Men, but Some of Us Are Brave: Black Women's Studies.* Old Westbury, N.Y.: Feminist Press.

Ibrahim, Fatima. 1992. "Sudanese Sisterhood." *Trouble and Strife,* winter, 32–35.

Ignagni, Esther, Deb Parent, Yvette Perreault, and Ana Willats (Toronto Rape Crisis Centre–Working Class Caucus). 1988. "Around the Kitchen Table." *Fireweed* 26 (winter/spring): 69–81.

ISIS ed. 1983. *Women in Development, A Resource Guide for Organization and Action.* Rome and Geneva: ISIS International.

Jackson, Stevi. 1992. "the amazing deconstructing woman." *Trouble and Strife,* winter, 25–31.

Jaggar, Alison. 1983. *Feminist Politics and Human Nature*. Totowa, N.J.: Rowman and Allanheld.

Jain, Devaki. 1978. "Can Feminism Be a Global Ideology?" *Quest: A Feminisst Quarterly* 4, no. 2 (winter): 9–15.

James, Adeola, ed. 1990. *In Their Own Voices: African Women Writers Talk*. London: James Currey.

Janeway, Elizabeth. 1974. *Between Myth and Morning: Women Awakening*. New York: Morrow.

———. 1976. "Opening Remarks." *The Scholar and the Feminist III: The Search for Origins*. Conference sponsored by Barnard College Women's Center, 23 April, 1977. Barnard College Women's Center 9–12.

Jayawardena, Kumari. n.d. *Feminism in Sri Lanka, 1975–1985*. Reprinted by NY: Women's International Resource Exchange (WIRE) Service.

Jean, Michèle. 1977. "Québecitude ou féminitude?" *Les têtes de pioche* 1, no. 9 (February): 5, 7.

Jean, Michèle, and France Théoret. 1976. "Le matriarcat québecois: Analyse par les Reines du Foyer." *Les têtes de pioche* 1, no. 1 (March): 1, 3, 8.

Jenness, Linda ed. 1972. *Feminism and Socialism*. New York: Pathfinders Press.

Jordan, June. 1977. "Second Thoughts of a Black Feminist." *Ms.*, February, 113–115.

———. 1992. *Technical Difficulties: African American Notes on the State of the Union*. New York: Pantheon.

Juteau, Danielle. 1990. "From Fragmentation to Unity: Articulating the Social Relations Which Produce 'Race,' 'Sex,' and 'Class.'" Paper given to the International Sociological Association, Madrid.

Juteau-Lee, Danielle. 1983. "La production de l'éthnicité ou La part réelle de l'idéel." *Sociologie et sociétés* 15, no. 2:39–55.

Kakwenzire, Joan. 1991. "Women and Human Rights in Uganda,." *Arise,* (April–June), 12–15.

Kalemara, Rose. 1988. "On a Feminist Crusade: Interview with Nawal El Sadaawi." *Sauti Ya Siti* No. 1 (March): 16–17.

Kaye/Kantrowitz, Melanie. 1992. *The Issue Is Power: Essays on Women, Jews, Violence, and Resistance*. San Francisco: Aunt Lute.

Kaye/Kantrowitz, Melanie, and Irene Lepfisz, eds. 1986. *Tribe of Dina: A Jewish Women's Anthology*. Montpelier, Vt.: Sinister Wisdom Press.

Kelly, Liz. 1991. "Unspeakable Acts." *Trouble and Strife* 21 (summer): 13–20.

Kelly, Petra. 1989. "Introduction." In Plant 1989. ix–xi.

Kelly-Gadol, Joan. 1976. "The Social Relations of the Sexes: Methodological Implications of Women's History." *Signs* 1, no. 4 (summer): 809–23.

Kerr, Joanna, ed. 1993. *Ours by Right: Women's Rights as Human Rights*. London: Zed Press with the North-South Institute.

Keysers, Loes. 1985. "International Women and Health Meeting No. IV, Women's International Tribunal and Meeting on Reproductive Rights, July 22–28, 1984, Amsterdam." *Sisterhood Newsletter: Divided in Culture/United in Struggle* 3 (March): 26–31.

Kihoro, Wanjiru. 1992. "Now *listen* to *me!*" *New Internationalist*, January, 20–21.

King, Ynestra. 1981. "Feminism and the Revolt of Nature." *Heresies* 13 (fall): 12–16.

———. 1989. "The Ecology of Feminism and the Feminism of Ecology." In Plant 1989. 18–28.

Kingston, Maxine Hong. 1977. *The Woman Warrior: Memories of a Girlhood among Ghosts*. New York: Random House, Vintage.

Kishwar, Madhu, and Ruth Vanita, eds. 1984. *In Search of Answers: Indian Women's Voices from* Manushi. London: Zed.

Koedt, Anne. 1973. "The Myth of the Vaginal Orgasm." In Koedt, Levine, and Rapone 1973. 198–207.

Koedt, Anne, Ellen Levine, and Anita Rapone, eds. 1973. *Radical Feminism.* New York: Quadrangle.

Koso-Thomas, Olayinka. 1987. *The Circumcision of Women: A Strategy for Eradication.* London: Zed.

LaChapelle, Caroline. 1982. "Beyond Barriers: Native Women and the Women's Movement." In *Still Ain't Satisfied: Canadian Feminism Today,* ed.Maureen Fitzgerald, Connie Guberman, and Margie Wolfe. Toronto: Women's Press.

Lahey, Kathleen A. 1989. "Celebration and Struggle: Feminism and the Law." In Miles and Finn 1989. 203–31.

Lamoureaux, Diane. 1986. *Fragments et collages: Essai sur le féminisme québecois des années '70.* Montreal: Les Éditions du Remue-Ménage.

Latinamerican Coalition to End Violence against Women and Children. 1992. *Working toward the Eradication of Violence in the Latinamerican Community.* Report published by the Latinamerican Coalition.

Lauretis, Teresa de. 1989. "The Essence of the Triangle; or, Taking the Risk of Essentialism Seriously: Feminist Theory in Italy, the U.S., and Britain." *Differences* 1, no. 2 (summer): 3–37.

———, ed. 1986. *Feminist Studies/Critical Studies.* Bloomington: Indiana University Press.

Lazarre, Jane. 1976. *The Motherknot.* New York: McGraw Hill.

Lazreg, Marnia. 1988. "Feminism and Difference: The Perils of Writing as a Woman on Women in Algeria." *Feminist Studies* 14:81–107.

Lecavalier, Nicole, Louise Laprade, and Pol Pelletier. 1978. *À ma mère, à ma mère, à ma mère, à ma voisine.* Montreal: Théatre Expérimental des Femmes.

Lederer, Laura, ed. 1980. *Take Back the Night: Women on Pornography.* New York: Morrow.

Leghorn, Lisa and Katherine Parker. 1981. *Woman's Worth: Sexual Economics and the World of Women.* London: Routledge.

Lehmann, Carolyn. 1987. "Casa Sofia: Where Wisdom and Friendship Dwell." *Woman of Power* 7 (summer): 10–12, 70.

Leidholdt, Dorchen and Janice G. Raymond, eds. 1990. *The Sexual Liberals and the Attack on Feminism.* New York: Pergamon.

Leon, Barbara. 1975. "Consequences of the Conditioning Line." In Redstockings 1975. 54–58.

Lewin, Ellen. 1977. "Feminism in Nursing." *Catalyst* 10/11:78–103.

Lopez, Sonia A. 1977. "The Role of the Chicana within the Student Movement." In *Essays on La Mujer,* ed. Rosaura Sánchez and Rosa Martinez Cruz. Los Angeles: Chicano Studies Center Publications, University of California. 16–29.

Lorde, Audre. 1978. "The Uses of the Erotic: The Erotic as Power." In Lorde 1984. 53–59.

———. 1982. "On a Night of the Full Moon." In Audre Lorde *Chosen Poems, Old and New.* New York: W. W. Norton & Co.: 20–21.

———. 1984. *Sister Outsider: Essays and Speeches by Audre Lorde,* Trumansberg, N.Y.: Crossing Press.

———. 1988. *A Burst of Light: Essays by Audre Lorde.* Ithaca, N.Y.: Firebrand Books.

Des luttes et des rires de femmes. 1979. "Religion sans indulgence." Special issue of *Des luttes et des rires de femmes* 12, no. 3 (February–March).

Maathai, Wangari. 1988. *The Green Belt Movement: Sharing the Approach and the Experience*. Nairobi, Kenya: Environment Liaison Centre International.

MacDonald, Eleanor. 1991. "The Trouble with Subjects: Feminism, Marxism, and the Questions of Poststructuralism." *Studies in Political Economy* 35 (winter): 43–71.

MacDonald, Ingrid. 1991. "We'll Deconstruct When They Deconstruct." *Resources for Feminist Research* 19, nos. 3–4 (September–December): 89–90.

MacKinnon, Catharine A. 1979. *Sexual Harassment of Working Women*. New Haven: Yale University Press.

———. 1983. "The Male Ideology of Privacy: A Feminist Perspective on Abortion." *Radical America* 17, no. 4 (July/August): 23–25.

———. 1991. "From Practice to Theory; or, What Is a White Woman Anyway?" *Yale Journal of Law and Feminism* 4, no. 4 (fall): 13–22.

Madre. 1992. Programme of the Mother Courage Peace Tour, self-published, no page numbers.

Madre. 1993. Programme of Mother Courage Peace Tour II, self-published, no page numbers.

Mainardi, Pat. 1970. "The Politics of Housework." In Tanner 1971. 336–42.

Mammandaran, Ngacobi. 1993. "Conference on African Women in Europe." *African World Review,* May–October), 46.

Mani, Lata. 1990. "Multiple Mediations: Feminist Scholarship in the Age of Multinational Reception." *Feminist Review* 35 (summer): 24–41.

Manushi. 1979. "Women's Politics: We Shall Re-examine Everything." Editorial from the inaugural issue of *Manushi* (January) in Kishwar and Vanita 1984. 242–45.

Maracle, Lee. 1988. *I Am Woman*. North Vancouver: Write-On Press.

Marks, Elaine. 1984. "Feminism's Wake." *Boundary* 2, no. 12 (winter): 99–110.

Martin, Biddy, and Chandra Talpede Mohanty. 1986. "Feminist Politics: What's Home Got to Do with It?" In Lauretis 1986. 191–212.

Match. 1992. "La Quinta Mesa (The Fifth Panel): A Victory for Salvadoran Women." *Match News: News about Women and Development* 16, no. 1 (summer) 4.

———. 1993a. "Editorial," *Match News: News about Women and Development* 16, no. 2 (fall): 1.

———. 1993b. "The Power of Thousands of Voices (Vienna, Austria): Report on the Second World Conference on Human Rights, June 1993." *Match News: News about Women and Development* 18, no. 1 (fall): 1, 2.

Match International Centre. 1990. *Linking Women's Global Struggles to End Violence*. Ottawa: Match.

Matthews, Nancy A. 1989. "Surmounting a Legacy: The Expansion of Racial Diversity in a Local Anti-Rape Movement." *Gender and Society* 3, no. 4 (December): 518–32.

Mayne, Anne and Rachel Wingfield. 1993. "Women Hurt in Systems of Prostitution" (an interview with Evelina Giobbe). *Trouble and Strife* 26 (summer): 22–30.

Mbilinyi, Marjorie and Ruth Meena, eds. 1991. "Reports from Four Women's Groups in Africa." *Signs* 16, no. 4 (summer): 846–69.

McFadden, Maggie. 1984. "Anatomy of Difference: Toward a Classification of Feminist Theory." *Women's Studies International Forum* 7, no. 6:495–504.

McIvor, Sharon. 1992. "Native Women's Association of Canada: McIvor Lays It Out." *Kinesis*, November.

Mehlman, Terrie, Debbie Swanner, and Midge Quant. 1984. "Obliteration as a Feminist Issue: A position paper by the Radical Feminist Organizing Committee." *Off Our Backs: A Women's Newsjournal* 14, no. 3 (March): 16, 17, 25.

Menkel-Meadows, Carrie. 1991. "Review of *Toward a Feminist Theory of the State* by Catharine A. MacKinnon and *Justice and Gender*by Deborah L. Rhode," *Signs* 16, no 3 (spring): 603–6.

Mernissi, Fatima. 1987. *Women and Islam: An Historical and Theological Enquiry.* Oxford, England: Basil Blackwell.

Mies, Maria. 1986. *Patriarchy and Accumulation on a World Scale: Women in the International Division of Labour.* London: Zed.

———. 1989. "Self-Determination: The End of Utopia?" *Resources for Feminist Research* 18, no. 3: 51–56.

———. 1992. "The Global Is the Local." In Oliviera and Corral 1992. 54–68.

Mies, Maria and Vandana Shiva. 1993. *Ecofeminism.* London: Zed.

Miles, Angela. 1985. "Feminism, Equality, and Liberation." *Canadian Journal of Women and the Law* 1, no. 1: 42–68.

———. 1991. "Reflections on Integrative Feminism and Rural Women: The Case of Antigonish Town and County." In Wine and Ristock. 1991. 56–74.

Miles, Angela and Geraldine Finn, eds. 1989. *Feminism: From Pressure to Politics.* (2d expanded ed. of *Feminism in Canada* 1982). Montreal: Black Rose Books.

Miller, Jean Baker. 1976. *Toward a New Psychology of Women.* Boston: Beacon Press.

Miller, Nancy. 1986. "Changing the Subject: Authorship, Writing, and the Reader." In Lauretis 1986. 102–20.

Millet, Kate. 1970. *Sexual Politics.* Garden City, N.Y.: Doubleday.

Minnich, Elizabeth. 1977. "Discussion." *The Scholar and the Feminist IV: Connecting Theory, Practice, and Values.* Report of A conference sponsored by Barnard College Women's Centre, 23 April.

Miranda, Carla, and Verónica Alemán. 1993. "National Feminist Committee: With Ideas of Their Own." *Barricada Internacional* 13, no. 365 (September): 20–21.

Mitchell, Juliet. 1967. "Reply to Discussion on Juliet Mitchell's 'Women: The Longest Revolution.'" *New Left Review* 41:81–83.

Mitter, Swasti. 1986. *Common Fate, Common Bond.* London: Pluto Press.

Modleski, Tania. 1991. *Feminism without Women: Culture and Criticism in a "Postfeminist Age."* New York: Routledge.

Molokomme, Athaliah. 1991. "Emang Basiada (Botswana)." *Signs* 16, no. 4 (summer): 848–51.

Moraga, Cherríe. 1983a. "La Guera." In Moraga and Anzaldúa 1983. 27–34.

———. 1983b. *Loving in the War Years: Lo que nunca pasó por sus labios.* Boston: South End Press.

———. 1983c. "Refugees of a World on Fire, Foreword to the Second Edition." In Moraga and Anzaldúa 1983. n.p.

———. 1993. *The Last Generation, Prose and Poetry.* Toronto: Women's Press.

Moraga, Cherríe, and Gloria Anzaldúa, eds. 1983. *This Bridge Called My Back: Writings By Radical Women of Color.* New York: Kitchen Table/Women of Colour Press. First ed.Watertown, Mass.: Persephone Press, 1981.

Morales, Aurora Levins and Rosario Morales. 1986. *Getting Home Alive.* Ithaca, N.Y.: Firebrand Books.

Morales, Rosario. 1979. "We're All in the Same Boat." In Moraga and Anzaldúa 1983: 91–93.

Morgan, Robin. 1970. "Goodbye to All That." In Morgan 1977: 121–130.

———. 1977. *Going Too Far: A Personal Chronicle of a Feminist.* New York: Random House.

———. 1990. *The Demon Lover: On the Sexuality of Terrorism.* New York: Norton.

———, ed. 1970. *Sisterhood Is Powerful: An Anthology of Writings from the Women's Liberation Movement*. New York: Random House, Vintage.

———, ed. 1984. *Sisterhood Is Global: The International Women's Movement Anthology*. Garden City, N.Y.: Anchor Press/Doubleday.

Morrison, Toni. 1971. "What the Black Woman Thinks about Women's Lib." *New York Times Magazine* (22 August), 14, 15, 63, 64, 66.

Moschkovich, Judith. 1983. "———But I Know You, American Woman." In Moraga and Anzaldúa 1983. 79–84.

Mukherjie, Arun ed. 1993. *Sharing Our Experience*. Ottawa: Canadian Advisory Council on the Status of Women.

Murray, Pauli. 1970. "The Liberation of Black Women." In Thompson 1970. 87–102.

Muvman Liberasyon Fam. 1983. "The Need for an Independent Women's Movement in Mauritius." In Davies 1983. 186–193.

Myron, Nancy, and Charlotte Bunch, eds. 1975. *Lesbianism and the Women's Movement*. Baltimore, Md.: Diana Press.

National Black Feminist Organization. 1974. "Statement of Purpose." *Ms.,* May, 99.

Necessary Bread Affinity Group. 1982. "Necessary Bread Disarmament Statement." *Feminist Studies* 8, no. 3: 690–92.

Newman, Louise M. 1991. "Critical Theory and the History of Women: What's at Stake in Deconstructing Women's History." *Journal of Women's History* 2, no. 3 (winter): 58–68.

New York Radical Feminists. 1970. "Politics of the Ego: A Manifesto for New York Radical Feminists." In Koedt, Levine, and Rapone 1973:379–83.

NiCharthaigh, Dearbhal. 1981. "NWSA as Metaphor for the United States." *Women's Studies Quarterly* 9, no. 3 (fall): 17–18.

Nicholson, Linda J, ed. 1990. *Feminism/Postmodernism*. New York: Routledge.

Nicholson, Linda J., and Nancy Fraser. 1990. "Social Criticism Without Philosophy: An Encounter between Feminism and Postmodernism." In Nicholson 1990. 19–38.

Norsigian, Judy, and Wendy C. Sandford 1979. "Ten Years in the 'Our Bodies Ourselves' Collective." *Radcliffe Quarterly* 65, no. 4: 16–18.

O'Brien, Mary 1976. "The Politics of Impotence." In Shea and King-Farlowe 1976. 147–63.

———. 1981. *The Politics of Reproduction*. London: Routledge.

Offen, Karen. 1988. "Defining Feminism: A Comparative Historical Approach." *Signs* 14, no. 1 (autumn): 119–57.

O'Leary, Véronique, and Louise Toupin, eds. 1981. *Québecoises deboutte! Tome I.* Montreal: Les éditions remue-ménage.

O'Leary, Véronique, and Louise Toupin, eds. 1982. *Québecoises deboutte! Tome II.* Montreal: Les éditions remue-ménage.

Oliviera, Rosiska Darcy de. 1992. "Women and Nature: An Ancestral Bond, a New Alliance." In Oliviera and Corral 1992. 70–83.

Oliviera, Rosiska Darcy de and Thais Corral, eds. (May/June 1992) *Terra Femina*, Brazil: IDAC (Institute of Cultural Action) and REDEH (Network in Defense of Human Species).

Omvedt, Gail, Chetna Gala, and Govind Kelkar. 1988. *Women and Struggle: A Report of the Nari Mukti Sangharsh Sammelan, Patna, 1988*. New Delhi: Kali for Women.

Osennontion, Marlyn Kane, and Sylvia Maracle Skonagenleh:rá. 1989. "Our World according to Osennontion and Skonagenleh:rá." *Canadian Woman Studies* 10, nos. 2 and 3 (summer/fall): 7–19.

Parkerson, Michelle. 1984. "Someplace That's Our Own: Interview with Barbara Smith." *Off Our Backs: A Women's Newsjournal* 14, no. 4 (April): 10, 26.

Parmar, Pratibha. 1989. "Other Kinds of Dreams." *Feminist Review* 31 (spring): 55–65.

Patel, Pragna. 1991. "Alert for Action." *Feminist Review* 37 (spring): 95–102.

Pelletier, Francine. 1985. "L'esprit de Nairobi." *La vie en rose,* September, 17–21.

Perpiñan, Soledad. 1986. "The Philippines: Prostitution and Sexual Exploitation." In Schuler 1986. 155–65.

———. 1993. "Peace: A Breakaway from Patriarchy." Paper presented to the Fifth International Interdisciplinary Congress on Women, San José, Costa Rica, 22–26 February.

Petchesky, Rosalind. 1979. "Dissolving the Hyphen: A Report on Marxist-Feminist Groups 1–5." In Eisenstein 1979. 373–89.

Peters, Barbara and Victoria Samuels eds. 1976. *Dialogue on Diversity: A New Agenda for American Women.* New York: Institute on Pluralism and Group Identity.

Phelan, Peggy. 1990. "Letter to the Editor." *Women's Review of Books* 8, no. 9 (June): 5.

Philippine Organizing Committee. 1992. *Proceedings of the Sixth International Women and Health Meeting, November 3–9, 1990.* Quezon City, Philippines: International Women and Health Network.

Piercy, Marge. 1969. *The Grand Coolie Damn.* Boston: New England Free Press.

———. 1971. "A Work of Artifice." In Babcox and Belkin 1971. 209. Also in *Circles on the Water,* Marge Piercy, New York: Alfred A. Knopf, 1982: 75.

Pietilä, Hilkka. 1993. "A New Picture of Human Economy: A Woman's Perspective." Paper presented to the Fifth Interdisciplinary Congress on Women. San José, Costa Rica, 22–26 February.

Plant, Judith, ed. 1989. *Healing the Wounds: The Promise of Ecofeminism.* Philadelphia: New Society Publishers.

Plaskow, Judith, and Carol P. Christ, eds. 1989. *Weaving the Visions: New Patterns of Feminist Spirituality.* San Francisco: Harper and Row.

popp, elena. 1988. "First Encuentro of Feminist Lesbians." *Off Our Backs: A Women's Newsjournal,* March: 32–33.

Powell, Linda C. 1979. "Black Macho and Black Feminism." In Smith 1983. 283–292.

Pratt, Minnie Bruce. 1988. "Identity: Skin Blood Heart." In *Yours in Struggle: Three Feminist Perspectives of Anti-Semitism and Racism,* ed. Elly Bulkin, Minnie Bruce Pratt, and Barbara Smith. Ithaca, N.Y.: Firebrand Books. 9–63.

Prettyman, Quandra. 1980. "Visibility and Difference: Black Women in History—Pieces of a Paper and Some Ruminations." In Eisenstein and Jardine 1980. 239–46.

Radford-Hill, Sheila. 1986. "Considering Feminism as a Model of Social Change." In Lauretis 1986. 157–72.

Radicalesbians. 1970. "The Woman Identified Woman." In Koedt, Levine, and Rapone 1973. 240–45.

Rahim, Chris, Cat Renay, and Margaret Matsuyama. 1992. "Report on the ALN (Asian Lesbian Network) Conference: Asian Lesbians Speak." *Kinesis,* September, 9.

Raymond, Janice G. 1989. "Putting the Politics Back into Lesbianism." *Women's Studies International Forum* 12, no. 2:149–56.

Reagan, Berenice Johnson. 1982. "My Black Mothers and Sisters; or, On Beginning a Cultural Anthropology." *Feminist Studies* 8, no. 1 (spring): 81–96.

———. 1983. "Coalition Politics: Turning the Century." In Smith 1983. 356–68.

Reddock, Rhoda. 1993. "Conceptualizing Identity, Culture, and Gender in Multi-Ethnic Societies: Intersections of Ethnicity, Class, and Gender in Trinidad and Tobago." Unpublished paper.

Redstockings. 1969. "Redstockings Manifesto." In Morgan 1973. 533–36.

———, ed. 1975. *Feminist Revolution*, New Paltz, N.Y.: Redstockings. Abridged edition with additional writings published by Random House, 1978.

Rich, Adrienne. 1976. *Of Woman Born: Motherhood as Experience and Institution*. New York: Norton.

———. 1978a. "Disloyal to Civilization: Feminism, Racism, and Gynephobia." *Chrysalis* 7:9–27.

———. 1978b. *The Dream of a Common Language: Poems 1974–1977*. New York: Morrow.

———. 1978c. "Natural Resources." In Rich 1978b. 60–67.

———. 1979a. *On Lies, Secrets, and Silences: Selected Prose, 1966–1978*. New York: Norton.

———. 1979b. "What Does a Woman Need to Know?" Commencement Address, Smith College, Northampton, Mass. In Rich 1986. 1–10.

———. 1980. "Compulsory Heterosexuality and Lesbian Experience" *Signs* 5, no. 4 (summer): 631–60.

———. 1986. *Blood, Bread and Poetry: Selected Prose, 1979–1985*. New York: Norton.

Riley, Denise. 1988. *Am I That Name? Feminism and the Category of "Women" in History*. Minneapolis: University of Minnesota Press.

Roberts, Barbara. 1988. *Smooth Sailing or Storm Warning? Canadian and Quebec Women's Groups and the Meech Lake Accord*. Ottawa: Canadian Research Institute for the Advancement of Women.

Rogers, Gerry. 1994. *The Vienna Tribunal: Women's Rights Are Human Rights*. Augusta Productions (with the National Film Board of Canada), 54 Mullock St., St. Johns, Newfoundland, A1C 2R8; tel. 709-753-1861 or 754-3202; fax 709-579-8090.

Rooney, Frances, and Pat Israel, eds. 1985. "Women and Disability" Special issue of *Resources for Feminist Research* 14, no. 1 (March).

Ruddick, Sara. 1980. "Maternal Thinking." *Feminist Studies*, 6, no. 2 (summer): 342–67..

Rupert, Linda. 1985–86. *Women in Peru: Voices from a Decade*. Ecumenical Committee on the Andes (Eco-Andes). Available from Eco-Andes, 198 Broadway, #302, New York, NY 10038.

Russell, Diana, and Nicole Van de Ven, eds. 1976. *Crimes Against Women: Proceedings of the International Tribunal*. Millbrae, Calif.: Les Femmes.

Russell, Michele. 1976. "The Black Woman." In Peters and Samuels 1976. 29–32.

———. 1981. "An Open Letter to the Academy." In *Building Feminist Theory: Essays from Quest: A Feminist Quarterly*, ed. Charlotte Bunch et al. New York: Longman. 101–10.

Saadawi, Nawal El. 1981. *The Hidden Face of Eve: Women in the Arab World*. Boston: Beacon Press.

Saadawi, Nawal El, Fatima Mernissi, and Mallica Vajarathon. 1978. "A Critical View of the Wellesley Conference." *Quest: A Feminist Quarterly* 4, no. 2 (winter): 101–8.

Sage. 1984. "Mothers and Daughters." Special issue of *Sage: A Scholarly Journal on Black Women* 1, no. 2.

Saint-Jean, Armande. 1980. "Preface." *Les têtes de pioche, collection complète*. Montreal: Les Éditions du Remue-Ménage: 5–10.

———. 1983. *Pour en finir avec le patriarcat*. Montreal: Les Éditions Primeur.

Sanchez, Carol Lee. 1989. "New World Tribal Communities: An Alternative Approach for Recreating Egalitarian Societies." In Plaskow and Christ 1989. 344–356.

Sanchez, Sonia. 1983. "Interview." In *Black Women Writers at Work*, ed. Claudia Tate. New York: Continuum Publishing. 132–48.

Sandoval, Chela. 1991. "U.S. Third World Feminism: The Theory and Method of Oppositional Consciousness in the Postmodern World." *Genders* 10 (spring): 1–24.

Sarachild, Kathie. 1975. "Consciousness-Raising: A Radical Weapon." In Redstockings 1975. 131–37.

Sargent, Lydia, ed. 1981. *Women and Revolution*. Boston: South End Press.

Sarna, Shirley. 1985. "Juives et arabes: Des soeurs ennemies se parlent." *La vie en rose* (April): 34–37.

Savane, Marie-Angelique. 1985. "Feminism: A Necessity in Africa." *ECHOE, AAWORD Newsletter* 2/3:9–11.

Schuler, Margaret, ed. 1986. *Empowerment and the Law: Strategies of Third World Women*. Washington, D.C.: OEF International.

———. 1990. *Women, Law, and Development: Action for Change*. New York: OEF International.

———. 1992. *Freedom from Violence: Women's Strategies from Around the World*. New York: OEF International, U.N. Development Fund for Women, Women Ink.

Scott, Joan. 1986. "Gender: A Useful Category of Historical Analysis." *American Historical Review* 91, no. 5 (December): 1053–75.

———. 1988. "Deconstructing Equality-versus-Difference; or, the Uses of Poststructuralist Theory for Feminism." *Feminist Studies* 14, no. 1:33–50.

Seager, Joni. 1993. *Earth Follies: Coming to Feminist Terms with the Global Environmental Crisis*. New York: Routledge.

See, Bernice. 1993. "Violence against Women: The Cordillera Experience." Testimony at the World Conference on Human Rights, Vienna, Austria, 15 June, 1993. *Chaneg* 4, no. 2 (April–June): 15–19.

Segal, Lynne. 1987. *Is the Future Female? Troubled Thoughts on Contemporary Feminism*. London: Virago.

Sen, Gita, and Caren Grown. 1987. *Development, Crises, and Alternative Visions: Third World Women's Perspectives*. New York: Monthly Review Press.

Senogles, Renee. 1992. "Women of the Americas Conference." *Indigenous Woman* 1, no. 3:28–30.

Sève, Micheline de. 1985. *Pour un féminisme libertaire*. Montreal: Les Éditions du Boréal Express.

———. 1989. "A Pacifist Politics." In *Women and Counter Power*, ed. Yolande Cohen. Montreal: Black Rose Books. 178–87.

Shadmi, Erella. 1993a. "Israeli Feminism Today." *Fireweed* 39/40 (summer): 16–25.

———. 1993b. "Occupation, Violence, and Women in Israeli Society." *Women in Black National Newsletter* 5 (spring): 6–8.

Shea, William R., and J. King-Farlowe, eds. 1976. *Contemporary Issues in Philosophy*. New York: Science History Publications.

Shiva, Vandana. 1989a. *Staying Alive: Women, Ecology, and Development*. London: Zed.

———. 1989b. "Women, Development, and Ecology," South Asian Workshop on Women and Development 1989: 34–39.

Signs. 1981. "Comments on Tinker's 'A Feminist View of Copenhagen.'" *Signs* 6, no. 4 (summer): 771–90.

———. 1986. "Reflections on Forum '85 in Nairobi, Kenya: Voices from the International Women's Studies Community." *Signs* 11, no. 3 (spring): 584–608.

Simms, Glenda. 1992. "Beyond the White Veil." In Backhouse and Flaherty 1992. 175–81.

———. 1993. "Feminism Is Global: Or Is It?" In *Women and Social Location: Our Lives, Our Research*, ed. Marilyn Assheton-Smith and Barbara Spronk. Charlottetown, P.E.I.: gynergy books. 189–97.

Sizemore, Barbara A. 1973. "Sexism and the Black Male." *Black Scholar* 4, nos. 6–7 (March–April): 2–11.

Smith, Barbara. 1980. "Racism and Women's Studies." *Frontiers* 5, no. 1:48–49.

———. 1983. *Home Girls: A Black Feminist Anthology*. New York: Kitchen Table–Women of Color Press.

Smith, Barbara, and Beverly Smith. 1983. "Across the Kitchen Table: A Sister to Sister Dialogue." In Moraga and Anzaldúa 1983. 113–27.

Smith, Beverly, Judith Stein and Priscilla Golding. 1981. "'The Possibility of Life between Us': A Dialogue between Black and Jewish Women." *Conditions* 3, no. 1 (spring): 25–46.

Smith, Dorothy E. 1975. "An Analysis of Ideological Structures and How Women Are Excluded: Considerations for Academic Women." *Canadian Review of Sociology and Anthropology* 12:353–69.

Snitow, Ann. 1989. "Pages from a Gender Diary: Basic Divisions in Feminism." *Dissent* (spring): 205–24. Longer version in Harris and King 1989. 35–74.

Snitow, Ann, Christine Stansell, and Sharon Thompson, eds. 1983. *Powers of Desire: The Politics of Sexuality*. New York: Monthly Review Press.

"South Asian Feminist Declaration." 1989. In South Asian Workshop on Women and Development 1989. 8–11.

South Asian Workshop on Women and Development. 1989. *Pressing against the Boundaries: Report of an FAO/FFHC/AD Workshop, Bangalore*. New Delhi: FAO.

SPARC (Society for Promotion of Area Resource Centres). 1992. "Pedagogy of Exchanges between the Poor: The South Africa-India Exchange Chronicle." An unpublished interim report (July). Available from P.O. Box 9389, Bombay-400 026, India.

Spelman, Elizabeth V. 1988. *Inessential Woman: Problems of Exclusion in Feminist Thought*. Boston: Beacon Press.

Spivak, Gayatri. 1987. *In Other Worlds: Essays in Cultural Politics*. New York: Methuen.

———. 1989. "In a Word: Interview with Ellen Rooney." *Differences* 1, no. 2 (summer): 124–56.

———. 1990. *The Post-Colonial Critic: Interviews, Strategies, Dialogues*, ed. Sarah Harasym. New York: Routledge.

Spretnak, Charlene. 1991. *States of Grace: The Recovery of Meaning in the Postmodern Age*. New York: Harper.

Stacey-Moore, Gail. 1993. "In Our Own Voice: Aboriginal Women Demand Justice." *Herizons*, (winter), 21–23.

Stephenson, Marylee. 1975. "Being in Women's Liberation: A Case Study in Social Change." Ph.D. thesis, University of British Columbia.

Sternbach, Nancy Saporta, Marysa Navarro-Aranguren, Patricia Chuchryk, and Sonia E. Alvarez. 1992. "Feminism in Latin America: From Bogotá to San Bernardo." *Signs* 17, no. 2 (winter): 393–434.

Stienstra, Deborah. 1994. *Women's Movements and International Organizations*. Basingstoke, U.K.: Macmillan.

Strobel, Margaret. 1994. "The Chicago Women's Liberation Union." In Ferree and Martin 1994.

Susan. 1970. "About My Consciousness Raising." In Tanner 1971. 238–43.

Susskind, Yifat. 1992/93. "Tourist Mentality Activism." *Women in Black National Newsletter*, winter, 8–9.

Tanner, Leslie, ed. 1971. *Voices from Women's Liberation*. New York: Mentor.

Tardy, Évelyne, Francine Descarries, Danielle Juteau, Chantal Collard, Roch Hurtubise and Micheline de Sève. 1986/87. "Un débat réussi sur *L'un est l'autre* d'Élisabeth Badinter." *Resources for Feminist Research* 15 (December/January): 31–40.

Tauli-Corpuz, Victoria. 1992. "Creating Alternative Culture against Foreign Domination and Towards the Liberation of Women." *Chaneg* 3, no. 1 (January–April): 17–20.

———. 1993. "Keynote Address: First Asian Indigenous Women's Conference." *Chaneg* 4, 1 (January–March): 9–14.

Taylor, Verta, and Leila J. Rupp. 1993. "Women's Culture and Lesbian Feminist Activism: A Reconsideration of Cultural Feminism." *Signs* 19, no. 1 (fall); 32–61.

Teather, Lynn. 1976. "The Feminist Mosaic." In *Women in the Canadian Mosaic*, ed. Gwen Matheson. Toronto: Peter Martin Associates. 301–346.

Telling It Collective. 1990. *Telling It: Women and Language across Cultures*. Vancouver: Press Gang.

Les têtes de pioche. 1977. "Editorial." *Les têtes de pioche* 2, no. 1:1.

Le Théâtre de Cuisine. 1976. *Môman travaille pas, a trop d'ouvrage* (*Mummy doesn't work, she has too much to do*). Play written and produced by Le Théâtre de Cuisine, Québec. Reported in *Les têtes de pioche*.

Thiele, Bev. 1989. "Dissolving Dualisms: O'Brien, Embodiment, and Social Construction." *Resources for Feminist Research* 18, no. 3: 7–12.

Thompson, Mary Lou, ed. 1970. *Voices of the New Feminism*. Boston: Beacon Press.

Touraine, Alain. 1971. *The Post-Industrial Society: Tomorrow's Social History: Classes, Conflicts, and Culture in the Programmed Society*. Trans. Leonard F. X. Mayhew. New York: Random House.

Trask, Haunani-Kay. 1984. "Fighting the Battle of Double Colonization: View of a Hawaiian Feminist." *Critical Perspectives* 2, no. 1 (fall): 196–212.

Trinh, T. Minh-ha. 1989. *Woman Native Other: Writing Postcoloniality and Feminism*. Bloomington: Indianapolis University Press.

Trujillo, Carla, ed. 1991. *Chicana Lesbians: The Girls Our Mothers Warned Us About*. Berkeley, Calif.: Third Woman Press.

Tynes, Maxine. 1987. *Borrowed Beauty*. Porter's Lake, Nova Scotia: Pottersfield Press.

Vidal, Mirta. 1972. "Chicanas Speak Out—New Voice of La Raza." In 1972. 48–57.

La vie en rose. 1981. Pour L'autonome." Editorial. *La vie en rose*, March, April, May.

———. 1984. "Women, the Church, and Religion." Special issue of *La vie en rose* 19 (September).

Vogel, Ursula. 1986. "Rationalism and Romanticism: Two Strategies for Women's Liberation." In *Feminism and Political Theory*, ed. Judith Evans, et al. London: Sage Publications. 17–46.

Walker, Alice. 1974. "In Search of Our Mothers' Gardens." *Ms.*, May, 64–70.

———. 1976. *Meridian*. New York: Washington Square Press.

———. 1983. *In Search of Our Mothers' Gardens*. New York: Harcourt Brace Jovanovich.

WAND/APCWD. 1980. *Developing Strategies for the Future: Feminist Perspectives*. Report of the International Feminist Workshop held at Stony Point, New York 20–25 April. (Includes the Report of the International Workshop (1979) "Feminist Ideology and Structures in the First Half of the Decade for Women," held in Bangkok 23–30 June), New York: International Women's Tribune Center.

Ware, Celestine. 1970. *Woman Power: The Movement for Women's Liberation*. New York: Tower Publications.

Waring, Marilyn. 1988. *If Women Counted: A New Feminist Economics*. San Francisco: Harper and Row.

Warren, Janine. 1977. "Le groupe de conscience des femmes issu de l'ex-comité des femmes du P.T.Q. [Parti des travailleurs du Québec]. *Les têtes de pioche* 2, no. 7 (November): 1, 2.

Warrior, Betsy. 1970. "Housework: Slavery or Labour of Love." In Koedt, Levine, and Rapone 1973. 208–212.

Weathers, Mary Ann. 1970. "An Argument for Black Women's Liberation as a Revolutionary Force." In Tanner 1971. 303–7.

Weedon, Chris. 1987. *Feminist Practice and Poststructuralist Theory.* Oxford, England: Basil Blackwell.

Welfare Warriors. 1991. "Letter to the Editor." *Off Our Backs: A Women's Newsjournal,* 20 (February).

WHISPER. 1985/86. Statement of Principles. *WHISPER* 1, no. 1 (winter): 1.

———. n.d. *When You Can't Stand Turning One More Trick, Turn to Us.* Pamphlet.

White, Evelyn C., ed. 1990. *Black Women's Health Book: Speaking for Ourselves.* Seattle, Wash.: Seal Press.

Willis, Ellen. 1992. *No More Nice Girls: Countercultural Essays.* Hanover, N.H.: Wesleyan University Press.

Wine, Jeri, and Janice L. Ristock, eds. 1991. *Women and Social Change: Feminist Activism in Canada.* Toronto: James Lorimer.

Women against Fundamentalism. 1990. "Women against Fundamentalism Statement." *Women against Fundamentalism Newsletter* 1, no. 1:2.

Women Living under Muslim Laws. n.d. "Statement of Principles." Published at the beginning of every issue of *Women Living under Muslim Laws Dossier.*

Women's Book Collective, Chinese Canadian National Council. 1992. *Jin Guo: Voices of Chinese Canadian Women.* Toronto: Women's Press.

Women's Global Network on Reproductive Rights. 1984. *Report of the International Tribunal and Meeting on Reproductive Rights.* Amsterdam: July 22–28, 1984. Amsterdam Women's Global Network on Reproductive Rights.

World University Service Women's Development Programme. 1992. *Women and Power: Implications for Development, Utilizing the Development and Political Process to Entrench the Rights of Women.* Conference Proceedings. Johannesburg, South Africa: World University Service.

World Women's Congress for a Healthy Planet. 1992. *Official Report, including Women's Action Agenda 21 and Findings of the Tribunals.* New York: Women's Environment and Development Organization (WEDO).

Woroniuk, Beth, and Josée Lafrenière. 1989. "What Do You Mean—'It Doesn't Affect Women'? Feminists Redefining Development." *Match News,* September/October, 1, 7.

Yates, Gayle Graham. 1975. *What Women Want: The Ideas of the Movement.* Cambridge, Mass.: Harvard University Press.

Yudelman, Sally W. 1987. *Hopeful Openings: A Study of Five Women's Development Organizations in Latin America and the Caribbean.* International Center for Research on Women Overseas Development Council, West Hartford, Conn.: Kumarian Press.

Zabaleta, Marta. 1983. "The Mothers Do Not Disappear." In Caldecott and Leland 1983. 152–54.